Taking Action!

3rd Edition

About IPSEA

IPSEA was established in 1983 and provides free advice to parents of children with special educational needs. Through its telephone advice lines and its network of volunteers covering England, Wales and Northern Ireland*, IPSEA offers a range of support to parents including:

- advice on the rights of children and young people with special educational needs and their parents

- free independent second professional opinions on children's special educational needs

- free advice and support for parents appealing to the Special Educational Needs Tribunal.

For further information write to:

IPSEA, 6 Carlow Mews, Woddbridge, Suffolk IP12 1EA.

IPSEA is a registered Charity (No 327691) and a Limited Comany (No 2198066), and relies on grants and donations for all of its work.

*Note: this guide does not apply to Scotland or Northern Ireland

Taking Action!

Appropriate education is every child's right

The essential guide to SEN law for teachers, parents, advocates and advice workers

John Wright and David Ruebain

3rd Edition

The Questions Publishing Company Ltd
Birmingham

First published in 1996 by
The Questions Publishing Company Ltd
Leonard House, 321 Bradford Street, Digbeth, Birmingham B5 6ET

© John Wright and David Ruebain 2002

Designed by Al Stewart
Cover design by James Davies

ISBN: 1-84190-081-8

Acknowledgements

Part 3, *Appealing to the Special Educational Needs Tribunal,* was written by Sally Capper.

Extracts from the Education Act 1996, The Education (Special Educational Needs) Regulations 2001, and The Special Educational Needs Tribunal Regulations 2001 are reproduced with the permission of the Controller of Her Majesty's Stationery Office.

The law: England

The advice in this book is based on:

Part IV of the Education Act 1996 and Schedule 26 and 27 of that Act;
The Education (Special Educational Needs Tribunal) Regulations 2001;
The Education (Special Educational Needs) (England) (Consolidated) Regulations 2001 (referred to in the text for ease as The Education (Special Educational Needs) Regulations 2001);
The Special Educational Needs Code of Practice.

The Tribunal regulations came into force on September 1st 2001. The other legislation and the Code of Practice came into force on January 1st 2002.

The law: Wales

The Education (Special Educational Needs Tribunal) Regulations 2001 came into force in Wales on September 1st 2001.
Part IV of the Education Act 1996 and Schedule 26 and 27 of that Act and the Education (Special Educational Needs) (Wales) Regulations 2002 came into force on April 1st 2002.
The Special Educational Needs Code of Practice for Wales came into force on April 1st 2002.
The cases in Part 2 of this book quote from the England regulations and the England Code of Practice. The regulations are almost identical to the Wales regulations, but important exceptions are

a. references to the Connexions Service, which do not appear in the Wales version as the service does not operate in Wales; and
b. references to the time limits for LEA's responding to tribunal orders and for carrying out actions when they concede appeals. For Wales, for a technical reason, these time limits are to be found in regulations published by the Department for Education and Skills, titled: The Special Education Tribunal (Time Limits) (Wales) Regulations 2001. The actual time limits are the same as those set out in the England regulations 25 and 26.

The Education (Special Educational Needs) (Wales) Regulations 2002 are available from HMSO shops and the HMSO web site. Parents in Wales and those advising them should obtain a copy of the regulations. They will be able to use the numbering of regulations in this book to guide them to the equivalent paragraphs in the Wales regulations.
The Code of Practice for Wales is very similar in the guidance it gives, but is occasionally worded differently. Rather than quoting paragraphs of the Code from Taking Action, parents in Wales or those advising them should obtain a copy of the Wales version (free, by calling 029 20826078). They will then be able to use the paragraph numbering in this book to guide them to the appropriate section in the Code for Wales.

Dedication

This book was written to help parents and carers who are struggling to get the special educational provision their children are legally entitled to. It is dedicated to them and to their children.

Contents

Notes on the text   viii

Part 1: First, find your problem   1

Part 2: The cases   7

Part 3: Appealing to the Special Educational Needs
         Tribunal   187

Part 4: Discrimination against disabled children in
         schools   193

Part 5: Judicial review and public funding for cases   203

Part 6: Case law   241

Part 7: Complaining to the Secretary of State, the
         Ombudsman and the Local Authority
         Monitoring Officer   269

Part 8: Support organisations and further reading   281

Part 9: The law   287
         The Education Act 1996   288
         The Education (Special Educational Needs)
         England Regulations 2001   321
         The Special Educational Needs Tribunal
         Regulations 2001   366

Part 10: Glossary   399

Part 11: Index   403

Notes on the text

The 'he's and 'she's

In English law, everyone is a 'he', therefore where we quote from special education law all children, parents and professionals will be male. Elsewhere in our text we have interchanged gender in order to avoid the risk of stereotyping and for the sake of variety. For the record, in IPSEA's case work the majority of children with special educational needs are boys and the majority of parents taking on the responsibility for sorting out problems with LEAs are their mothers.

Citations

The cases which are referred to in this book all include what are known as their citations. These are the letters and numbers that appear after the name of each case, which are used by lawyers to trace the judgements. When writing to a Local Education Authority or school, you do not usually need to quote the citation of the case, as well as the name, but sometimes it is useful to do so if you would like their lawyers to read the judgement. It is also useful for you to give the full case name, including the citation, to any solicitors who become involved on your behalf.

Part 1

First, find your problem

16. "The LEA say the school can meet our child's needs from their own resources, so there's no need for a statement. The school says they can't."

When the assessment is finished and you are sent the proposed statement ...

These are some of the problems you might face when you receive the proposed statement and copies of the professional advice.

17. "The psychologist told us verbally how much provision our son needs, but has said nothing about this in the written advice."

18. "The local school has made it plain they don't want our son and the LEA Officer says it's best not to force them. But that's the school we want for him."

19. "The proposed statement is fine, but the head says there'll be no help till the statement is finalised."

20. "The LEA is refusing to name a mainstream school for our son."

21. "Part 2 of the statement does not describe our daughter's needs in any detail at all."

22. "Part 3 of the statement does not give any detail of the provision our son is to get and it leaves the decision up to the school."

23. "We have been told we can't express a preference for an independent school, but that's exactly what we believe is needed."

24. "Speech therapy is listed in Part 2 as one of our daughter's special educational needs, but the provision is written under Part 6 as a 'non-educational provision'."

4

25. "The speech therapist's advice says our son's need for speech therapy is educational, not medical, but the statement lists it under Parts 5 and 6 as 'non-educational'."

26. "We want a school in the neighbouring LEA, but they've told our LEA that it's full."

When the LEA send the final statement ...

These are some of the problems you might face when the LEA finalise the statement.

27. "We disagree with the description of our son's needs in Part 2 and Part 3 is so vague we don't know what it means."

28. "The LEA have refused our request for a place in the school of our preference. Instead, they want to bus our daughter 52 miles a day."

29. "The statement names an LEA special school when we know that they cannot make the provision our daughter needs. This can only be made at a specialist independent school."

30. "We can't decide whether it is worthwhile appealing against our son's statement. We've heard that LEAs don't always obey tribunal decisions and that when they do, they really drag their feet."

Your child already has a statement of special educational needs ...

These are some of the problems you might face even though your child has a statement.

31. "We have lost our appeal to the Tribunal to have speech therapy moved to Part 3 of our son's statement – what else can we do?"

32. "My son is not getting the provision which Part 3 of his statement says he should get."

33. "The LEA have proposed an amendment to the statement saying that the first five hours of our son's help are to be paid for by the school. The school say they can't afford it."

34. "Our son refuses to go to school. We asked the LEA for a fresh assessment. They refused and sent an Attendance Order."

35. "Our daughter has been excluded from her special school. What now?"

36. "We moved 6 months ago but the new LEA still haven't given our son the provision the old LEA's statement says he should have."

37. "Our daughter is coming up to secondary transfer, and we are worried because no decision on her next school has been made."

38. "It's time for our son's statement review. How can we best influence the outcome of the review?"

39. "I would like to educate my daughter at home, but I've been told that this is not possible because she has a statement."

40. "Our son is coming up to 16 and the LEA say he must leave school and that his statement will lapse then – but what about his needs?"

If your problem is not here ...

Sorry ... turn to the list of support organisations in part 8 for advice. Also see the index on page 404.

Part 2

The cases

Case 1

66 Our daughter was born with spina bifida and, although she has just turned one year old, both the family doctor and our social worker have advised us to find out what help might be available from the LEA. But when we met with an Education Welfare Officer to discuss Clara's needs, we were told that the LEA had no responsibility towards children under 2 and that we were wasting our time by going to them. 99

The first step

The EWO was wrong. LEAs have a duty towards children with special educational needs from birth. Your first step should be to write to the Special Needs Officer asking for the LEA's published information about their special educational provision and asking for a meeting with the Officer to discuss what help they can offer Clara. Your letter could start like this:

Dear Sir or Madam,

I am writing as the parent of a child with special educational needs to ask for the information on special education provision which I understand every LEA has a legal duty to publish. Also, I would like to arrange a meeting with you, after I have had a chance to read through your published information, to discuss with you the particular needs of my daughter, Clara, who is 18 months old ... (then give some details about Clara, including the fact that the doctor and the social worker have suggested that you contact the LEA).

Yours sincerely

Ask your social worker to come with you to the meeting with the Special Needs Officer.

If that doesn't work

If you are not happy with the information you receive from the LEA, or if the meeting with the Officer gets you nowhere, you will have to decide whether or not to ask the LEA to do an assessment of Clara's special educational needs.

Case 1

But before doing this you should contact one of the support organisations listed in part 8 to discuss the pros and cons of having Clara assessed, and possibly 'statemented.'

An assessment of a child under 2 can take whatever form the LEA decides, and so can the statement (if they issue one). The Code of Practice sets out a bare minimum of information which LEA statements on children under 2 should contain, but there are no deadlines for LEAs completing assessments when children are under 2. Nor is there a right of appeal to the SEN Tribunal. For these reasons, it might be best to wait till Clara is 2. (See PS below).

What the law says

The Education (School Information) Regulations 1998 say:

'Information to be published by authorities:

14. The authority's detailed arrangements and policies in respect of –

(a) the identification and assessment of children with special educational needs and the involvement of parents in that process...
(b) special educational provision provided otherwise than at school...

16. The arrangements for parents who consider that their child may have special educational needs to obtain further advice and further information.'

Case 2

❝ Our son, Ashraf, is three and a half years old. He has Down's Syndrome and has been attending a nursery school, without specialist support, for around six months. The head of the nursery told us that they can't provide any additional help and suggested that we ask the LEA for an assessment under the 1996 Education Act. However, the educational psychologist says that the Authority's policy is to wait until children start school before doing special educational needs assessments. But we were hoping an assessment would lead to Ashraf being given extra support for his learning, now, in the nursery. ❞

The first step

The decision to assess a child is made by the Education Office of the LEA, not by an individual educational psychologist, although the LEA may seek his or her views before making their decision. You should write directly to the Chief Education Officer, asking for an assessment. Your letter could start like this:

Dear Sir or Madam,

I am writing as the parent of a child with special educational needs to ask for an assessment under section 323 of the 1996 Education Act. My child's name is Ashraf... and his date of birth is ... My reasons for wanting an assessment are ...

The LEA must reply to your letter within six weeks. They must agree to your request for an assessment, unless they believe that an assessment is not 'necessary'. This decision must be made with reference to Ashraf's special educational needs, not his age nor any policy which the LEA may have with regard to children not yet on the roll of a school.

If that doesn't work

If the LEA refuse to do an assessment, you will have the right to appeal to the Special Educational Needs Tribunal (see part 3 of this book for advice on this). You will need evidence that Ashraf has special educational needs which the nursery cannot meet from its own resources. Speak to the head of the nursery, who may be able to provide evidence and may also agree to appear as a witness for you at an appeal. If in doubt, speak to someone from one of the support organisations listed in part 8.

Case 2

What the law says

Section 329 of the 1996 Education Act says:

'(1) Where –

(a) the parent of a child for whom a local education authority are responsible but for whom no statement is maintained under section 324 asks the authority to arrange for an assessment to be made in respect of the child under section 323,

(a) no such assessment has been made within the period of six months ending with the date on which the request is made, and
(b) it is necessary for the authority to make an assessment under that section,

– the authority shall comply with the request.

(2) If in any case where subsection (1) (a) and (b) applies the authority determine not to comply with the request –

(a) they shall give notice in writing of that fact to the child's parent, and
(b) the parent may appeal to the Tribunal against the determination.'

2

Case

2

Regulation 12 of the Education (Special Educational Needs) Regulations 2001 says:

'(2) Where under sections 328(2) or 329(1) a parent asks the authority to arrange for an assessment to be made they shall within 6 weeks of the date of receipt of the request give notice to the child's parent ... of ... their decision to make an assessment (or) ... of their determination not to comply with the parent's request.'

What the Code of Practice says

'In deciding whether to make a statutory assessment, the critical question is whether there is convincing evidence that, despite the school, with the help of external specialists, taking relevant and purposeful action to meet the child's learning difficulties, those difficulties remain or have not been remedied sufficiently and may require the LEA to determine the child's special educational provision.'

(Paragraph 7:34)

Post Script

A statement of special educational needs is a two-edged sword.

On the one hand, a statement may be the only way that you can get your child the help he or she needs. You have the right to be consulted about the way your child's needs are described in a statement and, at the end of the day, the statement should guarantee that the help needed will in fact be given. If you are not happy with the statement, you can appeal to the Tribunal and, as a result, may get the statement rewritten.

On the other hand, some parents worry about their child being stigmatised by having a statement. And, if you end up with a statement which names a school which you think will not meet your child's needs, or may even perhaps be damaging for your child, you will have real problems deciding what to do if your appeal to the Tribunal fails.

So, it is important to think through the pros and cons of having a statement before asking your LEA to assess your child. It might help to discuss the situation with someone from one of the support organisations listed in part 8.

**Case
2**

Case 3

66 Our son is 7 and is making very little progress with his reading and number work. His teacher last year tried to give him extra help, but the teacher this year doesn't seem that worried. She says Will is just lazy and a 'daydreamer' and that if he made more effort to listen he would start to learn. She offered to send a note home on days when he tries hard, so that we can reward him. But we tried this with his teacher last year. How far behind does he have to fall before the school does something? 99

The first step

You have already taken the first step, by sharing your worries with Will's teacher. Now you need to ask the headteacher for a meeting, together with Will's class teacher and the school's special educational needs coordinator (SENCO). Ask if Will's class teacher from last year can also be there.

At the meeting, you should:

- Explain how Will has been having difficulties for a number of years. Take in some of his old school reports.
- Explain what Will is like at home and why you think his problem is not 'laziness'. Describe the ways you have tried to encourage him in the past which have not worked.
- Ask for Will to be placed on the school's Action or Action Plus stage and for him to receive extra help or support.
- Ask for targets to be set for his progress, and ask for a date to be fixed to review his progress.

If that doesn't work

If you get nowhere at the meeting, you should write to the school governors, who are responsible for the work of the school. Your letter could begin like this:

To: The Chair of the Governing Body,

Dear Sir or Madam,

I am writing to you as the parent of Will ... who is in Year 3. I believe that Will has special educational needs and that he should be receiving support. I have discussed this with my son's class teacher, and with the headteacher, without satisfaction.

I understand that the governors have a duty in law to 'use their best endeavours' to see that children with special educational needs have their needs met. My reasons for believing that Will has special educational needs are ...

2

Case 3

(Set out your reasons and include copies of any reports on Will which back you up)

If you need help wording this letter, talk to one of the support organisations listed in part 8. While you are waiting for a reply, ask your family doctor to check Will's hearing. Many children have problems in their early years at school because of 'glue ear.' This may be Will's problem. Your doctor will explain what it is and how it can be treated.

What the law says

The 1996 Education Act says:

'The governing body ... shall ... use their best endeavours ... to secure that, if any registered pupil has special educational needs, the special educational provision which his learning difficulty calls for is made.'

(Section 317 (1)(a))

'The Secretary of State shall issue ... a code of practice giving practical guidance in respect of the discharge by local education authorities and the governing bodies ... of their

2

Case

3

functions under this Part of the Act. It shall be the duty of local education authorities, and such governing bodies ... to have regard to the provisions of the code.'

(Section 313 (1) & (2))

What the Code of Practice says

'A child with special educational needs should have their needs met.'

(Paragraph 1:5)

'LEAs, schools and settings (should) work together to ensure that any child's special educational needs are identified early.'

(Paragraph 1:6)

Post Script

Try to be calm and polite in your dealings with the school. This is for three reasons:

First, whatever happens, Will is going to have to continue with the same class teacher and you are going to have to continue to talk to her and the head, whether they agree with you or not.

Second, there are a number of organisations which exist to help parents in your position. Many of them are listed in part 8 of this book. Rather than getting angry, use them.

Third, as a last resort, if at the end of the day you believe that Will has special educational needs which the school, for whatever reason, are not meeting, you will be able to ask the local educational authority for an assessment. The LEA will then ask the school what they are doing about Will's needs.

Case 4

Case 4

❝ We've just had the review of my daughter's progress under her Individual Education Plan. Josie is 9 and has problems with her reading and writing and spelling. Both her class teacher and the special needs coordinator agree that the targets set in her IEP have not been met, and this was its second review. I asked them to get an educational psychologist to see Josie to advise on a more specialised programme that might lead to some improvement. But the special needs coordinator says outside specialists can't be called in unless a child is on Action Plus. She also said that the LEA are so short of psychologists that by the time Josie is seen it would be time for the next IEP review anyway. ❞

The first step

If everyone agrees that the targets in Josie's Individual Education Plan have not been met, one of three things must be wrong: either she has not been getting the help, or she has not been getting enough of it, or it is the wrong kind of help.

The first step is to ask the headteacher to arrange a meeting between herself, yourself, Josie's class teacher and the Special Education Needs Coordinator. At the meeting you should ask these questions:

● Exactly how much help has Josie received under her Individual Education Plan since it was adopted?
● What does the school think is the reason for Josie not meeting her progress targets for the second review period running?
● Will the school now ask for an educational psychologist's advice on Josie's difficulties? If not, why not?

You may need to remind the staff that the Code of Practice says outside specialist advice can be requested at Action stage not just when a child is on Action Plus. If the headteacher

Case 5

66 We were having a chat with our 12 year old daughter about her school work and how she was getting on with her friends and teachers, that sort of thing, when she staggered us by saying that she has not seen her special support teacher since the beginning of term – around eight weeks ago. Shirley has an Individual Education Plan and under it is supposed to get one hour of special teaching a week. We have had no information at all from the school about this change. Perhaps Shirley doesn't need the help any more? 99

The first step

It is very unlikely that the help was dropped because Shirley did not need it. If that were the case, her progress would have been reported to you at a review meeting. It is more likely that the teacher has left suddenly, or is ill, and the school has failed to make alternative arrangements. The first step, then, is to find out exactly what has happened.

You should ask the headteacher for a meeting, together with the Special Education Needs Coordinator (SENCO). At this meeting you should:

- tell them Shirley's account of what has happened and ask for confirmation that she has had no special help for eight weeks;
- ask what the school plans to do in order to ensure that Shirley receives the help she is entitled to under her Individual Education Plan from this point on;
- ask what the school intends to do to help Shirley catch up with the help she has missed over the last term.

You should make the headteacher aware that you know that the governors of the school have a legal duty to 'use their best endeavours' to meet Shirley's needs, and ask whether the governors have been made aware of the situation, which presumably has affected other children as well as Shirley.

If that doesn't work

At the meeting you will almost certainly receive an apology for what has happened. But you may not get a promise of immediate help for Shirley or extra help to make up for what she has missed over the last term.

2

Case
5

In which case, you might consider writing direct to the chair of the school governors, pointing out their failure to fulfil their duty towards Shirley and asking formally for immediate action to resume her special help and for some extra help in the short term. Your letter could begin like this:

> *To: The Chair of the Governing Body,*
>
> *Dear Sir or Madam,*
>
> *I am writing as the parent of a pupil at your school, Shirley ..., who has special educational needs. I have only recently discovered that for the last eight weeks Shirley has not been receiving the special provision set out in her Individual Education Plan. This is because the teacher who is supposed to work with her has left. I have discussed the situation with the headteacher, but she is unable to give me a date when Shirley's help will be resumed and is unable to assure me that additional provision will be made available to Shirley in the short term to help overcome the effects of the help which has been lost to her.*
>
> *I am writing to ask you to take action which will fulfil your legal duty to 'use your best endeavours' to ensure that Shirley's needs (and the needs of other children who may be similarly affected) are met ...*

If this gets you nowhere, you could make a formal complaint to the Secretary of State on the grounds that the governing body is failing to fulfil its duty under the 1996 Education Act and under the Code of Practice. But before doing this, you should discuss the situation with one of the support organisations listed in part 8.

2

Case 5

What the law says

Section 317(1)(a) of the 1996 Education Act says:

'The governing body ... shall ... use their best endeavours, in exercising their functions in relation to the school, to secure that, if any registered pupil has special educational needs, the special educational provision which his learning difficulty calls for is made.'

What the Code of Practice says

'A child with special educational needs should have their needs met.'

(Paragraph 1:5)

PostScript

'Sorry' is not really good enough when a child has been denied the help she needs and to which she is legally entitled. So when you do have to complain to school, try to suggest something positive they can do which will actually help your child catch up on what she has missed.

This has benefits for your relationship with the school, as it offers a way for them to deal with a problem themselves, saving them the embarrassment of having a parent make a formal complaint to the Secretary of State. This might seem like a gentle form of blackmail ... but everyone stands to gain from a friendly conclusion to a dispute between parents and school, particularly the child involved.

Case 6

❝ Jasvinder is 8 and she was born with mild cerebral palsy. She has fine motor problems and needs coaching in using a ruler and protractor and with forming her letters and numbers. Her Individual Education Plan for last term gave her support in the classroom for three lessons a week by a non-teaching assistant. But Jasvinder has not been happy with this because she is embarrassed in front of the other children to be receiving individual help. It has not helped matters that her mother tongue is Punjabi and she is not very good at English. To make it worse, there is a small group of children in her class who taunt her, saying 'Where's your baby minder?' and calling her racist names.

Jasvinder is making very little progress and I think if she could have her help in a withdrawal situation for a while, away from the class, she might thrive. I've mentioned this on a number of occasions at the school, but of course I am just her mother, so no-one listens to my views. ❞

The first step

The Code of Practice says schools should take the views of parents and children seriously. And, if there is evidence that Jasvinder is failing to meet the targets set out in her individual education plan, they should already be questioning the arrangements for her help.

You should ask the headteacher for a meeting. Take someone with you who knows the points you want to make. At the meeting, explain:

- That you are very happy with the amount of help Jasvinder is receiving and with the efforts being made by her assistant, but ...
- That you do not believe that the best use is being made of the assistant's time because Jasvinder is not able to benefit from being helped in the classroom as much as you believe

25

2

Case

6

she would by being helped in a one-to-one situation away from the classroom. You should remind the headteacher that the school's basic duty is to ensure that where a child has special educational needs, 'the special educational provision which (his or her) learning difficulty calls for is made.' In-class support does not seem, at present, to be the provision which Jasvinder's learning difficulties 'call for'.

- That you agree it is important for Jasvinder to overcome her embarrassment about being given extra help, but that it is more important for her to be making real progress towards the objectives set out for her in her Individual Education Plan.

- That you are not asking for Jasvinder to be withdrawn as a solution to the abuse she is receiving from other children in the class, and that you would like to know what action the school takes to curb this kind of bullying between children.

If that doesn't work

If the meeting gets you nowhere, you should put your views and requests in writing and send them to the chair of the governors. For help with the wording of the letter, ring one of the support organisations listed in part 8. If the governors ignore your request, you are going to need more detailed advice and support from one of the Helpline organisations.

What the law says

Section 317(1)(a) of the 1996 Education Act says:

'The governing body ... shall ... use their best endeavours, in exercising their functions in relation to the school, to secure that, if any registered pupil has special educational needs, the special educational provision which his learning difficulty calls for is made.'

What the Code of Practice says

'A child with special educational needs should have their needs met.'

(Paragraph 1:5)

'Those responsible for special educational provision (should) take into account the wishes of the child concerned in the light of their age and understanding.'

(Paragraph 1:6)

'Special education professionals (should) take into account the views of individual parents in respect of their child's particular needs.'

(Paragraph 1:6)

Post Script

Remember that the main duty which the law on special education places on school governors is 'to use their best endeavours' to ensure that children with special needs get the help they need.

At the end of the day, this is a stronger duty than the duty to follow the particulars of the Code. So, although it is important for parents to keep the school up to scratch on its adherence to the Code of Practice, in terms of taking account of parents' and children's views, Jasvinder's mother's most important argument is that the in-class support is failing to enable Jasvinder to meet the targets set out in her Individual Education Plan. If there is clear evidence to show this, then on this basis alone, regardless of whether the school has followed the Code in detail, they should be prepared to re-examine the arrangements made for Jasvinder's help.

Case 7

❝❝ Lloyd has just turned 14 and has been getting into trouble at school for some time. He has a casual manner towards teachers which some of them find difficult to tolerate. Over the last year he has been given a series of punishments (detention, placed on report, temporary exclusion from school) which he considers petty and unjust. His respect for the teachers has taken a nose-dive and so has the school's tolerance of him.

I was called to a meeting last week by the head and informed that Lloyd had been the subject of a 'stormy' house case conference and that a majority of his teachers wanted the LEA to do an assessment of Lloyd's special educational needs under section 323 of the 1996 Education Act. Apparently they believe that Lloyd has emotional and behavioural difficulties and that he should be in a special school. When I objected, on the grounds that Lloyd does not have special educational needs, he said that he would ask for an educational psychologist to visit and see him, to give an expert opinion. I don't want Lloyd seen by a psychologist. What can I do? ❞❞

The first step

Parents cannot be forced to produce their children for examination by an educational psychologist unless an LEA is considering doing an assessment under section 323 of the 1996 Education Act.

Nor can a headteacher decide that an LEA assessment should be carried out. They can request this, but the decision is for the LEA to make.

So there are some things you need not worry about. However, it is clear that Lloyd and the school are not getting on and that won't help his education. You say that his attitude irritates 'some' of his teachers. Does that mean that there are other 'more positive' members of the teaching staff who might speak up for him? If so, I think you should have a word with one of them in confidence and ask their advice on what, if anything, can be done to overcome the problems between Lloyd and the other teachers.

It might also help if someone Lloyd trusts could have a heart to heart with him over his attitude to the school. For although the headteacher can't force the LEA to do an assessment, what he can do is exclude Lloyd from the school. It is important that both you and Lloyd understand the risk to his education if a solution to this problem cannot be found.

Try for another meeting with the head and ask for the Special Education Needs Coordinator to be present and, if possible, one of the teachers Lloyd *does* get on with. You should ask if Lloyd can also be present.

At the meeting you should try to get answers to these questions:

- How does the school see Lloyd's problems? Is he, for example, on the school's Action or Action Plus stages? Has the Special Education Needs Coordinator any responsibility for him?
- What extra help so far has the school been able to give Lloyd?
- Is there anything in addition that they believe might help Lloyd cope with the school, and vice versa?
- What do they believe you, as parent, can do to help Lloyd and the school?

Following this meeting, you should have a clearer idea of whether it is going to be possible for the school and Lloyd to overcome their problems. You will also know whether the school has good enough grounds for asking the LEA to do an assessment. For example, if Lloyd is not on the school's Action or Action Plus stages and has not received any special

Case 7

PostScript

Case 7

Some schools do use the threat of requesting a special needs assessment as a way of dealing with a discipline problem. And sometimes they follow through on that threat. Although it may be possible for a parent to argue against an assessment, the LEA have the legal power to undertake an assessment of any child over the age of 2 if they believe it is necessary. Either way, that still leaves the problems between the school and the child to be tackled. It is obviously no solution if the head immediately excludes a child. A parent faced with this situation needs to do two things: consider whether a transfer of school might not be in their child's best interests; and, get immediate advice on their rights and their child's rights from one of the support organisations listed in part 8.

Case 8

❝ The headteacher of my daughter's primary school attended the latest review of her Individual Education Plan and suggested that it would best for Ann if we agreed to an immediate transfer to a special unit, where she could be assessed for special education by the LEA. We have also asked the LEA to do an assessment, but we are not happy with Ann being moved to a special school for the assessment, as we always hoped that she would have her needs met in an ordinary school, whether statemented or not. What can we do? ❞

The first step

If you have not already done so, you should let the headteacher know that you are not in agreement with his proposal for a transfer to a special school. The law says that this cannot happen unless professionals *and* parents agree.

The simplest thing to do is to write a short letter to the headteacher, putting your views on record. Your letter could begin like this:

> *Dear ...,*
>
> *I am writing to you to put on record the fact that we do not agree to Ann being placed in a special school during her assessment for special educational provision. We understand that this cannot happen without our agreement as parents, and we are sending a copy of this letter to the Local Education Authority so that they also know our views.*

Case 9

6 6 My nephew, Tin Wo, is making slow progress at school. Tin Wo is 9 and came from Hong Kong to live with us last year when his father died. He spends most of his time learning English as a second language. The school refuse to accept that he may have a learning difficulty other than his need to learn English. We phoned the LEA but they refused our request for an assessment, saying they agreed with the school and that Tin Wo had to go through school Action and Action Plus before they would assess him. But we believe his language difficulties are hiding his special needs. His spoken Cantonese is limited and he can't read it. We believe that he would have learning difficulties whatever language he was taught in. 9 9

The first step

Your LEA seems to believe that Tin Wo's learning difficulties arise solely because the language in which he is being taught (English) is different from his 'home' language. On these grounds they can, quite legally, exclude him from special educational provision.

As a first step you should try to collect as much evidence as you can that Tin Wo's difficulties cannot be solely explained by language difference. This evidence could come, for example, from a Cantonese-speaking teacher who would know what level of language development to expect in a child of Tin Wo's age. This person may also be able to do some other assessment work with Tin Wo, observing his manipulative skills, trying out some maths, checking his general knowledge, etc. Ask the teacher to put his or her views in writing.

It might also help to ask your family doctor if he/she has any comments to make on Tin Wo's physical development and, if this seems helpful, again ask for it in writing.

In law, children do not have to be on, or have passed through, the Action or Action Plus stages before they can be considered for statutory assessment.

Ring one of the support organisations listed in part 8 for further advice on getting evidence on Tin Wo's learning difficulties. A second professional opinion may help.

2

Case 9

When you have as much information as you can collect, write (don't phone!) to the LEA, asking for an assessment, and send them all of your evidence. Your letter could start off like this:

To: The Chief Education Officer

Dear Sir or Madam,

I am writing as the guardian of Cheung Tin Wo to request an assessment under section 323 of the 1996 Education Act. I make this request as is my right under section 329 of the same Act and I understand that you have a duty to reply to this letter within 6 weeks.

My reasons for asking for an assessment are ...
... I have enclosed copies of letters and reports which support my opinion that Tin Wo has special educational needs which call for the LEA to undertake an assessment.

If that doesn't work

If the LEA refuse your written request, you will have the right to appeal to the Tribunal. Your argument would be based on the belief that Tin Wo has learning difficulties which have nothing to do with his mother-tongue language being different from the language of the school. The evidence you collected together in the hopes of persuading the LEA to do an assessment will be useful to you if you appeal, but you

Case 10

❝ The school told us they can't give George the help he needs so we asked the LEA to do an assessment. The LEA have written saying that George's needs are 'not severe and complex' and that he does not fall within the 2% of pupils who need statements. Surely the school knows better than the officer from the LEA whether George needs more help than they can give him? After all, they've been teaching him for four years now, whereas the officer hasn't even met him. ❞

The first step

LEAs have a duty to assess a child if a parent requests it, unless they consider that an assessment is not 'necessary.' In practice, an assessment is not necessary if a child does not have special educational needs, or if it is clear that the school can make the provision required to meet his or her needs. When the LEA inform parents that they do not believe an assessment is necessary, they must also inform them of their right to appeal to the Special Educational Needs Tribunal. In addition, the Code of Practice says that LEAs should write to parents and 'explain the reasons' for their decision not to assess a child. George's needs may not be 'severe and complex' and he may not be one of the 2% of children who have the greatest difficulties in our schools, but these reasons, on their own, do not justify the LEA deciding that they will not assess him. As well as seeking advice on appealing to the Tribunal, you should write back to the LEA and remind them what the Code says about giving full reasons and about the basis on which they should make decisions on whether to assess individual children. Your letter could start like this:

To: The Chief Education Officer

Dear Sir or Madam,

Your letter informing us of the decision not to assess our son, George ..., did not contain the information it should, according to paragraph 7:69 of the Code of Practice. It did not 'explain the reasons' for your decision. Would you please write to us again, this time setting out your reasons in detail.

Would you also please read that section of the Code of Practice which gives LEAs guidance on the criteria for deciding to make an assessment, that is paragraph 7:34. You will see that it makes no mention of a child's needs being 'severe or complex', nor that a child must be among the 2% of the most disabled children in our schools before an assessment can be done. Perhaps you are quoting from another section of the Code or from the 1996 Education Act or the Regulations? If so, we would be grateful if you would give us the references so that we can check for ourselves ...

Our reasons for believing that you have a duty to assess George are ...

2

Case 10

If that doesn't work

If the LEA refuse to give reasons for not deciding to assess George, you will be able to point this out to the Tribunal. Your own case will need to focus on George's needs and the evidence from the school that, despite the help they have given, he is not making progress. Any reports that you have from the school and from reviews of his Individual Education Plan may help you (see part 3 of this book).

What the law says

Section 323 of the 1996 Education Act says:

'(1) Where a local education authority are of the opinion that a child for whom they are responsible falls, or probably falls, within subsection (2), they shall serve a notice on the child's parent informing him –

(a) that they propose to make an assessment of the child's educational needs ...

(2) A child falls within this subsection if –

(a) he has special educational needs, and

(b) it is necessary for the authority to determine the special educational provision which any learning difficulty he may have calls for.'

What the Code of Practice says

'If the LEA decide it is not necessary to carry out a statutory assessment they **must** write to the parent and explain the reasons' (emphasis in the Code).

(Paragraph 7:69)

'In deciding whether to make a statutory assessment, the critical question is whether there is convincing evidence that, despite the school, with the help of external specialists, taking relevant and purposeful action to meet the child's learning difficulties, those difficulties remain or have not been remedied sufficiently and may require the LEA to determine the child's special educational provision.'

(Paragraph 7:34)

Post Script

LEAs should make the decision on assessing a child on the basis of that individual child's needs and the provision which is available to him in his or her school, without the benefit of the extra resources which a statement can bring. Whenever you hear an LEA laying down general rules about when they assess children or make statements – such as 'we only assess the severely disabled, or the 2%, or children over 5, or children who are on the Action Plus stage' – you should immediately suspect that they are acting against the intentions of the law on special education. When you suspect this, you should get immediate advice from one of the support organisations listed in part 8. See also the PS to case 1.

Case 11

❝ We have been waiting for six months for the LEA to start an assessment of our son Duane under the 1996 Education Act. The school says they sent in a request to the LEA immediately after the last review of his Individual Education Plan, but we have heard nothing and it is coming up to time for the next review. Duane is slipping further and further behind with his reading and writing and we are getting really desperate to get him some extra help. ❞

The first step

Either the school, the LEA or both are at fault here. The LEA should have responded long before now to the school's request for assessment within 6 weeks, either by writing to you proposing an assessment, or by informing you and the school that they did not think an assessment was necessary – in which case, you would have the right of appeal to the SEN Tribunal.

Ask the headteacher to give you the date when the request was sent to the LEA, and to copy you the letter. Perhaps things did not happen as promptly as they should have.

However, if it is clear that the LEA failed to respond to the head's request within 6 weeks, as the law says they must, you should write to the Chief Officer, like this:

To: The Chief Education Officer

Dear Sir or Madam,

I am writing to inform you that I believe your Authority are in breach of their legal duty to respond within 6 weeks to a request for statutory assessment of my son's special educational needs. This request was posted to you by the headteacher of Duane's school on February 26th, which is now almost 6 months ago.

Case

11

(b) a maintained nursery school,
(c) a pupil referral unit,
(d) an independent school,
(e) a school approved under section 342.

(13) 'The responsible body' means –

(a) in relation to a maintained nursery school or a pupil referral unit, the head teacher,
(b) in relation to any other relevant school, the proprietor or head teacher, and
(c) in relation to a provider of relevant nursery education, the person or body of persons responsible for the management of the provision of that nursery education.'

The Education (Special Educational Needs) Regulations 2001 say:

'Where section 329A applies an authority shall within 6 weeks of the date of receipt of a request from a responsible body that an assessment be made, give notice to that body –

(a) of their decision to make an assessment...or
(b) of their decision not to assess the educational needs of the child...

(4) Where section 329A applies an authority shall, within 6 weeks of the date of receipt of a request from a responsible body that an assessment be made, give notice to the child's parent –

(a) of –

    (i) their decision to make an assessment...or

(b) of –

    (i) their decision not to assess the educational needs of the child and their reasons for making that decision.

> (v) the parent's right to appeal to the Tribunal against the decision not to make an assessment.'
>
> (Regulation 12(3))

'Where under sections 328(2) or 329(1) a parent asks the authority to arrange for an assessment to be made they shall within 6 weeks of the date of receipt of the request give notice to the child's parent –

(a) of –

  (i) their decision to make an assessment ... or

(b) of –

  (i) their determination not to comply with the parent's request ...

  (v) The parent's right to appeal to the Tribunal against the determination not to make an assessment.'

(Regulation 12(2))

'An authority need not comply with the time limits referred to in paragraphs (1) to (4) if it is impractical to do so because –

(a) the authority have requested advice from the head-teacher of a school during a period beginning one week before any date on which that school was closed for a continuous period of not less than 4 weeks from that date and ending one week before the date on which it re-opens ...

(b) the authority have requested advice from the head of SEN in relation to or other person responsible for a child's education at an early education provider during a period beginning 1 week before any date on which that early education provider was closed for a continuous period of not less than 4 weeks from that date and ending 1 week before the date on which it re-opens;

2

Case 11

(c) exceptional personal circumstances affect the child or his parent during the 6 week period referred to in paragraphs (1) to (3); or

(d) the child or his parent are absent from the area of the authority for a continuous period of not less than 4 weeks during the 6 week period referred to in paragraphs (1) to (4).'

(Regulation 12(5))

What the Code of Practice says

'It is important that all requests and referrals for assessment are considered as quickly as possible regardless of their source.'

(Paragraph 7:8)

Post Script

It is always safer to request an assessment yourself, as a parent, rather than leaving it to the school.

However, it is helpful if a head teacher writes *in support of* a parent's request, so this is worth asking for.

An LEA's grounds for refusing an assessment are rarely that a child does not have special needs, but that the school already has the resources needed to meet those needs. What parents usually need to argue at an appeal, then, is that the school is not able to meet their child's needs. It is important to have evidence that progress is not being made, despite the help given by a school.

Case 12

❝ We are about to ask for our son to be assessed for the first time by the LEA, but we've heard that they are not keeping to the legal time limits on assessments. What are the time limits, and what can we do if the LEA ignore them? ❞

The first step

Here is a chart which shows the legal timetable for assessments:

You or a headteacher or head of nursery ask the LEA to assess your child or the LEA write proposing an assessment	*LEA have 6 weeks to decide whether or not to do an assessment*
LEA decide to assess your child	*LEA have 10 weeks to complete the assessment (that's 16 weeks so far)*
LEA complete assessment and decide if statement is needed	*LEA have 2 weeks to decide if statement is needed (that's 18 weeks so far)*
LEA decide not to make a statement, or issue proposed statement and invite parents' comments	*LEA have 8 weeks to consider parents' comments before finalising the statement (that's 26 weeks from assessment being requested)*

The first step is to mark the date on your calendar two working days after the request is posted (first class). Then count forward six weeks, and write: 'LEA refuse, or assessment begins.' Then count forward another ten weeks and write 'Assessment should end.' Two weeks later write 'Proposed statement.' Then eight weeks after that write 'Statement finalised.'

This is the timetable the LEA should work to. Of course, you can't assume that they have done something just because the date comes round on the calendar. If you have not heard anything by the beginning of the week after one of your marked dates, you should telephone to find out what is happening. Get new dates from them for the following deadlines and adjust your calendar. (You will also have to change your calendar if the LEA move more quickly through some of the stages.)

Case

12

If the deadlines are not met

LEAs do not have to keep to the first six-week deadline if it is impractical for them to do so because:

- they have requested advice from a headteacher or nursery head in the period from one week before the school/ nursery was about to close for four weeks (normally, the summer holiday) until one week before it was about to open again;
- there were exceptional personal circumstances affecting you or your child during the six weeks;
- you or your child were absent from the area for four weeks during the first six weeks.

LEAs do not have to keep to the ten-week deadline for assessment if it is impractical for them to do so because:

- the LEA decided they needed further advice on a child's needs, in an exceptional case;
- the LEA agreed to consider advice provided by the parents six weeks or more after the advice was requested;
- the LEA requested advice from a headteacher or nursery head in the period from one week before the school/ nursery was about to close for four weeks (normally, the summer holiday) until one week before it was about to open again;
- the health authority or the social services department have failed to provide their advice within the six-week deadline given them in law;
- there were exceptional personal circumstances affecting a parent or child during the ten weeks;
- a child or parent was absent from the area for four weeks during the first ten weeks;

Case 12

- the child failed to keep an appointment for an examination or test.

If your LEA fail to meet a deadline, you must give them the opportunity to explain. They must show not only that one of the situations listed above has occurred, but also that it has made the deadline *impractical*. If you are not happy with their explanation, you should contact one of the support organisations listed in part 8 of this book for advice. You may need to make a formal complaint to the Secretary of State for Education on the grounds that the LEA are failing to fulfil their legal duty towards your child. See page 270 for advice on complaining to the Secretary of State.

What the law says

*Regulations 12 and 17 of the Education (Special Educational Needs)
Regulations 2001 list all of the deadlines
(see pages 331–334 and 337–339).*

What the Code of Practice says

'It is important that all requests and referrals for assessment are considered as quickly as possible regardless of their source.'

(Paragraph 7:8)

'... the LEA should take all parental requests seriously and take appropriate action.'

(Paragraph 7:22)

Post Script

The deadlines do not prevent an LEA acting more quickly, if you feel that is needed. For example, if the school supports your request for assessment and sends in the information required at the same time as you ask as a parent, then the LEA may be able to reach their decision well before the six weeks are up. If your child needs help urgently, press your LEA to act before the deadline dates are reached wherever possible.

2

Case

12

The envelopes are important! For the purposes of the deadlines on assessments, the key dates are the ones on which letters and documents are posted, not when they are dated. So, it is important to keep the envelopes with letters. If a 2nd class stamp is used, documents are counted as having arrived four working days after the postmark on the envelope. If a 1st class stamp is used, documents are counted as arriving two working days after the postmark.

Many parents find it useful to keep all documents relating to their child's special educational needs in a file, in date order. This certainly helps when you ring an organisation for advice.

Case 13

66 The assessment of our son, Charles, has now taken almost six months. The special needs officer says that they are unable to complete it because neither the health authority nor the social services department have sent in their advice. Who can I complain to in order to get things moving? 99

The first step

The first thing you must do is get the facts straight about who did what, when.

Both the social services department and the health authority should have been notified about the possibility of Charles being assessed at the time you or the head asked for the assessment or when the LEA proposed it. Then, when the LEA decided to go ahead with the assessment, both bodies would have been asked to send written advice on Charles.

The law allows health authorities and social service departments six weeks to send advice to LEAs. However, there are circumstances which may make it impractical for them to meet the deadline:

- if exceptional personal circumstances affect the child or his parent during the six-week period;
- if the child or her parent are absent from the area for a period of four weeks during the six-week period;
- if the child fails to keep an appointment for an examination or a test made by either the health authority or the social services department during the six-week period;
- if the health authority and the social services department had no information on the child before they received the initial notification from the LEA.

If none of these circumstances apply, or if you still believe that it was practicable for the deadline to be met, you should write to the special needs officer and ask for answers to these questions:

- On what date were the health authority and social services departments notified that the assessment had been requested or proposed?
- On what date did the LEA send in the requests for advice?
- What are the names and addresses of the people in the health authority and the social services department to whom the requests for advice were sent?

When you have this information, write directly to the people responsible and ask for an explanation of the delay. Also ask to be told a firm date by which they intend to send their advice to the LEA.

If that doesn't work

If these letters fail to get things moving, you will need expert advice from an organisation with experience of complaints against health authorities and social services departments. Your local Citizens Advice Bureau or Local Law Centre will be able to advise you whom to contact.

What the law says

Regulation 12 of the Education (Special Educational Needs) Regulations 2001 says:

'(8) Subject to paragraphs (9), (10) and (11), where an authority have requested advice from a health authority or a social services authority under regulation 7(1)(c) or (e) respectively the health authority or social services authority shall comply with that request within 6 weeks of the date on which they receive it.

(9) A health authority or a social services authority need not comply with the time limit referred to in paragraph (8) if it is impractical to do so because –

(a) exceptional personal circumstances affect the child or his parent during the 6 week period referred to in paragraph (8);

(b) the child or his parent are absent from the area of the authority for a continuous period of not less than 4 weeks during the 6 week period referred to in paragraph (8); or

(c) the child fails to keep an appointment for an examination or a test made by the health authority or a social services authority respectively during the 6 week period referred to in paragraph (8).

(10) A health authority need not comply with the time limit referred to in paragraph (8) if they have not before the date on which a copy of a notice has been served on them in accordance with the regulation (6)(2), (6)(4) or (6)(5) produced or maintained any information or records relevant to the assessment of the child.

(11) A social services authority need not comply with the time limit referred to in paragraph (8) if they have not before the date on which a copy of a notice has been served on them in accordance with regulation (6)(2), (6)(4) or (6)(5) produced or maintained any information or records relevant to the assessment of the child.

What the Code of Practice says

'LEAs should always strive to ensure that any delay arising from the exceptions is kept to a minimum. As soon as the conditions which have led to an exception no longer apply, the LEA should endeavour to complete the process as quickly as possible.'

(Paragraph 7:93)

PostScript

If there has been a delay, this is the best possible argument for your LEA pressing on as quickly as they can once the problem has been overcome. Ask to be given, in writing, the date on which the assessment will be completed. Mark this new deadline on a calendar and make sure the LEA sticks to it.

2

Case

13

Case 14

66 We are getting increasingly anxious about the special education assessment we've requested for our son, Jamie. First the headteacher told us that we would be able to be present when Jamie was assessed. But now we've had a letter from the Psychologist saying that she does not believe in parents being present at examinations because it can distract children. We understand this, but Jamie is a very timid child and he is worried sick about being taken away on his own and given tests that he won't be able to do. We are all losing sleep over it now and we are beginning to think we've done the wrong thing by asking for an assessment. What exactly are our rights as parents? 99

The first step

Your rights with regard to your child being examined are as follows:

- If an LEA is considering making an assessment of Jamie under section 323 of the 1996 Education Act, you will be given a time and a date and a place to take him for psychological examination. If you fail to take him without a good reason, you *may* be prosecuted.
- However, it is only when LEAs are considering making an assessment under section 323 that you can be prosecuted for failing to produce your child for examination.
- The Code of Practice is wrong, however, when it says that LEAs can require parents to produce their children for examination as part of a statutory assessment. The law gives them no power to prosecute parents who do not cooperate in this situation.
- Parents have an absolute right in law to be present at any examination of their child which takes place when an LEA is considering making a section 323 assessment.
- The Code of Practice advises that sometimes a parent's presence can be off-putting for the child and cause her to

Case

14

behave differently than she otherwise would (paragraph 7:75). Therefore, the Code suggests, it might be best in some circumstances if parents are not present. However, the decision is for individual parents to make. If you believe that it is important for you to be present when your child is examined, then you have the legal right to insist on it.

Unfortunately, professionals do sometimes give parents wrong information about special education assessment. If you are in this situation, you should ask for a meeting with the Special Needs Officer. Inform him/her of the wrong information you have been given and ask for confirmation of the correct position.

If that doesn't work

If the officer will not meet you, you should write a letter, enclosing photocopies of the relevant parts of the law which are being misrepresented by the authority's professionals. Your letter could say something along these lines:

To: The Special Needs Officer

Dear...,

I am very concerned that parents whose children have special educational needs may be given wrong information about their rights in law by professionals employed by the authority, and I believe that this is a situation which requires some response from you as an officer for the authority.

Specifically, I have recently received the enclosed letter...

You should also contact one of the support organisations listed in part 8 and speak to someone about the problems you are having with your LEA.

What the law says

The 1996 Education Act says:

'Where a local authority are considering whether to make an assessment, they may serve a notice on the parent of the child concerned requiring the child's attendance for examination in accordance with the provision of the notice.'

(Schedule 26 paragraph 4(1))

Case 14

'The parent of a child examined under this paragraph may be present at the examination if he so desires.'

(Schedule 26 paragraph 4(2))

'Any parent who fails without reasonable excuse to comply with any requirements of a notice served on him under paragraph 4 above commits an offence if the notice relates to a child who is not over compulsory school age at the time stated in it as the time for holding the examination.'

(Schedule 26 paragraph 5(1))

What the Code of Practice says

'Parents **must** also be informed of their right to be present with their child at any interview, test, medical or other assessment which is being conducted and should be told of the time and place of appointments. They must also be told the name of an LEA officer from whom they can obtain further information, and that they have a right to submit information to the LEA if they want to. Parents should be told that, whilst it is their right to be present, in certain circumstances it may be counterproductive: for instance, where a classroom observation is carried out as part of an assessment, a child will behave differently if his or her parent is present, which would negate the purpose of the observation.'

(Paragraph 7:75)

PostScript

Much of the information in the Code of Practice is an explanation of what the law says and means. But the Code is not the law itself. When there is a contradiction between what the Code says and what the law says on a particular point, you must be guided by the law. In this situation, for example, the Code appears to be wrong in saying that parents must produce children for examination as part of statutory assessment, or risk prosecution. For what the law says is that this requirement (and threat) arises when LEAs are 'considering whether to assess', not actually doing an assessment.

Where the Code and the law say the same thing, quote directly from the law and not the Code. This is because LEAs have a stronger duty to obey the law than they do the Code.

In general, it is best not to rely too much on what professionals such as educational psychologists (EPs) tell you about the law on special education and your LEA's duties. They do not always know that much about it. To be safe, if you are in doubt about what you have been told about your rights as a parent or your child's rights, speak to someone from one of the support organisations listed in part 8 of this book.

Case 15

66 We feel we've been tricked. Our son's headteacher advised us to ask the LEA for an assessment in order that the school could have more help with managing his behaviour. We did this and the assessment is almost done. But today we've received a letter telling us that Reace has been excluded from school till the Easter holidays, which is almost 6 weeks away. The head says that the school does not have the resources to cope with Reace. We know that, that's why we asked for the assessment. Does this mean that the head won't have Reace in his school when the assessment is finished? Will any other school have him now? 99

The first step

The first step is for you to think very seriously about whether you want Reace to go back to this school when his statement is issued, and to involve Reace in this decision as much as possible. It may be that you feel so let down by the headteacher that you don't want anything to do with him or his school in the future. This would be understandable. However, try and put your frustration on one side and focus just on the question of a school for Reace.

If you want Reace to return to his existing school despite what has happened because you really feel that this school is the best one for your son, then you should try to meet with the headteacher as soon as possible. Ask him:

- why, now that the assessment is almost complete and extra help is hopefully at hand, did he have to exclude Reace? Was there really no alternative that could have been found as a short-term solution?
- did he speak to the LEA to see if there was any temporary support they could have offered Reace and the school, until the statement was issued?

- would he support you, now, if you approached the LEA to ask for temporary support to be made available? If the LEA will help, will he lift the exlcusion, given that you are going to be asking for his school to be named on Reace's statement?
- is he aware of the guidance in DfEE Circular 10/99 on exclusion and in particular what it has to say about children with special educational needs? (see below)

If the head does not respond positively at your meeting, you should put these points to the Governors when they (or their Discipline Committee) meet – as they must – to discuss this exclusion.

The meeting with the head and/or the governors is likely to be difficult. Contact one of the support organisations listed in part 8 to see if they can arrange for someone to go with you.

If that does not work

If neither the head, the governors nor the LEA are prepared to help, you should at least insist on work being sent home for Reace (see *What the courts have said*), but then arrange to meet your local Councillor as a matter of urgency. Ask them to approach the Chair of the Education Committee for your LEA with a strong request that they now complete Reace's assessment and issue a statement as a matter of absolute urgency, given that he is going to be out of school now for at least 8 weeks (the excluded period plus the Easter holiday). You will get the names of Councillors for your area from the Town Hall, the library or the Citizen's Advice Bureau. At the same time, get the name and address of your MP, and write to them about the situation you and Reace are now in.

You will be informed of your right to appeal to the Exclusion Appeal Committee, but this always takes time and as it is possible that the 6 weeks' exclusion will have passed before you get a decision, this is less useful to Reace than your putting pressure on the LEA to complete the assessment and issue the statement as quickly as possible and to put some interim support in the school in the meantime so that the head will reconsider the exclusion.

If you don't want Reace to return to the same school, but want him to go to another mainstream school, it will still be important to get the LEA to complete the assessment as a matter of urgency and your local Councillor and MP may be able to help with this.

However, you must also try to find another school which you and Reace would be happy with and which would be happy to take him. It is best to visit and talk face to face with staff (particularly headteachers and SENCOs when a child has special educational needs). Be absolutely open about what has happened with regard to the assessment being underway and what led to the exclusion. Heads talk to each other on the phone, so there is nothing to be gained by withholding information.

If you want Reace to go to a special school, again it is important for the assessment to be completed quickly, but, in this case, if you know the actual special school you want to be named on the statement, you should write to the LEA and ask if they will arrange for Reace to attend immediately, while the assessment is being completed.

If that doesn't work (either)

Do not feel guilty or useless as a parent if this situation is both puzzling and frustrating. Schools have their reasons for excluding children, of course, but it can be the cruelest and least helpful action imaginable for a child with special educational needs and their parents. You will probably need detailed advice and advocacy and someone who can attend probably three or four meetings with you, before matters are resolved. Contact one of the support organisations in part 8.

2

Case 15

You should bear in mind that once the proposed statement is sent, you will have the right to express a preference for school to be named in part 4 and the head and governors of whatever school is named on the statement will have a legal duty to accept Reace. At the end of the day, then, it will be the LEA's decision which school Reace attends, not the school's. (see 'What the courts have said').

Case

15

What the law says

The 1996 Education Act says:

'(2) Section 316(2) does not require a child to be educated in a mainstream school during any period in which – ...

(c) he is admitted to a special school, following a change in his circumstances, with the agreement of –

    (i)   the local education authority,

    (ii) the headteacher of the school, or if the school is in Wales, the governing body, and

    (iii) his parent.'

(Section 316A)

'If the name of a maintained school is specified in the statement, the governing body of the school shall admit the child to the school.'

(Section 324(5)(b))

What the courts have said

In a judgement known as *R v Chair of Governors and Headteacher of A and S School ex parte T [2000] ELR 274*, the mother of a boy with a statement sought Judicial Review when the governors of the school named on the statement refused to accept her son. The court ruling made clear that governors' duty in law under section 324(5)(b) was absolute.

In the case of *R v East Sussex County Council ex parte T [1998] ELR 251,* the House of Lords ruled that when an LEA make provision at home for a child who cannot attend school, under Section 19 of the Education Act 1996, they must provide what is necessary, not just what they feel they can afford.

Case 15

Although the girl involved in this case did not have a Statement of Special Educational Needs the judgement is potentially useful in situations where children with Statements are excluded or are out of school because of a dispute between their parents and the LEA.

In the final judgement the House of Lords ruled:

'There is nothing in the Act to suggest that resource considerations are relevant to the question of what is "suitable education". On their face those words connote a standard to be determined purely by educational considerations. This view is much strengthened by the definition of "suitable education" in section 298(7) (now section 19(7) EA 1996) which spells out expressly the factors which are relevant to the determination of suitability, viz. the education must be "efficient" and "suitable to his age, ability and aptitude" and also suitable "to any special education needs he may have". All these express factors relate to educational considerations and nothing else. There is nothing to indicate that the resources available are relevant ... '

What the Code of Practice says

'In exceptional cases it may be necessary to make an emergency placement for a child, for example where ... the parents, school, relevant professionals and the LEA agree that a sudden and serious deterioration in the child's behaviour make the child's current placement untenable or unsafe.'

(Paragraph 8:23)

2

**Case
15**

What DfEE Circular 10/99 says:

6.10 The level of exclusions for pupils with a statement of SEN is extremely high; the most recent data show that the permanent exclusion rate for such pupils was seven times higher than for pupils without a statement. Other than in the most exceptional circumstances, schools should avoid permanently excluding pupils with statements. In most cases, the head teacher will be aware that the school, whether mainstream or special, is having difficulty managing a statemented pupil's behaviour well before the situation has escalated. Schools should try every practicable means to maintain placements, including seeking LEA and other professional advice as appropriate. Where this process has been exhausted, the school should liaise with the LEA about initiating an 'interim' annual review of the statement.

6.11 Where a child is excluded from a special school during the period between the head teacher's initial decision and the meeting of the governing body, the head teacher should work with the LEA to see whether more support can be made available, or whether the statement can be changed to name a new school. If either of these options is possible, the head teacher should normally withdraw the exclusion.

6.12 There is some evidence that a significant number of pupils are being excluded from mainstream schools part way through the assessment process. Head teachers should make every effort to avoid this. Although a large and increasing number of exclusions are from schools catering for pupils with EBD, there is evidence that the most effective special schools are very reluctant to exclude their pupils.

PostScript

Remember that the time limits on LEAs for completing assessments are *outside* time limits i.e. LEAs may not take longer than the time limits. But this does not mean that they cannot complete assessments in much shorter times, when they want to or are pushed to. This is why it is always worthwhile in really difficult circumstances – exclusion, for example – to try and get your local Councillor and MP to put pressure on to get things speeded up.

Case 15

Also, it is obvious that when parents simply have no alternative but to go to work, exclusion can put enormous strains on their ability to act in their child's best interests. But remember, if you feel that you have no practical option but to ask for your child to be placed in a special school so that you can continue working while an assessment is completed, this will not remove or in any way lessen your right to argue for a mainstream school to be named on the statement, when the assessment is concluded.

Case 16

❝ We have just received a letter from the LEA telling us that they do not intend to issue a statement for our daughter, following the assessment of her special educational needs. They have also sent us a document called 'A note in lieu of a statement' and copies of all of the advice collected during Sui Ling's assessment. The 'note in lieu' describes her special needs and says that she should have 'occasional non-teaching support as necessary to assist with her personal welfare.' But we do not understand who is going to provide this. The head said the school can't, because the welfare workers are too busy with other children. That's the reason the school asked for Sui Ling to be assessed in the first place. ❞

The first step

You must appeal against the LEA's decision. You have two months to write the notice of appeal and get it to the Special Educational Needs Tribunal. Mark the date on a calendar, to remind you of the deadline, but do your notice of appeal as soon as possible. See part 3 of this guide for advice on appealing and speak to someone from one of the support organisations listed in part 8.

Then, ask the named officer if he or she will arrange a meeting between the school, the LEA and yourself in order to discuss the note in lieu, as suggested in the Code of Practice (paragraph 8:17). If you can, take someone along to this meeting as support and to take notes on what might be said. One of the support organisations may be able to arrange this for you.

What you should try to bring into the open at the meeting is the headteacher's opinion that the school cannot make the provision Sui Ling needs from its own resources. At the meeting, ask the headteacher:

- What is the school's budget for special educational needs provision and what provision is made out of this budget?
- What help has the school been giving Sui Ling over the last year, and how much, roughly, has this cost?
- Are there any unspent funds under the special needs budget which the school can draw upon to make the provision specified in the 'note in lieu of a statement'?

Take careful note of the answers and (if it would help your case) ask the headteacher to put her views in writing for you. Send a copy to the LEA, with a letter asking them to reconsider their decision not to issue a statement.

If that doesn't work

If they agree, you will be able to withdraw your appeal. If not, you will have to go ahead with it. Perhaps the head will be prepared to appear as a witness on your side? Contact one of the support organisations listed in part 8 for advice.

What the law says

Section 325 of the 1996 Education Act says:

'(1) If, after making an assessment ... of the educational needs of any child for whom no statement is maintained ... the local education authority do not propose to make such a statement, they shall give notice in writing of their decision ...

(2) In such a case, the child's parent may appeal to the Tribunal ...'

What the Code of Practice Says

'The decision not to issue a statement may be disappointing to parents and be seen as a denial of additional resources for their child. The LEA should ensure that the parents (and the school) are aware of the resources available within all maintained schools to meet special educational needs...'

(Paragraph 8:16)

Case 16

PostScript

Headteachers are not used to being asked detailed questions about their school's budget by parents. If she refuses, it might help to remind her that the Tribunal has the power to order that this information is disclosed. This might sound a bit threatening, but it is true. The Tribunal has similar powers to a court of law in terms of summoning witnesses and requiring relevant documents and information to be produced.

Case 17

❝ We had always wanted our son, Jacob, to go to the local primary school along with his sisters. But Jacob has Attention Deficit Disorder and he is a very slow learner. He has just been assessed by the LEA and we have just received the proposed statement and the professional advice. We are very concerned about the psychologist's report. When we spoke to him, after he examined Jacob, he told us that he thought he was going to need more specialist teaching support than the LEA would probably be prepared to give him in a mainstream school. He said: 'If Jacob were my child I'd be looking around at special schools.' But we've combed through his report and he says nothing at all about the amount of help he thinks Jacob needs, or about the kind of school that might be best for him. Does this mean he's changed his mind, or has he been 'leaned on'? ❞

The first step

Now that you have the proposed statement you have the right to ask for a meeting with the officer who is responsible for the statement. You must write and ask for this meeting within 15 days. You also have a right to ask for a meeting with the psychologist to discuss his report. Strictly speaking, you are expected to meet with the officer before requesting a meeting with the psychologist, but as the officer cannot, on his or her own, deal with the problem you have here it would be wise to try and get both the psychologist and the officer together in a room for the first meeting.

This will be a difficult meeting and you should consider taking someone along with you for support (see part 8 for details of organisations which can help). You should also consider writing down the exact points you want to make and the questions you want to ask, so that you can be sure you don't miss out anything you want to say at the meeting. You can also leave the officer and the psychologist with a copy of your points, as a reminder to them.

These are the points you need to raise:

- The law says that written advice must include a professional's opinion on 'the provision which is appropriate for the child.' The EP's advice says nothing about the amount of help Jacob needs, but we know he has an opinion on this because he discussed it with us. Will the EP now say, and put on record, the amount of support - teaching and non-teaching - that he believes Jacob requires? *(If he does, ask that it be written down and attached to the advice.)*
- In law, the type of school is considered to be an aspect of the special education provision. Again, the EP's report contains no opinion on the type of school which might be best for Jacob, although we know the EP does have an opinion on this. Will he now make this clear so that it can be placed on record? *(Again, ask for it to be written down and attached to the original advice.)*

By this point you should, at least, have made sure that EP's full opinion will form part of his written advice and that, therefore, the LEA will have to take account of it when they make their decision about the amount of provision to be specified in Part 3 of the statement and the type of school to be named in Part 4. It should also help you, as parents, to argue for an appropriate amount of help for Jacob in the mainstream school of your preference. And, if the LEA ignore the EP's views and your own views, you will be in a stronger position with regard to a tribunal appeal, having got the EP to 'go on record.'

If that doesn't work

It may be that the meeting gets you no further forward. The officer may say: 'In our authority, we ask professionals to report on children's needs, not on the provision required to meet them. That's *my* decision.' The EP may say: 'I am not allowed to include my opinion on types of school in my professional advice.' Neither of these is in line with the law or the Code of Practice (see below), however you are unlikely to be able to persuade them during the meeting itself to get out their copies of the law and the Code and read them again!

Instead, you should inform them that you will be raising these issues as part of your Tribunal appeal, should it be necessary for you to appeal against the statement when it is finalised. But also, you should let them know that you will be writing to them, within 15 days of the meeting, to let them know exactly how much help and support you want the statement to specify for Jacob in part 3. You should get advice on this (see part 8).

What the law says

Section 7 of the Education (Special Educational Needs) Regulations 2001 says:

'(2) The advice ... shall be written advice relating to –

(a) the educational, medical, psychological or other features of the case ... which appear to be relevant to the child's educational needs (including his likely future needs);
(b) how those features could affect the child's educational needs; and
(c) the provision which is appropriate for the child in light of those features of the child's case, whether by way of special educational provision or non-educational provision, but not relating to any matter which is to be specified in a statement by virtue of Section 324(4)b.'

N.B. Section 324(4)b of the 1996 Education Act refers to 'the name of any school or institution', but this does not prevent advice referring to a 'type' of school or institution.

What the Code of Practice says

'Those giving advice may comment on the amount of provision they consider appropriate. Thus, LEAs should not have blanket policies that prevent those giving advice from commenting on the amount of provision they consider a child requires.'

(Paragraph 7:79)

'... discussions between advisers and parents about the child's needs and the adviser's written advice may include consideration of various options including the scope for mainstream education for the child and the type of school in which the child's needs might best be met, for example mainstream, special or residential ...'

(Paragraph 7:80)

PostScript

The law gives parents the right to express a preference for the type of school and the individual named school, which they 'prefer' for their child. When a child has special educational needs, parents inevitably decide their preference on the basis of which school can give their child the right kind of help and a sufficient amount of help to meet their needs. When LEA officers and professionals refuse to inform parents how much help their child needs, following a statutory assessment which is intended, in the main, to find this out, they prevent parents acting in their child's best interests.

For comments on the role of educational psychologists, see the PS to case 14.

Case 18

" I've visited the local secondary school, which is the school we want our son, Toby, to attend. Toby has Down's Syndrome, and the head made it clear that he does not want him. At our meeting with the special needs officer to discuss the proposed statement, she said it would not be in Toby's best interests to force the school to take him, but we do believe he thrives best in a mainstream setting. And, just as important as his formal education, we want him to grow up in, and as part of, his local community. "

The first step

The LEA is under a legal duty to place Toby in the school you name as your preference, provided that:

- it is suitable to his age, ability or aptitude and his special educational needs;
- his attendance will not affect the education of other children there;
- there is an efficient use of resources.

The LEA must consult the school you name as your preference, but the decision is made by the LEA, not the school. Once a school is named on a statement, it must accept your child (see 'What the Courts have said').

Your first step is to study Toby's statement, in particular part 2 (which describes his needs) and part 3 (which sets out the provision necessary to meet his needs). If you believe that the provision necessary to meet his needs can be arranged at the local school, then go ahead and ask for it to be named on the statement.

You have the right to ask for meetings with any of the professionals who have provided written advice on Toby for the assessment. If any of these have recommended a mainstream place for Toby in their advice, but not been specific about the help Toby would need to make progress, you should ask for a meeting with them. Ask them face to face what kind of help – and how much – Toby would need to be supported in the mainstream school. Make careful note of their answers.

If that doesn't work

If the LEA decide not to name the mainstream school of your preference on Toby's statement, they should name another mainstream school unless this would be incompatible with the efficient education of other children. Remember, however, that once the LEA have finalised the statement, you only have two months to prepare and submit your notice of appeal to the Tribunal. So, given your clear wish for Toby to attend your local community school, you should immediately get in touch with an organisation which can give you advice on appealing – see part 8.

Study the LEA's reasons for not allowing you the school of your preference. Basically, the onus is on them to prove that at least one of the three conditions listed above cannot be met in Toby's case. If you think a second professional opinion might help, now is the time to try and arrange it (see the support organisations in part 8).

As soon as the LEA finalise the statement, send in your notice of appeal. You can always withdraw it if the LEA change their mind. See part 3 of this guide for advice on appealing.

What the law says

The 1996 Education Act says:

'(1) Every local education authority shall make arrangements for enabling a parent –

(a) on whom a copy of a proposed statement has been served under paragraph 2,

(b) on whom a copy of a proposed amended statement has been served under paragraph 2A, or

(c) on whom an amendment notice has been served under paragraph 2A which contains a proposed amendment about –

    (i) the type or name of a school or institution, or

    (ii) the provision made for the child concerned under arrangements made under section 319,

to be specified in the statement,

to express a preference as to [the maintained school] at which he wishes education to be provided for his child and to give reasons for his preference.

(2) Any such preference must be expressed or made within the period of 15 days beginning –

(a) with the date on which the written notice mentioned in [paragraph 2B], was served on the parent, or

(b) if a meeting has (or meetings have) been arranged under paragraph 4(1)(b) or (2), with the date fixed for that meeting (or the last of those meetings).

(3) Where a local education authority make a statement in a case where the parent of the child concerned has expressed a preference in pursuance of such arrangements as to the school at which he wishes education to be provided for his child, they shall specify the name of that school in the statement unless –

(a) the school is unsuitable to the child's age, ability or aptitude or to his special educational needs, or

(b) the attendance of the child at the school would be incompatible with the provision of efficient education for the children with whom he would be educated or the efficient use of resources.'

(Schedule 27(3))

2

Case

18

Duty to educate children with
special educational needs in mainstream schools

Case 18

'(1) This section applies to a child with special educational needs who should be educated in a school.

(2) If no statement is maintained under section 324 for the child, he must be educated in a mainstream school.

(3) If a statement is maintained under section 324 for the child, he must be educated in a mainstream school unless that is incompatible with –

(a) the wishes of his parent, or
(b) the provision of efficient education for other children.

(4) In this section and section 316A 'mainstream school' means any school other than –

(a) a special school, or
(b) an independent school which is not –

    (i)   a city technology college,

    (ii) a city college for the technology of the arts, or

    (iii) a city academy.'

(Section 316)

'(4) If a local education authority decide –

(a) to make a statement for a child under section 324, but
(b) not to name in the statement the school for which a parent has expressed a preference under paragraph 3 of Schedule 27,

they shall, in making the statement, comply with section 316(3).'

(Section 316A)

What the courts have said

In a judgement known as *R v Chair of Governors and Headteacher of A and S School ex parte T [2000] ELR 274*, the mother of a boy with a statement sought Judicial Review when the governors of the school named on the statement refused to accept her son. The court ruling made clear that governors' duty in law under section 324(5)(b) was absolute.

Case 18

In the case known as *C vs Lancashire County Council [1997] ELR 377*, the parents appealed to the High Court on a point of law against the decision of the Tribunal to place their child in a special school, rather than in the mainstream school of their choice. One of the reasons put forward by the LEA, and accepted by the Tribunal, was that placing a child in a mainstream school was not an efficient use of resources. On this point, the judge ruled that the decision was not entirely a question of which option was the least expensive for an LEA:

'... one has to look at the figures, decide whether there is an additional cost, and then do a balancing exercise weighing the additional cost against the parents' preference ... it is partly a factual exercise and partly a balancing exercise.'

'If the name of a maintained, grant-maintained or grant-maintained special school is specified in the Statement, the governing body of the school shall admit the child to the school.'

(Section 324(5)(b))

Inclusive Schooling: Statutory Guidance re. DfES/0774/2001

'It is reasonable to expect a local education authority to be able to provide a mainstream education for nearly all children with special educational needs. However, it is not reasonable or practical to expect all schools to provide for every possible type of special educational needs. When making decisions about individual schools the Government believes that it is right to consider: what parents want; individual school's suitability to provide for the needs of the pupil; the impact their inclusion would have on resources and the efficient education of others.'

(Paragraph 29)

Case 18

PostScript

If you feel that the headteacher of a school is less than enthusiastic about your child attending his school, remember that his prejudices will not necessarily be shared by all members of the school staff. For example, there may be teachers and other workers in the school who are also parents of children with special educational needs and who believe, as strongly as you do, in inclusive education in inclusive local communities. Remember, also, that at the end of the day the onus is on the LEA to prove why Toby cannot attend the school of your preference. If they fail to convince the Tribunal, you will get the school you want.

Case 19

❝ The LEA have sent us a proposed statement and we are very happy with the level of support specified in it and so is the headteacher of our son's school. However, he says that nothing will happen in practice until the statement is finalised. Is there anything we can do to speed things up, or at least ensure that the LEA do not drag their heels at this point? ❞

The first step

In law the LEA have to finalise a statement eight weeks after it has been sent to parents in proposed form. They are allowed to go beyond this eight-week period if it is impractical for them to keep to the deadline because:

- exceptional personal circumstances have affected the child or parent during the eight weeks;
- the child and parent are absent from the area for four consecutive weeks during the eight-week period;
- parents ask to make representations about the content of the proposed statement after the expiry of the 15-day deadline for these;
- parents ask for a second meeting with an officer or a meeting with a professional who has submitted advice;
- the LEA are waiting for a reply from the Secretary of State to a request for a child to be placed in an independent school which is not on the DfES' approved list.

This does not mean that the LEA can automatically ignore the deadline of eight weeks if, for example, you ask for a second meeting with an officer. They must show that this second meeting has made it 'impractical' for the deadline to be met, which is not the same thing.

In your case, however, you do not need one meeting with an officer, let alone two, so you should write immediately saying that you do not want to make representations or meet with anyone, and ask for the statement to be finalised immediately.

If that doesn't work

Case 19

If this does not work, you will probably have to wait the full eight weeks before the LEA finalise the statement. In the meantime, however, you should check with the school that arrangements are in hand to get the extra support to your son as soon as the statement comes into force. For example, if an extra support teacher is to be employed, the plans for doing this should be under way now. Waiting until the statement is finalised before advertising or appointing someone will inevitably mean a further delay after the statement is finalised before the provision is made.

If the statement is not finalised by the ninth week, you should contact one of the support organisations listed in part 8 of this guide for advice.

What the law says

Regulation 17 of the Education (Special Educational Needs) Regulations 2001 says:

'(3) Subject to paragraph (4), where an authority have served a copy of a proposed statement on the child's parent under paragraphs 2(1) or 2A(2) of schedule 27 to the Act they shall within 8 weeks of the date on which the proposed statement or proposed amended statement was served, serve a copy of the completed statement or completed amended statement and a written notice on the child's parent under paragraphs 6(1) and 6(2) respectively of Schedule 27.

(4) The authority need not comply with the time limit referred to in paragraph (3) if it is impractical to do so because –

(a) exceptional personal circumstances affect the child or his parent during the 8 week period referred to in paragraph (3);

(b) the child or his parent are absent from the area of the authority for a continuous period of not less that 4 weeks during the 8 week period referred to in paragraph (3);

(c) the child's parent indicates that he wishes to make representations to the authority about the content of the statement under paragraph 4(1) (a) of schedule 27 to the Act after the expiry of the 15 day period for making such representations provided for in paragraph 4(4) of that schedule;

(d) a meeting between the child's parent and an officer of the authority has been held pursuant to paragraph 4(1) of schedule 27 to the Act and the child's parent has required that another such meeting be arranged or under paragraph 4(2) of that schedule has required a meeting with the appropriate person under to be arranged; or

(e) the authority have sent a written request to the Secretary of State seeking his consent under section 347(5) to the child being educated at an independent school which is not approved by him and such consent has not been received by the authority within two weeks of the date on which the request was sent.'

Post Script

In this situation, as with others, the headteacher of your child's school is a potential ally. He or she will be as anxious as you to get extra support in place, not just for your son but for the staff as well. Heads cannot make decisions in relation to when statements will come into effect, or when the provision will be made for a child, but they can find out, and let parents know if delay is likely. If you have good reason to believe your LEA might be dragging their feet then you should seek advice from one of the support organisations listed in part 8, rather than waiting until the actual deadline has been breached.

Case

19

Case 20

❝ We expressed a preference for our local mainstream school when we received the proposed statement but we've been turned down. Now the LEA are telling us that they do not believe Clive can be educated in any of their mainstream schools, and they are going to name a special school. We don't want this. What can we do? ❞

The first step

First, you should bear in mind that you do not have to give up on having Clive placed in the mainstream school of your preference. The onus is on your LEA to prove why this cannot be done (see case 18) and you will be able to appeal to the Tribunal for the school you want once the statement is finalised.

However, when an LEA turns down a parent's request for a particular mainstream school, they must, in law, offer them another mainstream school, provided this is compatible with the efficient education of other children. If they refuse to name *any* mainstream school on the statement they must also, in law, show why it is not possible for 'reasonable' steps to be taken which would make the placement compatible with the efficient education of other children.

The Government have issued guidance to LEAs on what grounds they are able to cite when saying that a child's placement in a mainstream school would not be compatible with the efficient education of other children. This guidance also gives examples of the reasonable steps which LEAs could take to overcome the problem. These are quoted in the section below headed: '*Inclusive Schooling: Statutory Guidance re. DfES/0774/2001*'. If, having looked at these examples, you think that your LEA have not followed the guidance and have made a wrong decision, then you should seek a meeting with the officer responsible for Clive's statement as soon as possible. Contact one of the organisations listed in part 8 to see if they can arrange for someone to attend the meeting with you.

If that does not work

If you are not able to get the LEA to name the school you want, or at least another mainstream school, on Clive's statement when they finalise it, you will probably want to appeal to the Tribunal (see part 3). Remember, you will be able to make 2 appeals:

Case 20

 (i) first, for the school of your preference (see case 18);

 (ii) second, for an alternative mainstream school.

What the law says

The Education Act 1996 says:

(1) Every local education authority shall make arrangements for enabling a parent –

(a) on whom a copy of a proposed statement has been served under paragraph 2,

(b) on whom a copy of a proposed amended statement has been served under paragraph 2A, or

(c) on whom an amendment notice has been served under paragraph 2A which contains a proposed amendment about –

 (i) the type or name of a school or institution, or

 (ii) the provision made for the child concerned under arrangements made under section 319,

 to be specified in the statement,

to express a preference as to [the maintained school] at which he wishes education to be provided for his child and to give reasons for his preference.

(2) Any such preference must be expressed or made within the period of 15 days beginning –

(a) with the date on which the written notice mentioned in [paragraph 2B], was served on the parent, or
(b) if a meeting has (or meetings have) been arranged under paragraph 4(1)(b) or (2), with the date fixed for that meeting (or the last of those meetings).

(3) Where a local education authority make a statement in a case where the parent of the child concerned has expressed a preference in pursuance of such arrangements as to the school at which he wishes education to be provided for his child, they shall specify the name of that school in the statement unless –

(a) the school is unsuitable to the child's age, ability or aptitude or to his special educational needs, or
(b) the attendance of the child at the school would be incompatible with the provision of efficient education for the children with whom he would be educated or the efficient use of resources.

(Schedule 27(3))

Duty to educate children with special educational needs in mainstream schools

(1) This section applies to a child with special educational needs who should be educated in a school.

(2) If no statement is maintained under section 324 for the child, he must be educated in a mainstream school.

(3) If a statement is maintained under section 324 for the child, he must be educated in a mainstream school unless that is incompatible with –

(a) the wishes of his parent, or
(b) the provision of efficient education for other children.

(4) In this section and section 316A 'mainstream school' means any school other than –

(a) a special school, or
(b) an independent school which is not –

    (i) a city technology college,

    (ii) a city college for the technology of the arts, or

    (iii) a city academy.]

(Section 316)

2

Case

20

(4) If a local education authority decide –

(a) to make a statement for a child under section 324, but
(b) not to name in the statement the school for which a parent has expressed a preference under paragraph 3 of Schedule 27,

they shall, in making the statement, comply with section 316(3).

(5) A local education authority may, in relation to their mainstream schools taken as a whole, rely on the exception in section 316(3)(b) only if it shows that there are no reasonable steps that it or another authority in relation to the school could take to prevent the incompatibility.

(Section 316A)

Inclusive Schooling: Statutory Guidance re. DfES/0774/2001

'Efficient education

(40) **Where a child has a statement mainstream education can only be refused, against parental wishes, where the child's inclusion would be incompatible with the efficient education of other children.** Efficient education means providing for each child a suitable and

appropriate education in terms of a child's age, ability, aptitude and any special educational needs he/she may or may not have. Paragraphs 48–52 consider instances when it may not be possible to include specific children. Whilst it stresses that cases must be considered on their individual merits it explains that this may include pupils whose behaviour systematically, persistently and significantly threatens the safety of and impedes the learning of others. However, all reasonable steps must be taken to enable pupils to be included without compromising the efficient education of other pupils.

(41) When a local education authority is considering whether mainstream education is appropriate (i.e. it is not considering the appropriateness of an individual school) the term 'other children' means children with whom the child with the statement would be likely to come into contact with on a regular day to day basis.

(42) When considering individual schools **'other children' is intended to mean the children with whom the child who has a statement will directly come into contact with on a regular day-to-day basis.** For example in a primary school it would often be the child's class or literacy/numeracy group. It would not necessarily mean children in other classes or year groups. In a secondary school it may include the pupil's form or tutor group, pupils in the pupil's subject classes or groups or exceptionally even the entire year group. **'Other children' does not mean children in other schools or pupils who will only occasionally come into contact with the child.**

(43) The efficient education caveat – within section 316 – must not be abused. OFSTED will be monitoring how schools and local education authorities operate the new inclusion framework. The Secretary of State will also not hesitate to act if she or he believes a maintained school or local education authority was acting unreasonably and using the caveat inappropriately.

(44) Trivial and inappropriate reasons should not be used to deny children who should and could benefit from a mainstream education from gaining one. The three

cases set out below are just some of the examples where minor reasons have been used to block a child's inclusion. The examples also explain how the barriers to learning and participation were overcome.

Case 20

A young child with brittle bones who walks using a rollator had been successfully included in a mainstream nursery. She and her parents wanted her to transfer to a mainstream primary school. The school's Victorian accommodation had narrow walkways. For her own safety, her parents asked if she could leave class five minutes before the end of lessons in order to miss the rush in the corridors. It was claimed that this would disrupt lessons and therefore her inclusion at the school would be incompatible with the efficient education of other children. Refusing the child mainstream education on these grounds would be an abuse of the efficient education caveat. It is reasonable to allow the children in these circumstances to leave lessons five minutes early. Reasonable steps can be taken to prevent the disruption this might cause. In this case the school carefully timetabled classes, breaks and meals to ensure the young girl was able to avoided crowded corridors. They also created safe environments for her to mix with her peers during lunch and other breaks. The child's inclusion has been successful.

A child with Downs Syndrome had been attending a mainstream secondary school successfully. However, following an annual review it was agreed that a teaching assistant should support the girl in some of her lessons. One of the girl's subject teachers claimed that having another adult in the classroom would be disruptive and make the child's inclusion incompatible with the efficient education of other children. Refusing the child mainstream education on these grounds would be an abuse of the efficient education caveat. Where a child's statement specifies they should receive support from a teaching assistant the assistant must be allowed into the classroom. Reasonable steps can be taken to ensure the teacher and assistant work effectively together and support each other. The child was included successfully.

Case 20

A child with a hearing impairment who had been successfully included in a mainstream primary school moved into a new local education authority area. The boy and his parents wanted the child to continue education in a mainstream school. They expressed a preference for the school nearest to their home. In order to allow the child to access lessons his classroom teacher needed to wear a microphone. The school claimed that this would be disruptive and would compromise the efficient education of other children. Refusing the child mainstream education on these grounds would be an abuse of the efficient education caveat. In this case the local education authority argued that wearing the microphone would not disrupt other pupils. Rather it required the teacher to take a modest reasonable step to allow the child to access mainstream education. The authority provided training to staff at the school. They also arranged for someone from a local organisation for the deaf to come and talk to the class and explain why their teacher would now be using a microphone. This allowed pupils to discuss the issues in a supportive environment. The child was welcomed into the school and has been included successfully.

Reasonable steps

(45) Mainstream education can only be refused on the grounds that a child's inclusion would be incompatible with the efficient education of others where there are no reasonable steps maintained schools or local education authorities could take to prevent the incompatibility. Education law does not set out what should be taken into account when deciding if a step is reasonable. Of course, what constitutes a reasonable step or

steps depends on all of the circumstances of the individual case. Also what can be reasonably expected of schools and local education authorities now will be very different in years to come as they become more able to meet the needs of diverse groups of children. However, without intending to be exhaustive, the following are some of the factors which might be taken into account when considering what is reasonable:

Case 20

(a) whether taking the step would be effective in overcoming the incompatibility;

(b) the extent to which it is practical for the maintained school or local authority to take the step;

(c) the extent to which steps have already been taken to facilitate the child's inclusion and their effectiveness;

(d) the financial and other resource implications of taking the step; and

(e) the extent of any disruption taking the step would cause.

(46) When it comes to considering what is reasonable – i.e. what are the reasonable steps which could be taken by either a maintained school or local education authority or both – the cost implications will be a factor. It will often be reasonable to spend some money. However, it will not always be reasonable to spend large amounts of money. Set out below are some examples of the sorts of reasonable steps school and local education authorities could take to prevent a child's inclusion being incompatible with the efficient education of other children. Pupils with disabilities within the meaning of the Disability Discrimination 1995 will have further protection from September 2002 when the amendments to the Act come into force. Until then pupils with SEN and a disability will only be covered by this inclusion guidance. It is expected that the reasonable steps under the Disability Discrimination Act will be similar to those set out below. This is in no way an exhaustive or definitive list. Rather the examples are designed to help

Case 20

schools and local education authorities think about the sorts of reasonable steps they could take.

The reasonable steps to ensure that the inclusion of a child with learning difficulties is not incompatible with the efficient education of other children may include:

- praising the pupil's strengths and areas of success so that self esteem is maintained and enhanced;
- using flexible grouping arrangements including ones where the pupil can work with more able peers;
- providing for all pupils experiences which will be of benefit to most pupils but particularly to the pupil with learning difficulties;
- considering carefully the use of language in the classroom and strategies to promote the learning of need vocabulary;
- setting appropriate targets so that personal progress can be tracked as well as progress towards externally determined goals;
- considering carefully the pupil's learning styles and ensuring that this is reflected in the styles of teaching; and;
- developing a partnership with the parents to support the pupil and the curriculum.

The reasonable steps to ensure that the inclusion of a primary aged pupil who has severe temper tantrums is not incompatible with efficient education of other children **may** include:

- addressing factors within the *class* that may be contributing to the problem – e.g. addressing teasing by using circle time as a forum for discussing teasing and how to respond to it;
- teaching the child alternative behaviours – i.e. taking quiet time in a specially designated area at times of stress;

- providing the child with a channel of communication other than tantrums – i.e. fetching another child identified as their listening partner, or completing a 'think bubble sheet' to identify the stressor, the accompanying feelings and his or her possible courses of action;
- using a carefully designed system of behaviour targets drawn up together with the child, and linked to a powerful reward system which, wherever possible, involves parents/carers;
- ensuring that all staff who deal with the child have been briefed on potential triggers for outbursts, and effective ways of heading off trouble at an early stage – i.e. an agreed school-wide system where the child is asked to take a colour-coded object to another member of staff as soon as the emotional temperature is rising;
- drawing up a contingency plan for what will happen if there is a confrontation in class: in conjunction with the child, identifying a key helper who will be summoned to remove the child or the rest of the class from the situation, identifying how they will know the need is urgent, and setting out what the later consequences will be for the child if this system has to be used; and
- ensuring that if there is any possibility that positive handling may need to be used to prevent injury to others or damage to property, that relevant staff have had training in appropriate techniques, that these have been carefully explained to the child, and that the circumstances under which they may be used have been recorded on a written plan agreed with and signed by the child and his or her parents/carers.

2

Case 20

The reasonable steps to ensure that the inclusion of a secondary aged pupil with Downs Syndrome working towards level 1 of the National Curriculum is not incompatible with efficient education of other children **may** include:

- identifying a named member of staff to oversee the social and curriculum aspects of the pupil's inclusion, and liaise with parents and outside agencies;
- planning an individualised and differentiated curriculum, by identifying links between the content of whole class work and the learning objectives appropriate at pre-Level 1;
- adjusting the balance of the curriculum to allow for additional time to be spent on such areas as expressive and receptive language, personal, social and life skills;
- arranging for in-class support from a teaching assistant and securing appropriate training for the teaching assistant, from the local education authority or other sources;
- training subject teachers in using teaching styles which include visual prompts to support curriculum delivery, delivering instructions in short chunks and checking for understanding, giving the pupil time to process language and respond;
- providing for alternative means of access to tasks involving reading and writing;
- ensuring access to appropriate CT – for example talking word processor software;
- encouraging peer support – for example, by setting up a circle of friends who have chosen to plan ways in which they can help the pupil access the curriculum and the social opportunities provided by the school;
- adhere to teaching timetables, routines and school rules explicitly, and allowing the pupil time to learn them; and
- arranging for a key worker to meet regularly with the pupil to discuss positives and difficulties build on successes and sustain meaningful links with home.'

(See part 8 for information on obtaining
a free copy of this guidance.)

Post Script

Remember that at the proposed statement stage the LEA are not supposed to make up their minds on placement until you have expressed your preference for a particular school. Then, the onus will be on the LEA to show why your preference cannot be met. If that preference is for a mainstream school, and they turn you down, the LEA must offer you a place in another one – unless 'reasonable steps' cannot be taken to protect the education of other children.

There are three reasons why you should take full advantage of your rights in law to ask for meetings with officers and professionals at the proposed statement stage:

First, changes can be made quickly at this stage, and the LEA officer will be anxious to compromise, provided you have strong evidence to back you up. In this way, the LEA can avoid Tribunal appeals which they are likely to lose.

The second reason is that you can collect a lot of information which can be of use to you if you have to go to appeal at the next stage. Make careful note of the questions you ask and the answers given. Ask for answers to be confirmed in writing after a meeting.

The third reason is that LEA officers are not always aware of the law on special education. You should remind the special needs officer that when you name a school as your preference, the onus will be on the LEA to show that it is not suitable. Also, officers may not have considered all of the examples given in *Inclusive Schooling*. You may be doing them a favour by drawing their attention to these.

Case 21

❝ We have just received our daughter's proposed statement and we are not happy with the way her needs have been described in Part 2. All it says is that Jenny is a friendly and attractive little girl (which we already knew!) with 'a general delay with her learning.' In fact she has a specific problem with reading and writing. In other areas her development is fine. ❞

The first step

You have 15 days to write back and ask for a meeting with the special needs officer. Do this. Do not put your views in writing at this stage – simply ask for a meeting to discuss the proposed statement.

Before the meeting, read through all of the professional advice which you will have received along with the proposed statement. There are bound to be more specific descriptions of Jenny's learning difficulties than the one contained in Part 2 of the statement.

If you agree with the descriptions of Jenny's needs in the advice, then at your meeting with the officer ask that the proposed statement is amended in order to include the specific descriptions of her needs as they appear in the professional advice. Remind the officer that in law Part 2 of the statement must refer to the needs identified during Jenny's assessment.

If you disagree with the way Jenny's needs are described in the professional advice, you should consider getting a second professional opinion – see part 8 of this guide for the name of an organisation which may be able to help you with this. If the second opinion backs you up, send a copy of it to the LEA and ask for part 2 of the statement to be amended in order to include more specific reference to Jenny's needs as these have been identified by the second professional opinion.

When you ask the officer to amend the statement, give him/ her a copy of what it is you want the statement to say under Part 2. Prepare this before the meeting. Leave a copy with the officer and keep one for yourself.

2

If that doesn't work

Case 21

If the LEA finalises the statement as it was originally proposed, and without amending it according to your request, then you will have to decide whether to appeal or not. Someone from one of the support organisations can help you make this decision (see part 8 for telephone numbers).

What the law says

Section 324 of the Education Act 1996 says:

'(3) In particular, the statement shall –

(a) give details of the authority's assessment of the child's special educational needs.'

Regulation 16 of the Education (Special Educational Needs) Regulations 2001 says:

'A statement shall (a) be in a form substantially corresponding to that set out in Schedule 2 to these Regulations; (b) contain the information therein specified …'

Schedule 2 to the 2001 Regulations says:

'Part 2: Special Educational Needs [Here set out the child's special educational needs, in terms of the child's learning difficulties which call for special educational provision, as assessed by the authority.]'

What the courts have said

In a judgement known as *R vs The Secretary of State for Education and Science ex parte E [1992] 1 ELR 377*, the Court of Appeal ruled that Part 2 of a statement ('special educational needs') must set out all of a child's special educational needs identified during an assessment. In addition, Part 3 (b) of a statement must specify the provision required to meet each of the needs identified in Part 2, whether that provision was to be made by the LEA or by the child's own school. For more information on this judgement, see page 242.

What the Code of Practice says

'Part 2 of the statement should describe **all** the child's learning difficulties identified during the statutory assessment. It should also include a description of the child's current functioning – what the child can and cannot do. The description in Part 2 should draw on and may refer to the professional advice attached in the appendices. Where the LEA adopt that advice in their description of the child's learning difficulties, they should say that they have done so. But merely stating that they are adopting the advice in the appendices is not sufficient. The appendices may contain conflicting opinions or opinions open to interpretation, which the LEA must resolve, giving reasons for the conclusions they have reached. Part 2 should be set out in a fashion which can relate directly to the description of provision set out in Part 3 (b).'

(Paragraph 8:32)

PostScript

It is important to get Part 2 of your child's statement right. This is because the LEA must specify, under Part 3, provision to meet each and every one of the needs identified in Part 2. If Part 2 fails to mention one of your child's needs, the child may not get the provision required to meet that need. If you are not happy with the provision for your child (set out under

Part 3 of the statement) when it is finalised, then it is vital to check to make sure whether you need to appeal against Part 2 as well as Part 3 of the statement. Read case 22 immediately, and contact one of the support organisations in part 8 if you need to discuss the situation with someone.

Case 21

Case 22

66 We are unhappy with the special education provision in Part 3 of our son's proposed statement. It is not specific enough. There is no indication of what kind of help he should get, nor how much. Also, the statement says that the school will decide on the help he needs – whereas we thought that the LEA made this decision when they decided what a statement should say. 99

The first step

You are right in thinking that Part 3 of a statement should be specific. You are also right in thinking that when an LEA makes a statement, they are accepting that they – rather than anyone else, including the school – must make the decision on what a child's needs are and what provision is necessary to meet them (see *What the courts have said* below).

It seems that one of three things might have gone wrong here:

- Part 2 of the statement (special educational needs) does not set out all of Joe's needs. As a result, Part 3 does not specify the provision necessary to meet all of his needs. If this is the problem, read case 21 as well as this one.
- Part 2 sets out all of Joe's needs, but the provision in Part 3 does not match up with all the needs identified in Part 2.
- The provision in Part 3 has not been sufficiently specified.

You have 15 days to write asking for a meeting with an officer to discuss the proposed statement. Study all of the professional advice before meeting the officer. You may find that the educational advice and the psychological advice both contain full descriptions of Joe's needs and of the provision necessary to meet them. If so, when you go to the meeting with the officer, you should ask:

'Why have you ignored your own professional advice in writing the statement? Please amend the statement to include specific reference to the needs identified in the professional advice and to the provision which the advice says is necessary.'

If the statement refers to the kind of provision Joe needs but fails to specify how much, you will need to draw the officer's attention to paragraph 8:37 of the Code of Practice and the judgement in 'L vs Clarke and Somerset County Council [1998] ELR 129' (see *What the courts have said* below).

Case 22

You should also draw the officer's attention to the judgement in *C v Special Educational Needs Tribunal and London Borough of Greenwich* [1999] ELR 5 with reference to decisions being delegated to 'other bodies' such as schools (see *What the courts have said*).

Write down that *you* think Joe's statement should say in Parts 2 and 3 and leave a copy of this with the officer at the end of the meeting.

If you disagree with the way Joe's needs are described in the professional advice, you should consider getting a second professional opinion – see part 8 for the name of an organisation which may be able to help you with this. If the second opinion supports your views, copy it to the LEA with a letter asking for Parts 2 and 3 of the statement to be amended in order to include more specific reference to Joe's needs and the provision necessary to meet them, as these have been identified in the second professional opinion.

If the LEA's professional advice fails to say what provision Joe needs, then also read case 17 before meeting the officer.

If that doesn't work

If the LEA finalises the statement without amending it, then you will probably want to appeal. See part 3 of this book for advice on how to do so.

What the law says

The 1996 Education Act says:

2

Case

22

'(1) A parent on whom a copy of a proposed statement has been served under paragraph 2 above may –

(a) make representations (or further representations) to the local education authority about the content of the statement, and

(b) require the authority to arrange a meeting between him and an officer of the authority at which the statement can be discussed.'

(Schedule 27(4))

'(3) In particular, the statement shall –

(b) ... specify the special educational provision to be made for the purpose of meeting those needs ...'

(Section 324)

Schedule 2 of the Education (Special Educational Needs) Regulations 2001 says:

'Statement of Special Educational Needs ...

Part 3: Educational Provision to meet needs and objectives ... Here specify the special educational provision which the authority consider appropriate to meet the needs specified in Part 2 and to meet the objectives specified in this Part, and in particular specify –

(a) any appropriate facilities and equipment, staffing arrangements and curriculum,

(b) any appropriate modifications to the application of the National Curriculum,

(c) any appropriate exclusions from the application of the National Curriculum, in detail, and the provision which it is proposed to substitute for any such exclusions in

102

order to maintain a balanced and broadly based curriculum, and

(d) where residential accommodation is appropriate, that fact.'

What the courts have said

In a judgement known as *R vs The Secretary of State for Education and Science ex parte E [1992] 1 ELR 377*, the High Court ruled that Part 2 of a statement ('special educational needs') must set out all of a child's special educational needs identified during an assessment. In addition, Part 3 of a statement must specify the provision required to meet each of the needs identified in Part 2, whether that provision was to be made by the LEA or by the child's own school.

A statement which says in Part 2, for example, 'Joe has a variety of special educational needs, but is a very happy child' has not been written in accordance with the judgement in 'ex parte E' and therefore is legally challengeable. Similarly, a statement which says 'The special educational needs coordinator at Joe's school will decide on the level of support required to meet Joe's needs' has not been written in accordance with 'ex parte E' and, again, is legally challengeable.

In a judgement known as *L vs Clarke and Somerset County Council [1998] ELR 129*, the court ruled on the duty of an LEA to be specific when writing part 3 of a statement of special educational needs:

'A requirement that the help to be given should be specified in the statement in terms of hours per week was not an absolute and universal precondition of the legality of any statement ... however ... in very many cases it will not be possible to fulfil the requirement to specify the special educational provision considered appropriate to meet the child's needs, including specification of staffing arrangements and curriculum, unless hours per week are set out.'

Case

22

In a judgement known as *C v Special Educational Needs Tribunal and London Borough of Greenwich* [1999] ELR 5 the High Court was critical of a tribunal which had failed to make a decision about the curriculum needs of a child and had delegated this decision to a Pupil Referral Unit. This case can be cited to argue that an LEA must make the assessment decision when writing a statement, not delegate this responsibility to someone else, such as a school. For more information about this judgement see page 260.

What the Code of Practice says

'Provision should normally be quantified (e.g. in terms of hours of provision, staffing arrangements.) although there will be cases where some flexibility should be retained in order to meet the changing special educational needs of the child concerned.'

(Paragraph 8:37)

Post Script

One of the comments reported in 'ex parte E' was that Part 2 of a statement was like a doctor's diagnosis of what was wrong with you, and Part 3 was like the prescription. Sometimes LEAs write both Parts 2 and 3 of their statements like diagnoses – writing long lists of a child's needs, but never getting around to saying what provision they intend to make to meet those needs.

Another way of thinking of Parts 2 and 3 of a statement is to imagine them as pieces of a jigsaw puzzle which must fit exactly together. For example, if Part 2 lists seven special educational needs, then Part 3 should refer to special educational provision to meet each and every one of these seven needs. These two Parts of the statement should then lock together.

Case 23

"We have received the proposed statement and all the professional advice. We have been told that we can express a preference for an LEA maintained school. However, we believe our son needs intensive special help of the kind which can only be provided in a specialist independent school for autistic pupils. But if we can't express a preference for an independent school, what are we going to do? "

The first step

The law says that you can only express a preference for a maintained (i.e. LEA) school, but this does not mean that you can not **ask for and argue for** a place at an independent school.

The difference is this:

When you 'express a preference' for an LEA school, the LEA has to comply with your request. If they don't, the onus is on them to prove why it is not possible.

However, when you ask for an independent school as part of your 'representations' on the proposed statement, the onus is on you to prove that none of the schools the LEA is offering can meet your child's needs – and that, therefore, they must place your child in the independent school.

Within 15 days of receiving the proposed statement, you must ask for a meeting with the special needs officer. At that meeting, explain why you do not believe that the schools the LEA can offer can meet your child's special educational needs. If you can convince them of this, then they may consider an independent school. But if you cannot persuade them, they are under no obligation to look at independent provision – and it does not matter that the independent school you have in mind is an excellent school and clearly better suited to your child's needs than the school the LEA has in mind. LEAs are not bound to offer a child with special needs 'the best' provision to meet their needs (see *What the courts have said*, below) – only what is necessary to meet their needs.

Case

23

It may be that the professional advice gives you the evidence you need to prove that your child's needs cannot be met by any school the LEA can offer him. If not, you might have to consider getting a second professional opinion – see part 8 of this book for organisations which may be able to help you with this.

If that doesn't work

If you are unable to persuade the LEA at the proposed statement stage to name the independent school you want, then you will have to consider appealing to the Tribunal when the statement is finalised.

What the law says

Schedule 27 of the 1996 Education Act says:

'(4) (1) A parent on whom a copy of a proposed statement has been served ... may –

(a) make representations (or further representations) to the local education authority ... and
(b) require the authority to arrange a meeting between him and an officer of the authority at which the statement ... can be discussed.'

What the courts have said

In a judgement known as *R vs Surrey County Council Education Committee ex parte H [1985] 83 LGR 219*, the High Court ruled: 'There is no question of Parliament having placed the local education authority under an obligation to provide a child with the best possible education ... or to educate him or her to his or her maximum potential.'

What the Code of Practice says

'Parents may express a preference for any maintained school they wish their child to attend, or make representations for a placement in any other school ... LEAs must consider parental representations and arrange any meting(s) with LEA officers or advisers parents seek, before issuing the final statement. When considering parental representations for a place at a school or institution which is not a maintained school, LEAs must establish that the school or institution proposed can make the special educational provision necessary to meet the child's special educational needs, and the provisions of section 9 of the Education Act 1996: that is, they must have regard to the parent's wishes, so far as that is compatible with the efficient instruction and training of the child and the avoidance of unreasonable public expenditure.'

(Paragraph 8:60)

Inclusive Schooling: Statutory Guidance re. DfES/0774/2001

'Parents whose children have statements, and those for whom a statement is being drawn up, continue to be able to make representations for their child's statement to name an independent or non-maintained school. The local education authority must give full consideration to the parent's representations ...'

(Paragraph 54)

'... Where a local education authority disagrees with what parents want and does not name the independent or non-maintained school in the child's statement the parents have the right of appeal to the SEN Tribunal.'

(Paragraph 55)

PostScript

Remember, the most important point you must prove is not that the independent school is better than the LEA school, but that the school offered by the LEA cannot meet your child's needs. It would help your case to have a report which backs your opinion from an independent professional who has met and assessed your child and visited the school in question.

It is very unlikely that the school itself, or the LEA, will object to an independent professional making a visit – but it has been known! If it happens to you, contact one of the support organisations listed in part 8 for advice on dealing with the situation.

Case 24

66 The LEA has sent us a proposed statement on Emily, our daughter, which lists speech therapy as one of her special educational needs under Part 2, but then lists the speech therapy provision for her under Part 6 as 'Non-educational provision.' Surely it should be included under Part 3 as 'special educational provision'?

We had a meeting with the officer to discuss the proposed statement but she was not convinced that there was any need to change it. She just kept telling us that we would be able to appeal to the Tribunal if we weren't happy. But surely parents shouldn't have to appeal to the Tribunal just to get the LEA to write a statement properly? 99

The first step

You are right in saying that it should not be necessary to have to go through an appeal to the Special Educational Needs Tribunal just to get the LEA to write their statement in accordance with the law. However, even though it should not be necessary, it often is!

As your daughter's statement is still at the proposed stage, it might be worth raising the issue in writing with the Chief Education Officer. In your letter, set out the grounds for believing that the statement has not been properly written and ask for it to be amended. Your letter could say something like this:

To: The Chief Education Officer

Dear Sir or Madam,

We are writing to request that you amend the proposed statement of special educational needs on our daughter on the grounds that it is not written in

2

Case 24

accordance with the law. Emily's need for speech therapy is educational, not medical, and this is confirmed by the fact that the statement lists her need for therapy under Part 2, headed 'Special Educational Needs.'

As you will be aware, following the court ruling in the 'ex parte E' case, Part 3 of a statement must contain a reference to provision to meet any need identified in Part 2. Would you please amend the statement to bring it in line with the law, removing the reference to speech therapy in Part 6 and specifying the speech therapy provision as 'Special Education Provision' in Part 3.

If you are not prepared to make the changes I have asked for, then would you please finalise the statement immediately and I will prepare my case for the Special Educational Needs Tribunal ...

If that doesn't work

If your letter to the Chief Education Officer gets no results then you must appeal to the Special Educational Needs Tribunal as soon as the statement is finalised. You have an excellent case, but see Part 3 of this guide for advice on appealing to the Tribunal.

What the law says

Regulation 16 of the Education (Special Educational Needs) Regulations 2001 says:

'A statement shall (a) be in a form substantially corresponding to that set out in schedule 2 to these Regulations; (b) contain the information therein specified ...

Schedule 2 – Statement of Special Educational Needs, says:

'Part 3: Special Educational Provision [Here specify the special educational provision which the authority consider appropriate to meet the needs specified in Part 2].'

What the courts have said

In a judgement known as *R vs The Secretary of State for Education and Science, ex parte E [1992] 1 ELR 377*, the Court of Appeal ruled that Part 2 of a statement ('special educational needs') must set out all of a child's special educational needs identified during an assessment; and, that Part 3 of a statement must specify the provision required to meet each of the needs identified in Part 2, whether that provision was to be made by the LEA or by the child's own school. (For more information on this judgement, see page 242.)

Case 24

What the Code of Practice says

Case law has established that speech and language therapy can be regarded as either educational or non-educational provision, depending upon the health and developmental history of each child. It could therefore appear in either Part 3 or Part 6 of the statement or in both. However, since communication is so fundamental in learning and progression, addressing speech and language impairment should normally be recorded as educational provision unless there are **exceptional** reasons for not doing so.' (Emphasis in the Code.)

(Paragraph 8:49)

Post Script

It is only if speech therapy is specified as a special educational provision under Part 3 of a statement that your child has a legal right to receive the provision. This is because LEAs have a strict duty to arrange the provision set out in Part 3. They are entitled to get another body, such as the health authority, to actually provide or pay for speech therapists. But if, for whatever reason, the health authority won't or can't make the provision, then the LEA *must* do so.

111

2

Case 24

If speech therapy is set out only under Part 6 of a statement, as a non-educational provision, however, then no-one – neither the LEA nor the health authority – has a legal duty to make the provision a child needs.

Whenever you believe that your LEA is not following the law, you should try to get an opinion on the situation from one of the support organisations listed in part 8 of this guide, or from a solicitor familiar with educational law.

Case 25

❝ The LEA have sent us a proposed statement on our son, Tony, who has language and communication problems. The speech therapist's advice says his need for speech therapy is educational and that it should be provided for him in an educational setting. However, the draft statement lists 'Speech therapy' under Part 5 as 'Non-educational needs' and under Part 6 as 'Non-educational provision.' We understand that the LEA have a duty to make special educational provision, but not 'non-educational' provision. What can we do to make sure that Tony's needs are written in his statement under the right part and that the LEA accepts responsibility for meeting them? ❞

The first step

You should write immediately to the officer, asking for a meeting to discuss the proposed statement. You have to write within 15 days of receiving the proposed statement.

At your meeting, ask the officer:

- What evidence have you got for saying that Tony's need for speech therapy is non-educational rather than educational?
- On what grounds are you ignoring the speech therapist's advice?
- Will you agree to amend the proposed statement in order to list Tony's need for speech therapy under Part 2, as a special educational need, and then specify the provision necessary under Part 3 as a special educational provision?

Write your questions on a sheet of paper which you can leave with the officer at the end of the meeting as a reminder. Ask for the answers to be confirmed in writing as soon as possible in order that you can decide what further action you might want to take.

If that doesn't work

2

Case 25

If the LEA refuse to amend the statement, you will probably have to appeal against it to the Special Educational Needs Tribunal. You cannot appeal against the fact that speech therapy is referred to in Parts 5 and 6 of the statement, because there is no appeal against Parts 5 and 6; however, you can appeal on the grounds that Part 2 fails to include a reference to Tony's language and communication problems and that Part 3 is incomplete by failing to specify speech therapy as a special educational provision necessary to meet his needs.

See part 3 of this book for advice on appealing to the Tribunal. At this stage it might help to speak to someone from one of the support organisations listed in part 8.

What the law says

Regulation 16 of the Education (Special Educational Needs) Regulations 2001 says:

'A statement shall (a) be in a form substantially corresponding to that set out in Schedule 2 of these Regulations; (b) contain the information therein specified ...'

Schedule 2 – Statement of Special Educational Needs, says:

'Part 3: Special educational provision [Here specify the special educational provision which the authority consider appropriate to meet the needs specified in part 2].'

What the courts have said

The judgement in the case of *R vs Lancashire County Council ex parte M [1989] 2 ELR 279* included this comment:

'To teach an adult who has lost his larynx because of cancer might be considered as treatment rather than education. But to teach a child who has never been able to communicate by language, whether because of some chromosomal disorder ... or because of social cause ... seems to us just as much educational provision as to teach a child to communicate in writing.' (For more information, see page 245.)

(For more information, see page 245.)

Case 25

What the Code of Practice says

Case law has established that speech and language therapy can be regarded as either educational or non-educational provision, depending upon the health and developmental history of each child, It could therefore appear in either Part 3 or Part 6 of the statement or in both. However, since communication is so fundamental in learning and progression, addressing speech and language impairment should normally be recorded as educational provision unless there are **exceptional** reasons for not doing so.' (Emphasis in the Code, Paragraph 8:49.)

Post Script

There may come a point, when you are arguing over your child's proposed statement with the LEA, when you realise that they are not going to change it. To continue to ask for meetings with professionals after this point will only delay finalising the statement and therefore the point when you can appeal. So, once you sense you are wasting your time, ask the LEA to finalise the statement so that you can appeal to the Tribunal.

If the LEA's own professional advice is on your side, you have a strong case and will not need additional independent professional advice. You are not able to appeal against Parts 5 and 6 of a statement, as these deal with 'non-educational needs and provision.' Your appeal must be based on the fact that speech therapy has not been referred to in Parts 2 and 3 as 'educational needs and provision'.

If in doubt about wording your Notice of Appeal, contact one of the support organisations listed in part 8.

Case

25

Note that physiotherapy and occupational therapy, like speech therapy, may be educational or medical, depending on the individual child's needs (see *B vs Isle of Wight Council [1997] ELR 279* and *London Borough of Bromley and Special Educational Needs Tribunal and Others*, QBD and CA [1999] ELR 260, on page 259).

Case 26

66 We're at the proposed statement stage and have found a mainstream school we really like for our son, Saul. At our meeting with the special needs officer to discuss the proposed statement, we expressed a preference for this school, but we were told we'd be wasting our time as it is in a neighbouring LEA's area and that LEA have said that the school is full. 99

The first step

Your own LEA are under a legal duty to place Saul in the school of your preference, provided it is a maintained school (i.e. not a private school) and provided that:

● it is suitable to his age, ability or aptitude and his special educational needs;
● his attendance there will not affect the education of other children;
● there is an efficient use of resources.

This is the law, regardless of which LEA are responsible for the school you prefer. It is true that your own LEA must consult the governing body of the school and consult the neighbouring LEA but, after this consultation, the decision has to be made by *your* LEA – not the school itself or the neighbouring LEA.

The first step is to write to your own LEA reminding them that they (and no-one else) have the duty in law to make the decision (see *What the law says* below).

Also, you need to ask your LEA to explain in writing exactly why they are denying you a place for Saul in the school of your preference. Is it because they believe his needs cannot be met in that school, or that other children's education will suffer, or that it would not be an efficient use of resources?

Your letter could go something like this:

To: The Chief Education Officer,

Dear Sir or Madam,

Case 26

We are writing to you as the parents of Saul Williams, who has a proposed statement of special educational needs. We wish to express a preference for ... School, in ..., and want this school to be named in Saul's statement. We understand that under the 1996 Education Act, your Authority must make the decision about whether to name this school on Saul's statement, even though a different LEA maintain the school.

We also understand that you are under a legal duty to name ... School on Saul's statement, this being our preference as parents, unless you can show that the school cannot meet his needs, or that other children's education would be prejudiced or that there would be an inefficient use of resources. We do not believe that any of these conditions would arise if Saul were to go to ... School, and we ask you to set out in writing which conditions you believe would arise and to provide us with your reasons and evidence for believing this ...

If that doesn't work

If you are unhappy with the reply you receive to this letter, and the LEA go ahead and finalise Saul's statement without naming the school of your preference, you will be able to appeal to the Special Educational Needs Tribunal. It is advisable to consider appealing against Parts 2 and 4 of a statement, as well as Part 4 (which names the school). You should get advice on this straight away (see part 8 of this guide).

What the law says

The 1996 Education Act says:

Case 26

'(3) (1) Every local education authority shall make arrangements for enabling a parent ... on whom a copy of a proposed statement has been served under paragraph 2 ... to express a preference as to the maintained school at which he wishes education to be provided for his child and to give reasons for his preference.

(2) Any such preference must be expressed or made within the period of 15 days beginning –

(a) with the date on which the written notice mentioned in paragraph 2B above was served on the parent, or
(b) if a meeting has (or meetings have) been arranged under paragraph 4(1)(b) or (2) with the date fixed for that meeting (or the last of those meetings).

(3) Where a local education authority make a statement in a case where the parent of the child concerned has expressed a preference in pursuance of such arrangements as to the school at which he wishes education to be provided for his child, they shall specify the name of that school in the statement unless –

(a) the school is unsuitable to the child's age, ability or aptitude or to his special educational needs, or
(b) the attendance of the child at the school would be incompatible with the provision of efficient education for the children with whom he would be educated or the efficient use of resources.'

(Schedule 27(3))

'if the name of a maintained school is specified in the statement, the governing body of the school shall admit the child to the school.'

(Section 324(5)(b))

Case

26

PostScript

There is no definition in law of what it means for a school to be 'full.' LEAs are able to name schools which say they are 'full' in statements – and may have no choice when the Special Educational Needs Tribunal orders them to. In order to convince the Tribunal that the school the parents want simply cannot take another child, the LEA have to show that because of the high numbers of pupils in the school, the child's needs won't be met, or that other children's needs would not be met, or that there would be an inefficient use of resources (for example, as a result of them having to appoint another teacher or build another classroom).

Case 27

❝ The statement has been finalised and we disagree with the description of our son's needs in Part 2. All it says is that he has cerebral palsy and that he needs a modified curriculum suitable for a child with severe and developmental learning difficulties. There is no mention in Part 2 of his need for Occupational Therapy and Speech Therapy. We are also worried about Part 3 of the statement, which does not mention either Occupational or Physiotherapy. When we raised these issues at the proposed statement stage, the Officer told us that Occupational Therapy and Physiotherapy were regarded as medical provisions by his LEA and that they would be referred to in Parts 5 and 6 of the statement. We feel this can't be right, but do not know how to make our case. ❞

The first step

The arguments you must use to appeal against the way your child's special educational needs have been described in the finalised statement are the same as the ones you would use when a statement is first proposed – see case 21. This time, however, instead of putting your case to an LEA officer, you need to put it to the Special Educational Needs Tribunal (see part 3).

It may be that your child's needs are fully described in the professional advice, but that the LEA have ignored the details in the reports. Or it could be that the professional advice is not detailed enough, in which case you should consider whether you need an independent second professional opinion on his needs (see the support numbers in part 8 for advice on this).

You also need to appeal against the provision in Part 3 of the statement. The arguments that you need to make are the same as the arguments you would use at the proposed stage (see case 22). In particular, you should study the professional advice and see if there is any support for what you want in Part 3 (Special Educational Provision) in the advice. The law says that professionals should include their views on the provision a child needs in their advice (see case 17).

You have two months to send in a Notice of Appeal to the Special Educational Needs Tribunal. Your grounds for appeal could be like this:

> *'Part 2 of the statement does not set out Troy's special educational needs in sufficient detail to make it clear what his actual needs are. We believe there should be specific reference to Troy's need for Occupational and Physiotherapy in Part 2.'*

Part 3 of the statement does not specify Troy's special educational provision in sufficient detail. It makes no reference at all to Occupational Therapy or Physiotherapy. We want the statement to say that he should receive daily twenty minute sessions of Occupational Therapy and Physiotherapy ...

Along with the form send a copy of the statement and all of the professional advice attached to it.

You might also want to appeal against the other special education provision in Part 3 of the statement, on the grounds that it is not quantified (see case 22).

The Officer is wrong to say that the therapies are medical provision. They can be either medical or educational depending on the needs of the individual child (see *What the Courts have said*). It does not matter if the therapies are listed as non-educational needs and provision in Parts 5 and 6, as long as they are also listed as educational needs and provision in Parts 2 and 3 (see case 24).

It is important that you get advice on appealing to the Tribunal if you are at all unsure of the arguments you should be making. See part 3 of this guide for how to do this.

What the law says

The 1996 Education Act says:

'(1) The parent of a child for whom a local education authority maintain a statement under section 324 may –

(a) when the statement is first made,
(b) where the description in the statement of the authority's assessment of the child's special educational needs, or the special educational provision specified in the statement, is amended, or
(c) where, after conducting an assessment of the educational needs of the child under section 323, the local education authority determine not to amend the statement,

appeal to the Tribunal against the description in the statement of the authority's assessment of the child's special educational needs, the special educational provision specified in the statement or, if no school is named in the statement, that fact.'

(Section 326)

'(3) In particular, the statement shall –

(a) give details of the authority's assessment of the child's special educational needs, and
(b) specify the special educational provision to be made for the purpose of meeting those needs.'

(Section 324)

The Education (Special Educational Needs) Regulations 2001 say:
'A statement shall (a) be in a form substantially corresponding to that set out in Schedule 2 to the Regulations; (b) contain the information therein specified:'

(Regulation 13)

'Part 2 ... Here set out the child's special educational needs, in terms of the child's learning difficulties which call for special educational provision, as assessed by the authority.'

123

'Part 3 ... Here specify the special educational provision which the authority consider appropriate to meet the needs specified in Part 2 ...'

(Schedule 2: Statement of special educational needs)

2

Case 27

What the courts have said

In a judgement known as *R vs The Secretary of State for Education and Science, ex parte E [1992] 1 ELR 377*, the court ruled that Part 2 of a statement ('special educational needs') must set out all of a child's special educational needs identified during an assessment; and, that Part 3 of a statement must specify the provision required to meet each of the needs identified in Part 2, whether that provision was to be made by the LEA or by the child's own school. A statement which simply says in Part 2, for example, 'Troy has severe learning difficulties' has not been written in accordance with the judgement in 'ex parte E.' Similarly, a statement which says 'Troy needs a moderate learning difficulties curriculum' has not been written in accordance with 'ex parte E.' In both of these cases the statement is open to legal challenge.

In a judgement known as *L vs Clarke and Somerset County Council [1998] ELR 129*, the court ruled on the duty of an LEA to be specific when writing Part 3 of a statement of special educational needs:

'A requirement that the help to be given should be specified in the statement in terms of hours per week was not an absolute and universal precondition of the legality of any statement ... however ... in very many cases it will not be possible to fulfil the requirement to specify the special educational provision considered appropriate to meet the child's needs, including specification of staffing arrangements and curriculum, unless hours per week are set out.'

In a judgement known as *R vs Cumbria County Council ex parte P [1995] COD 267*, the court ruled that although it was not illegal to refer to a funding level (e.g. 'Band C') in Part 3 of a statement, or a specific amount of money, this did not satisfy the legal duty to 'specify' the provision to be arranged for a child.

In a judgement known as *London Borough of Bromley v Special Educational Needs Tribunal and Others QBD and CA/1999/ELR 260*, the Queens Bench Division and the Court of Appeal ruled that a child's need for Occupational, Physio and Speech Therapy could be educational needs, depending on the individual child (see page 259).

2

Case 27

What the Code of Practice says

'Part 2 of the statement should describe **all** the child's learning difficulties identified during the statutory assessment. It should also include a description of the child's current functioning – what the child can and cannot do. The description in Part 2 should draw on and may refer to the professional advice attached in the appendices. Where the LEA adopt that advice in their description of the child's learning difficulties, they should say that they have done so. But merely stating that they are adopting the advice in the appendices is not sufficient. The advice received may contain conflicting opinions or opinions open to interpretation, which the LEA must resolve, giving reasons for the conclusions they have reached.'

(Paragraph 8:32)

'... the second subsection (of Part 3) should specify all of the special educational provision the LEA consider appropriate for **all** the learning difficulties in Part 2 even where some of the provision will be made by direct intervention on the part of the authority, some will be made by the child's school from within its own resources, and some may be made by the health authority. It is the LEA that is responsible for arranging the provision in the statement, irrespective of who actually delivers it, unless the LEA is satisfied that the child's parents have themselves made suitable arrangements.'

(Paragraph 8:34(b))

'... Provision should normally be quantified (e.g. in terms of hours of provision, staffing arrangements) although there will be cases where some flexibility should be retained in order to meet the changing special educational needs of the child concerned.'

(Paragraph 8:37)

Case 27

PostScript

When children are referred to special schools, their statements often do not contain much detail in parts 2 or 3 because it is assumed by everyone that they will receive whatever provision other children at the school get. This can be dangerous if there are changes in the resourcing of the school and it is always in a child's best interests for their statement to be as detailed as possible when it is first issued. This is true whether a child is in a special school or a mainstream school. Even if you know what provision your child will receive and you are happy with this, you should insist on your child's educational needs being accurately and fully described in Part 2 of the statement, and with the provision being clearly specified and quantified in Part 3.

If you believe that there is information missing from the professional advice which, in law, should be there, then you should ask the president of the Tribunal to issue a direction telling the LEA to go back to the professional or professionals concerned and obtain the missing information.

You have to explain why you want the direction. In the case of an incomplete professional report, the reason is obvious: how can you be sure what your child needs if the professional reports do not spell it out for you? How can you argue effectively against the LEA at the Tribunal unless you know exactly what the professionals think is the appropriate provision for your child? For further information on appealing to the Tribunal, see part 3.

Case 28

❝ The statement is finalised but we've been refused a place in the LEA school of our preference. We have visited the school the LEA have named in the statement, and it is a good school, but it is 26 miles away. Mandy is nervous about travelling and is car sick. We do not think she can take 52 miles a day in a taxi. How do we appeal against this decision? Can we keep her at home if we lose the appeal? ❞

The first step

The LEA's grounds for refusing your choice of school must be one of the following:

- that the school of your preference is not suitable to your daughter's age, ability, aptitude or special educational needs;
- that your daughter's attendance will prejudice the provision of efficient education for other children;
- that your daughter's attendance at the school would not be an efficient use of resources.

Basically, your appeal will be against whichever of these reasons the LEA have put forward for refusing your child a place in the school of your choice. If your preference was for a mainstream school, the LEA must by law offer you another mainstream school, unless they have evidence that your daughter's presence would prejudice the efficient education of other pupils there, and that there are no reasonable steps which could be taken to avoid this (see case 20, and *What the law says*, below).

If your preference was for a special school, the LEA should consider offering you a place in another special school (see *Inclusive Schooling: children with special educational needs*, below).

But, whatever your views about the alternative school you have been offered, you have a right to appeal to the Special

Educational Needs Tribunal on the grounds of not getting a place in the school of your preference – and the LEA must prove why this has not been possible (see case 18).

You have two months to send in a Notice of Appeal to the Special Educational Needs Tribunal. Your grounds for appeal might read like this:

We are appealing against the LEA's decision not to allow our daughter to attend the local community school of our preference, on the grounds that:

1. The LEA's letter to us of May 7th fails to show that Mandy's needs could not be met in the school of our preference.

2. The LEA have produced no evidence that other children's education would be prejudiced by Mandy's presence in the school.

3. The LEA have produced no figures or costings showing that placing Mandy in the school of our preference would represent an inefficient use of resources.

Along with the form send a copy of the statement and all of the professional advice attached to it. You might also want to appeal against the way Mandy's needs have been described in Part 2 and the way the provision has been specified in Part 3 (see case 27).

An additional ground for your appeal could be that the travelling involved would be so stressful that Mandy would be unable to benefit from the educational provision available at the school (see *What the courts have said* below).

It is important that you get advice on appealing to the Tribunal if you are at all unsure of the arguments you should be making. See part 8 for the numbers of support organisations.

For more information on appealing to the Tribunal, see part 3 of this guide.

What happens after that

Legally, the LEA do not have to offer Mandy a place in a school other than the one named on the finalised statement, although in practice many LEAs allow children to remain at their present school or nursery when parents are appealing against a statement. You should speak to the head of the school or nursery about this and write to the Chief Education Officer making a formal request, if this is what you think would be best for her.

Legally, you are entitled to educate Mandy at home, but the LEA have a duty to check up to ensure that her needs are being met. However, this does not mean that you have a legal duty to arrange all of the provision specified in Part 3 of the statement. If you are considering home education, speak to one of the support organisations first. If the LEA are not satisfied that you are providing for Mandy's needs at home, it is possible that they may serve an Attendance Order on you, which could end up in your being prosecuted in a magistrate's court, and fined. If your LEA send you a notice of Attendance Order, you must seek immediate legal advice from a solicitor.

What the law says

The 1996 Education Act says:

'(1) Every local education authority shall make arrangements for enabling a parent –

(a) on whom a copy of a proposed statement has been served under paragraph 2,

(b) on whom a copy of a proposed amended statement has been served under paragraph 2A, or

(c) on whom an amendment notice has been served under paragraph 2A which contains a proposed amendment about –

  (i) the type or name of a school or institution, or

  (ii) the provision made for the child concerned under arrangements made under section 319, to be specified in the statement,]

to express a preference as to the maintained school at which he wishes education to be provided for his child and to give reasons for his preference.

(2) Any such preference must be expressed or made within the period of 15 days beginning –

(a) with the date on which the written notice mentioned in paragraph 2B was served on the parent, or
(b) if a meeting has (or meetings have) been arranged under paragraph 4(1)(b) or (2), with the date fixed for that meeting (or the last of those meetings).

(3) Where a local education authority make a statement in a case where the parent of the child concerned has expressed a preference in pursuance of such arrangements as to the school at which he wishes education to be provided for his child, they shall specify the name of that school in the statement unless –

(a) the school is unsuitable to the child's age, ability or aptitude or to his special educational needs, or
(b) the attendance of the child at the school would be incompatible with the provision of efficient education for the children with whom he would be educated or the efficient use of resources.'

(Schedule 27(3))

Duty to educate children with
special educational needs in mainstream schools

'(1) This section applies to a child with special educational needs who should be educated in a school.

2

**Case
28**

(2) If no statement is maintained under section 324 for the child, he must be educated in a mainstream school.

(3) If a statement is maintained under section 324 for the child, he must be educated in a mainstream school unless that is incompatible with –

(a) the wishes of his parent, or
(b) the provision of efficient education for other children.

(4) In this section and section 316A 'mainstream school' means any school other than –

(a) a special school, or
(b) an independent school which is not –

    (i)   a city technology college,

    (ii) a city college for the technology of the arts, or

    (iii) a city academy.'

(Section 316)

'(5) If a local education authority decide –

(a) to make a statement for a child under section 324, but
(b) not to name in the statement the school for which a parent has expressed a preference under paragraph 3 of Schedule 27,

they shall, in making the statement, comply with section 316(3).'

(Section 316A)

'(1) The parent of a child for whom a local education authority maintain a statement under section 324 may –

(a) when the statement is first made,
(b) where the description in the statement of the authority's assessment of the child's special educational needs, or the special educational provision specified in the statement, is amended, or
(c) where, after conducting an assessment of the educational needs of the child under section 323, the local education authority determine not to amend the statement,

– appeal to the Tribunal against the description in the statement of the authority's assessment of the child's special educational needs, the special educational provision specified in the statement or, if no school is named in the statement, that fact.'

(Section 326)

'In exercising or performing all their respective powers and duties under the Education Acts, the Secretary of State, local education authorities and the funding authorities shall have regard to the general principle that pupils are to be educated in accordance with the wishes of their parents, so far as that is compatible with the provision of efficient instruction and training and the avoidance of unreasonable public expenditure.'

(Section 9)

What the courts have said

In the case known as *C vs Lancashire County Council [1997] ELR 377*, the parents appealed to the High Court on a point of law against the decision of the Tribunal to place their child in a special school, rather than in the mainstream school of their choice. One of the reasons put forward by the LEA, and accepted by the Tribunal, was that placing a child in a mainstream school was not an efficient use of resources. On this point, the judge ruled that the decision was not entirely a question of which option was the least expensive for an LEA:

'... one has to look at the figures, decide whether there is an additional cost, and then do a balancing exercise weighing the additional cost against the parents' preference ... it is partly a factual exercise and partly a balancing exercise.'

Case 28

In the case known as *R vs Hereford and Worcester County Council ex parte P [1992] 2 ELR 732,* the judge ruled as follows:

'It is implicit in section 55(1) of the Education Act 1944 that the LEA is under a duty to make such arrangements as it considers necessary for a child to reach school without due stress, strain or difficulty such as would prevent him from benefiting from the education the school has to offer ... It follows that where a child with special educational needs requires transport to get him to school, the transport which the LEA proposes to make available must therefore be non-stressful transport ...'

Inclusive Schooling: Statutory Guidance re. DfES/0774/2001

'Where the parents preferred choice of maintained special school is not named in the child's statement the local education authority must consider the request for special school education. In doing this the local education authority must have regard to the general duty imposed by section 9 (see above). In addition they must also have regard to the need to arrange suitable special educational provision imposed by section 324 of the Education Act 1996. The authority decides which school (special or mainstream) is named on the child's statement. Parents can appeal against the local education authority's decision.'

(Paragraph 36)

PostScript

You may be feeling very angry when you go to the Tribunal if you believe that your LEA have ignored their duty to consider seriously your preference for a particular school. Although you should certainly draw the Tribunal's attention to this, do not rest the whole of your case on criticising the LEA.

Try to show how, in practice, your child could receive appropriate education in the school of your choice, without other children's education being prejudiced and without resources being used inefficiently. If you believe a second professional opinion will help you show this, speak to one of the support organisations listed in part 8 immediately.

Case 29

Case 29

❝ Our daughter has cerebral palsy and her statement has just been finalised. We have no problem with Part 2, which says clearly that our daughter will benefit from a programme based on conductive education, or with Part 3, which says that she will be taught by a conductor trained in Peto methods. The problem comes with Part 4, where the LEA names one of its own special schools. We have visited this school and spoken to the head. Four of the teachers attended an evening lecture on Peto methods last year, and it is on this basis that the LEA now claims that the school offers conductive education for children. The real training consists of a four-year course, and is only offered by the Peto Institute in Hungary. The school we want is staffed by conductors who are Peto trained, but it is a private school. How do we prepare our appeal? ❞

The first step

The first step is to put on one side the arguments about the training and qualifications of the teachers at the special school. These are important, but not the most important part of the case you have to argue. In order to be successful at appeal, you will have to show that your daughter's special educational needs include the need for the range of activities, tasks and experiences which are embodied within the conductive education programme. Spell these out in detail. Do not just rely on Tribunal members understanding what you mean by the label 'conductive education.'

Having defined your daughter's needs in these terms, describe the provision required to meet them, again in a series of detailed points. Don't rely on phrases like 'needs to be taught by a Peto-trained conductor', because people may not know what that means. For each need in Part 2, try to specify – and quantify – the provision required to meet it in Part 3 (see *What the courts have said* below).

135

2

**Case
29**

You will also need to present evidence that the LEA special school is not able to make the provision necessary to meet your daughter's needs as you have described them. You may need a second professional opinion on the provision available in the LEA school to prove your point. See part 8 of this book.

You have two months to send in a Notice of Appeal to the Special Educational Needs Tribunal. Your grounds for appeal need to stick close to the points outlined above.

It will not be enough to prove that the school you want is better than the LEA school. You will have to show that their school cannot make the provision necessary to meet your daughter's needs (see *What the courts have said* below).

What happens after that?

The Tribunal will send a copy of the Notice of Appeal to your LEA, and give you and them 30 working days to prepare a 'Statement of Case.'

At this point you should decide whether you want to ask the president of the Tribunal to 'direct':

- that any particular witnesses should appear;
- that any particular information or documents should be disclosed by the LEA.

You will be asked to fill in an attendance form, giving the names of your own witnesses and your representative, if you have one.

For more information on how the Tribunal works, see part 3 of this guide.

What the law says

Section 326 of the 1993 Education Act says:

'(1) The parent of a child for whom a local education authority maintain a statement under section 324 may –

(a) when the statement is first made,
(b) where the description in the statement of the authority's assessment of the child's special educational needs, or the special educational provision specified in the statement, is amended, or
(c) where, after conducting an assessment of the educational needs of the child under section 323, the local education authority determine not to amend the statement,

– appeal to the Tribunal against the description in the statement of the authority's assessment of the child's special educational needs, the special educational provision specified in the statement or, if no school is named in the statement, that fact.'

What the courts have said

According to the judgement in the case known as *R vs Surrey CC Education Committee ex parte H (1983) 83 LGR 219*: 'There is no question of Parliament having placed the local education authority under an obligation to provide a child with the best possible education … or to educate him or her to his or her maximum potential.'

In a judgement known as *R vs The Secretary of State for Education and Science, ex parte E [1992] 1 ELR 377*, the court ruled that Part 2 of a statement ('special educational needs') must set out all of a child's special educational needs identified during an assessment; and, that Part 3 of a statement must specify the provision required to meet each of the needs identified in Part 2, whether that provision was to be made by the LEA or by the child's own school.

2

Case

29

In a judgement known as *L vs Clarke and Somerset County Council [1998] ELR 129*, the court ruled on the duty of an LEA to be specific when writing Part 3 of a statement of special educational needs:

'A requirement that the help to be given should be specified in the statement in terms of hours per week was not an absolute and universal precondition of the legality of any statement ... however ... in very many cases it will not be possible to fulfil the requirement to specify the special educational provision considered appropriate to meet the child's needs, including specification of staffing arrangements and curriculum, unless hours per week are set out.'

Case 29

Post Script

When you are preparing your arguments and your evidence for appeal, remember the basic principles underlying the law on special education. These are that individual children's needs are identified, assessed, described in a statement and then provided for. Your starting point must be trying to get as full a description of your child's needs as possible in Part 2 of a statement. Then, in Part 3, specify in as much detail as possible the exact provision or help necessary to meet each one of her needs.

If you can then show that the LEA's choice of school cannot, in practice, make that provision, you have the basis of a good case. On the other hand, if your only arguments are that your daughter needs 'conductive education' and that only a four-year Peto-trained professional can provide this, then you are not likely to be successful at appeal – not because you are wrong, but because the Tribunal members may not understand the terms well enough to appreciate what you are saying. To be sure, spell it all out in detail – both your daughter's needs and the provision required to meet them.

Case 30

❝ We have a finalised statement which we are not happy with, but we are finding it difficult to make our minds up about appealing to the Tribunal. This is because my sister-in-law won her appeal about 6 months ago and the LEA as yet have done nothing. Do they have to obey tribunal Orders? Are there any deadlines by which they must carry out Orders? ❞

LEAs have a legal duty to obey the Orders of the Special Educational Needs Tribunal. You should get your sister-in-law to ring one of the support organisations listed in part 8 for advice on what to do. Normally, a formal complaint to the Secretary of State for Education and Skills will get things moving (see page 270 for help with making complaints).

So, from the point of view of enforcement, yes, it is worthwhile appealing to the Tribunal if you are unhappy with your son's final statement.

As from January 1st 2002, there are legal deadlines by which LEAs must implement tribunal decisions. These differ according to what LEAs are being told to do, and take effect the day after the Order is issued.

Order	Deadline
To make an assessment	Must start within 4 weeks
To issue a statement after assessment	5 weeks
To reconsider decision on issuing a statement after assessment	2 weeks
To amend a statement	LEA must send parents an amendment notice within 5 weeks
To continue to maintain a statement	With immediate effect

To continue to maintain a statement, but with amendment	*Continue to maintain with immediate effect, with 5 weeks to send a parent the amendment notice*
To change the school named to a maintained school	*2 weeks*

Case 30

Note: When a parent loses their appeal against a decision to cease to maintain a statement, the statement ceases immediately, or on a day chosen by the LEA, whichever is the later.

What if it does not happen

There are exceptional circumstances which allow an LEA to take longer than the legal deadline to implement a tribunal Order. But, to do this an LEA must show: *first*, that the exceptional circumstance has arisen, and *second*, that this circumstance has made it impractical for them to meet the deadline.

The circumstances are:

- that exceptional circumstances affect the child or parent during the period
- that the child or parent are absent from the area for 2 weeks during the period
- the parent wants to make representations on a proposed statement beyond the initial 15 day period
- a meeting has been held to discuss a proposed or proposed amended statement and the parent asks for a further meeting
- the LEA have requested the Secretary of State's consent to a placement in an independent school but have not received this within 3 weeks of making the request.

If your LEA has breached the deadline for implementing the tribunal order and none of the above circumstances have arisen, then you need to get advice on making a complaint. Contact one of the support organisations listed in part 8.

If one of the exceptional circumstances has arisen but you do not feel that this has made it impractical for the deadline to be met, then, again, you should get advice on complaining.

What the law says

Regulation 25 of The Education (Special Educational Needs) Regulations 2001 says:

(1) Subject to paragraph (4), if the Tribunal, following an appeal to it by a parent, makes an order requiring an authority to perform an action referred to in paragraph (2) the authority shall perform that action within the period specified in paragraph (2).

(2) In the case of an order –

(a) to make an assessment, the authority shall notify the child's parent that it will make an assessment under section 323(4) or 329A(7) as the case may be within 4 weeks;

(b) to make and maintain a statement, the authority shall make a statement within 5 weeks;

(c) remitting a case back to the authority under section 325(3)(c), the authority shall take the action referred to in regulation 17(1)(a) or 17(1)(b) within 2 weeks;

(d) to amend a statement, the authority shall serve an amendment notice on the child's parent under paragraph 2A of Schedule 27 within 5 weeks;

(e) to continue to maintain a statement, the authority shall continue to maintain the statement with immediate effect;

(f) to continue to maintain and to amend a statement, the authority shall continue to maintain the statement with immediate effect and shall serve an amendment notice on the child's parent under paragraph 2A of Schedule 27 within 5 weeks;

(g) to substitute the name of the school or other institution specified in a child's statement with the name of a school

2

Case

30

specified by a parent, the authority shall specify the school specified by the parent within 2 weeks, and

(h) dismissing an appeal against a determination to cease to maintain a statement, the authority shall cease to maintain that statement immediately or on a date proposed by the authority, whichever is the later.

(3) In each case the period shall begin on the day after the issue of the Order in question.

(4) The authority need not comply with the time limits referred to in paragraph (2) if it is impractical to do so because –

(a) exceptional personal circumstances affect the child or his parent during the relevant time period;

(b) the child or his parent are absent from the area of the authority for a continuous period of not less than 2 weeks during the relevant time period;

(c) the child's parent indicates that he wishes to make representations to the authority about the content of the statement under paragraph 4(1) of Schedule 27 after the expiry of the 15-day period for making such representations provided for in paragraph 4(4) of that Schedule;

(d) a meeting between the child's parent and an officer of the authority has been held pursuant to paragraph 4(1) of Schedule 27 and the child's parent under paragraph 4(2) of that Schedule either required that another such meeting be arranged or has required that a meeting with the appropriate person be arranged, or

(e) the authority have sent a written request to the Secretary of State seeking his consent under section 347(5) to the child being educated at an independent school which is not approved by him and such consent has not been received by the authority within 3 weeks of the day on which the request was sent.

PostScript

You should always give your LEA an opportunity to explain, in writing, why a delay is happening. But, if you are not satisfied with their explanation, you should always get advice on action you can take which will get things moving again.

Case 30

Case 31

❝ Our son's speech therapy needs are listed under Part 5 (non-educational needs) and the provision is set out under part 6 (non-educational provision). We have just heard that we have lost our appeal to the Tribunal, where we tried to get the provision moved to Part 3 of the statement. Now we are worried about how specific the wording of Parts 5 and 6 should be. All the statement says under Part 5 is that he 'needs speech therapy;' all it says under Part 6 is 'regular speech therapy.' Will that be good enough? **❞**

The first step

You should get immediate advice on the Tribunal's decision. You can ask for a review of the decision within ten days, or appeal on a point of law within 28 days. Contact one of the support organisations listed in Part 8 for advice on approaching a solicitor.

If that doesn't work

If the Tribunal refuse to review the decision and you are not able to challenge the Tribunal's decision on a point of law, you should ask for an urgent meeting with the Special Needs Officer.

At the meeting, ask the officer these questions:

- What arrangements will be made for the provision of speech therapy?
- What are the objectives of the speech therapy provision?
- What are the arrangements for monitoring progress towards meeting those objectives?

Remind the officer that all this information should, by law, be included in Part 6 of the statement of special educational needs. Ask for an assurance that the statement will be amended in order to bring it into line with the requirements of the law.

Also, if you believe that the LEA should arrange the provision specified under Part 6, then ask. The law allows them to, if they choose.

At the end of the meeting, leave the officer with a written copy of your questions, and ask for the answers to be provided in writing as soon as possible.

If the LEA refuse to bring the wording of the statement in line with the law, contact one of the support organisations. You may be able to challenge the LEA for the way they have worded Parts 5 and 6 of the statement (see part 4 of this guide, which deals with judicial review and legal help). Again, you will need advice on contacting a solicitor who knows something about special education law.

What the law says

The Education (Special Educational Needs) Regulations 2001 say:

'A statement shall (a) be in a form substantially corresponding to that set out in Schedule 2 to these Regulations; (b) contain the information therein specified.'

'Part 6: Non-educational provision
[Here specify any non-educational provision which the authority propose to make available or which they are satisfied will be made available by a health authority, a social services authority or some other body, *including the arrangements for its provision. Also specify the objectives of the provision, and the arrangements for monitoring progress in meeting those objectives.*]' (our emphasis)

(Schedule 2: Statement of Special Educational Needs)

2

Case 31

What the Code of Practice says

'The designated officer for social services should work with the LEA to confirm social services provision and the medical officer for special educational needs should liaise as necessary to ensure that the health service contribution has been confirmed.

Part 6 should also state the objectives to be achieved by such non-educational provision and should set out the arrangements which have been agreed by the LEA and the providing body for its delivery.'

(Paragraph 8:44)

'When describing a child's educational and non-educational needs and provision, the LEA should ensure that the needs are clearly and accurately described and that there is full agreement on the nature and quantity of the provision necessary to meet those needs, consulting the relevant responsible professionals as necessary.'

(Paragraph 8:46)

Post Script

You do not need to let the matter rest when you lose an appeal. Even if there are no grounds for taking legal action, you should try to speak to the LEA again about the situation. You could, for example, ask for an early review of the statement (see case 38 for advice on influencing reviews).

If you feel strongly that your child's needs are not being met, talk the situation through with someone from one of the support organisations listed in part 8 of this book.

Case 32

❝ Our son's statement was issued last year and things went fine to begin with. Part 3 of the statement said he should have two hours individual specialist teaching, one to one, every week from a member of the learning support team. This teacher has just unexpectedly resigned, leaving Mark without his teaching. The school say they have no-one who can take the first teacher's place. The LEA says that, because Mark's statement is due for review in six months time, the need for continued support will be looked at afresh then. Is there anything I can do in this situation which will get Mark back his help quickly? I have been told I cannot appeal to the Special Educational Needs Tribunal. ❞

The first step

You can't appeal to the Tribunal in this situation, but luckily the law is very clear. Your local education authority has a binding duty to 'arrange' that the special educational provision set out in Mark's statement (under Part 3) is made. They can ask the school to provide Mark's specialist teaching, or they can ask for another member of the learning support team to take over. But if neither of these happens the LEA will have to take action on its own to provide Mark with his special education provision.

The LEA will be fully aware of their duty to 'arrange' Mark's special educational provision. After all, this is the whole point and purpose of statements of special educational needs. You should not delay in reminding them of their legal duty, by writing a letter to the Chief Education Officer. It could go like this:

Dear Chief Education Officer,

I am writing to inform you that your LEA are in breach of their duty to arrange the special education provision

Case

32

for my son, Mark ..., which is set out under Part 3 of his statement of special educational needs. This is specified as 'two hours per week one-to-one tuition with a member of the learning support service.'

The provision was discontinued with the resignation of the original teacher, and the Special Needs Officer has informed me that the LEA intend to wait until Mark's review (not due for six months) before deciding whether to replace the teacher.

I am sorry to have to inform you that if I do not receive assurance from you within five days of my delivering this letter that the provision specified for Mark will be immediately re-instated, I shall be placing the matter in the hands of a solicitor.

Deliver this letter by hand and get a written receipt from the receptionist at the Education Department when you hand it in, or post it by recorded delivery. Keep a copy.

If that doesn't work

See a solicitor. If you don't know a solicitor who specialises in education law, ask one of the support organisations listed in part 8 if they can recommend one.

What the law says

Section 324 of the 1996 Education Act says:

'(5) Where a local education authority maintain a statement under this section, then –

(a) unless the child's parent has made suitable arrangements, the authority –

(i) shall arrange that the special educational provision specified in the statement is made for the child, and

(ii) may arrange that any non-educational provision specified in the statement is made for him in such manner as they consider appropriate, and

(b) if the name of a maintained school is specified in the statement, the governing body of the school shall admit the child to the school.'

Case 32

What the courts have said

LEAs have been known, in the past, to argue that they have no legal duty to 'arrange' the provision under Part 3 of a statement when it relies on professionals employed by the Health Authority. One LEA, the London Borough of Harrow, were taken to court over this issue. They argued that because they had made the request to the Health Authority, their own duty had been fulfilled. The court disagreed and in a judgement known as *R v London Borough of Harrow ex parte M [1997] ELR 62* the judges ruled:

'In clear terms the obligation upon a LEA under s 168 (5) [1993] (now s 324 (5) EA 1996. ed) is simply expressed and subject to no qualification whether express or implied.'

Post Script

It is best to discuss any problems with your child's teacher and headteacher first, to see if a quick solution can be found. However, if your child is not receiving the special educational provision specified in his or her statement, you should seek legal advice quickly. You can see from this problem how important it is that Part 3 of a statement is worded in specific terms. If it had just said: 'extra provision to be determined and provided by the school's special needs department' then the legal position would have been much less clear – and your chances of putting the matter right much less strong.

Case 33

❝ We've just had a notice from the LEA telling us they propose to amend our son's statement. It says that agreement has been reached with the school for them to provide the first five hours of his 12 hours of learning support to be paid for from the school's own special needs budget. I've spoken to the head and she says there is no way the school can meet this cost and she has advised me to appeal. Is that right? ❞

The first step

You don't have a right of appeal yet, if all that has happened is that the LEA have proposed the amendment. Their letter should have told you that you have 15 days to ask for a meeting or to 'make representations.' This means writing to them and letting them know what you think. You should ask for a meeting with the Special Needs Officer. Take someone with you to the meeting, to support you and take notes on what is said.

At the meeting, ask the officer:

- Did you get any professional advice on the school's ability to fund five hours of Alan's welfare support, before you proposed this amendment?
- If so, could I have copies of those reports, in line with paragraph 8:128 of the Code of Practice?
- Will you confirm that it is still the LEA's view that Alan's needs call for the level of help which is being made for him at present and which is specified in Part 3 of the statement i.e. 12 hours of non-teaching assistance?
- Do you accept that section 324 of the 1996 Education Act places a duty on the LEA to 'arrange' the special education provision set out in Part 3 of Alan's statement?
- If the school informs you that they are not able to fund the first five hours of this provision, will the LEA withdraw the proposed amendment?

Take a written copy of these questions to the meeting. After the meeting, leave a copy with the officer and ask him to write to you to confirm his answers.

Then ask the headteacher these questions:

Case 33

- Is there money unspent under the school's special educational needs budget?
- If not, where will the school get the money to pay for five hours of welfare support? Will it come from provision being made presently for children with special needs who do not have statements?

After the meeting, write to the head asking her to confirm in writing whether the school intends to agree with the LEA's proposal and accept responsibility for funding five hours of welfare support for Alan.

If that doesn't work

If the LEA presses ahead and confirms that the statement has been amended, despite whatever was said at your meeting or in letters afterwards, you will need to appeal to the Special Educational Needs Tribunal, which is your right under special education law (see part 3 of this guide). Contact one of the support organisations listed in part 8 for advice on this.

What the law says

The 1996 Education Act says:

'(5) Where a local education authority maintain a statement under this section, then –

(a) unless the child's parent has made suitable arrangements, the authority –

    (i)   shall arrange that the special educational provision specified in the statement is made for the child, and

(ii) may arrange that any non-educational provision specified in the statement is made for him in such manner as they consider appropriate, and

(b) if the name of a maintained school is specified in the statement the governing body of the school shall admit the child to the school.'

(Section 324)

'(4) If, following a periodic review, a local education authority propose to amend a statement, they shall serve on the parent of the child concerned –

(a) a copy of the existing statement, and
(b) an amendment notice.

(5) If, at any other time, a local education authority propose to amend a statement, they shall proceed as if the proposed amendment were an amendment proposed after a periodic review.

(6) An amendment notice is a notice in writing giving details of the amendments to the statement proposed by the authority.'

(Schedule 27 (2A))

Regulation 17(6) of the Education (Special Education Needs) Regulations 2001 says:

'Where under paragraph 2A(4) of Schedule 27 of the Act an authority serve an amendment notice on the child's parent informing him of their proposal to amend a statement, they shall amend the statement before the expiry of 8 weeks from the date on which the notice was served.'

What the courts have said

In the case of *R vs Oxfordshire County Council ex parte P [1996] ELR 153*, the judge ruled that it was not unlawful for the LEA to obtain agreement from a school, after a statement had been finalised, that part of the cost of the special educational provision set out on the statement should be met from the school's own budget. The judge said:

Case 33

'... the (LEA's) decision ... could, of course, only be put into effect with the concurrence of the school ... But if ... the school were suddenly to turn round and say that they were no longer prepared to apply any part of their budget to the cost of the 20 hours extra support, it is undoubted that the (LEA) would immediately have to meet the full cost. The provision would in any event be secure.'

What the Code of Practice says

'For amendments following a review, other than after a reassessment, LEAs must send the parents an amendment notice that sets out the details of their proposed amendments. The amendment notice should be appended to the Notice to Parents set out at Part B of Schedule 1 at Annex A. They must explain the reasons for the proposals and ensure that the parents have copies of any evidence that prompted the proposal. Where a proposal to amend the statement arises from the annual review, the parents should have already received copies of the review report and the school's recommendations.'

(Paragraph 8:128)

Post Script

The law gives parents the right to insist on a meeting with an officer when an amendment to a statement is proposed.

After the meeting, leave the officer with a written record of the questions you have asked. Also, ask people to confirm in writing what they have said at a meeting as soon as possible afterwards.

Case

33

If a notice of amendment proposes a change to Part 4 of the statement (to change the school or type of school or 'education otherwise' arrangements), you have the right to express a preference for a maintained school.

Case 34

❝ Our 10-year-old son, Gerry, has refused to go to school now for the past month. He's had a statement since he started nursery, but of late he has not been making progress and his behaviour has gone from bad to worse both at school and at home. On Monday last week we wrote to the LEA asking for a fresh assessment of his needs. On Thursday we received a letter from them threatening us with an Attendance Order and court if Gerry didn't return to school. Do they not understand Gerry's problems? Or do they just not care? ❞

The first step

This could well be a case of the left hand not knowing what the right hand is doing. The first step, then, is to write and tell the person or department who threatened you with the attendance order that Gerry has special educational needs and that you have asked for a fresh assessment of his needs. Suggest to them that serving an Attendance Order would be premature, given that a fresh assessment may well identify a different school for Gerry.

The second step is to follow up on your request for assessment and find out when the LEA intend to reply to you. You should tell them about the threatened Attendance Order and ask them, in these circumstances, to reach a decision about an assessment as a matter of urgency, rather than waiting the full six weeks allowed in law.

If you want, you could also ask for an emergency placement to be arranged for Gerry in a special school for the purposes of a fresh assessment.

Hopefully, once everyone involved realises that Gerry's non-attendance is to do with his special needs rather than with you deliberately keeping him away from school, the decision to reassess will be taken quickly and the threat of issuing an Attendance Order will be withdrawn.

If that doesn't work

If the LEA continue with the threat of serving an Attendance Order, or actually serve it, you will need to speak to a solicitor who is familiar with education law. You should contact one of the organisations listed in part 8 of this book.

If the LEA refuse your request for a fresh assessment, you should get advice on appealing to the Special Educational Needs Tribunal (see part 3).

What the law says

The 1996 Education Act says:

'(1) If a parent on whom a school attendance order is served fails to comply with the requirements of the order, he is guilty of an offence, unless he proves that he is causing the child to receive suitable education otherwise than at school ...

(4) A person guilty of an offence under this section is liable on summary conviction to a fine not exceeding level 3 on the standard scale.'

(Section 443)

(2) Section 316(2) does not require a child to be educated in a mainstream school during any period in which –

(a) he is admitted to a special school for the purposes of an assessment under section 323 of his educational needs and his admission to that school is with the agreement of –

    (i) the local education authority,

    (ii) the head teacher of the school or, if the school is in Wales, its governing body,

    (iii) his parent, and

2

Case 34

(iv) any person whose advice is to be sought in accordance with regulations made under paragraph 2 of Schedule 26;

(Section 316A)

Regulation 12 of the Education (Special Educational Needs) Regulations 2001 says:

2

Case 34

'(2) Where under sections 328(2) or 329(1) a parent asks the authority to arrange for an assessment to be made, they shall within 6 weeks of the date of receipt of the request give notice to the child's parent –

(a) of –

    (i) their decision to make an assessment ...

(b) of –

    (i) their determination not to comply with the parent's request ...

    (v) the parent's right to appeal to the Tribunal against the determination not to make an assessment.'

Post Script

If you make a positive decision to educate your child at home, and can show that you have made adequate arrangements to do this, then it is unlikely that your LEA would serve an Attendance Order, or that a court would convict you. However, you should get independent advice on home education before you make a decision – see part 8 for details of relevant support organisations.

Case 35

66 Jane is nine. She's just been permanently excluded from her special school. We've been arguing for some time now that this would happen if she didn't get more help, but no one listened. We think this is unfair on her and us, but what can we do about it? 99

The first step

Where you go from here depends on what has gone wrong in the past and what you want for Jane from this point on.

For example, if you want Jane to go back to the school which has excluded her, you should write to the governing body and ask to be invited to the Governors' Discipline Committee meeting which has to be arranged to consider the exclusion. (See part 8 for a support organisation which can help you argue for Jane's re-instatement.)

If you do not want Jane to go back to that school, but still want to register a complaint because of the unfairness of the exclusion, you should write to the governing body with your complaint. In this case, however, make it clear that you are complaining about the unfairness of the exclusion, but *not* asking them to reinstate Jane.

Perhaps Jane's statement was not well enough written in the first place, i.e. her needs may not be fully described; or perhaps there is not enough provision specified on the statement. In this case, you may need to think about asking the LEA for another assessment of her special educational needs.

Perhaps the statement is well enough written but Jane has not been getting the provision specified in Part 3. In this case, you may need legal advice to get the LEA to fulfil their duty towards Jane by arranging that she does get the provision specified in the statement. (See case 32).

Perhaps the statement is well enough written and Jane has been getting the help as specified in Part 3, but you believe there should be a change of school for her. In this case, you could ask the LEA to change the statement to name a different maintained school in Part 4.

Case 35

Whichever of these applies to you, remember that the LEA continues to have a duty to 'arrange' the special education provision in Part 3 of Jane's statement even though she has been excluded. In practice, what this means is that they should be trying their best to resolve the situation as quickly as they can in order that her special educational provision continues. So, you could, if you wish, contact the LEA straight away and ask what it intends to do to fulfil its duty to 'arrange' Jane's special educational provision (see *What the courts have said*).

If that doesn't work

If you still want Jane to return to her school, but fail to persuade the Governors' Discipline Committee to direct the head to re-instate her, you will have the right of appeal to the Exclusion Appeals Panel (an independent panel set up by the LEA under the School Standards and Framework Act 1998). Seek advice on this from one of the support organisations listed in part 8.

If you want a different school of the same type, you could ask the LEA to change the name of the school on Jane's statement provided you have not done this in the previous 12 months, and provided the statement is more than one year old. (See *What the law says*). There is a snag with asking for the name of the school to be changed, and it is this. Although you have a right of appeal to the Tribunal if the LEA turns down your request, the Tribunal hearing your appeal is only able to alter the name of the school in part 4 (or not, if you lose the appeal). They cannot amend Part 3 of the statement. So, if Part 3 indicates a type of school other than the one you want them to order into Part 4, they are unlikely to do it. This is because it would create an inconsistency between Parts 3 and 4 of the statement. Before going down the avenue of appealing, it would be wise to get some advice on the wording of the statement from one of the organisations listed in part 8. For, it may be that you should be asking for a fresh statutory assessment. (see *What the law says.*)

The main danger in this situation is that things are allowed to drift, with Jane missing more and more school. Unless you are absolutely clear what you want, and how to achieve it, you should ring the appropriate support organisation in part 8 and get advice.

What the law says

The 1996 Education Act says:

'(5) Where a local education authority maintain a statement under this section, then –

(a) unless the child's parent has made suitable arrangements, the authority –

(i) shall arrange that the special educational provision specified in the statement is made for the child …'

(Section 324)

'(1) Sub-paragraph (2) below applies where –

(a) the parent of a child for whom a statement is maintained which specifies the name of a school or institution asks the local education authority to substitute for that name the name of a maintained school specified by the parent, and

(b) the request is not made less than twelve months after –

(i)   an earlier request under this paragraph,

(ii) the service of a copy of the statement or amended statement under paragraph 6,

(iii) if the parent has appealed to the Tribunal under section 326 or this paragraph, the date when the appeal is concluded, whichever is the later.

2

Case 35

(2) The local education authority shall comply with the request unless –

(a) the school is unsuitable to the child's age, ability or aptitude or to his special educational needs, or

(b) the attendance of the child at the school would be incompatible with the provision of efficient education for the children with whom he would be educated or the efficient use of resources.

(3) Where the local education authority determine not to comply with the request –

(a) they shall give notice in writing of that fact and of the effect of paragraph (b) below to the parent of the child, and

(b) the parent of the child may appeal to the Tribunal against the determination.'

(Schedule 27(8))

'(2) Where –

(a) the parent of a child for whom a statement is maintained under section 324 asks the local education authority to arrange for an assessment to be made in respect of the child under section 323,

(b) no such assessment has been made within the period of six months ending with the date on which the request is made, and

(c) it is necessary for the authority to make a further assessment under section 323,

– the authority shall comply with the request.'

(Section 328)

What the courts have said

In the case of *R v East Sussex County Council ex parte T [1998] ELR 251*, the House of Lords ruled that when an LEA makes provision at home for a child who cannot attend school, under Section 129 of the Education Act 1996, it must provide what is necessary, not just what it feels it can afford.

Although the girl involved in this case did not have a statement of special educational needs, the judgement is potentially useful in situations where children with statements are excluded or are out of school because of a dispute between their parents and the LEA.

In the final judgement the House of Lords ruled:

'There is nothing in the Act to suggest that resource considerations are relevant to the question of what is "suitable education". On their face those words connote a standard to be determined purely by educational considerations. This view is much strengthened by the definition of "suitable education" in section 298(7) (now section 19(7) EA 1996) which spells out expressly the suitability, viz. the education must be "efficient" and "suitable to his age, ability and aptitude" and also suitable "to any special educational needs he may have". All these express factors relate to educational considerations and nothing else. There is nothing to indicate that the resources available are relevant ...'

Post Script

It can help to inform a local councillor of what is going on and, hopefully, get them on your side. If the LEA moves quickly to find another school for Jane which you feel is suitable then you won't need the help of a councillor. However, if weeks turn to months and Jane is still out of school, there is a danger that she will get into the habit of not going to school! You might also find it useful to read cases 29, 34 and 39, which discuss the issue of home education for children who are out of school.

Case 35

Case 36

66 We moved home about two months ago. Six weeks after we moved we got a letter from the new LEA telling us that they had received a copy of Roger's statement from the old authority and that they would be reviewing it in three months time. The letter also said that the LEA had no plans to reassess Roger. Before we moved, he was getting four hours of specialist teaching support a week. Since we moved he has been getting nothing, despite the fact that we have spoken to the headteacher about his problems on a number of occasions. Do we have to wait for the review before anything happens? 99

The first step

No. Once the statement has been transferred to your new LEA they have the same duties in law as if it they had issued it themselves. The most important duty is to arrange that Roger gets the four hours special education provision specified in Part 3 of the statement. The fact that the LEA have decided to review the statement in three months time is irrelevant. They should be making the special education provision set out in the statement right now.

You should write immediately to the Chief Education Officer, along these lines:

To: The Chief Education Officer

Dear Sir or Madam,

I am writing to inform you that my son, Roger, has a statement of special educational needs, but that he is not getting the special educational provision specified in Part 3 of that statement, i.e. four hours a week teaching support. I understand that it is your legal duty to arrange that he gets this provision, and I would be grateful if you would reply to this letter immediately, informing me of your proposals for fulfilling your duty towards Roger.

Our family moved into your authority's area last October, and we received a letter on November 25th informing us that Roger's statement has been transferred from the old LEA to your education office. However, he has not received help of any kind with his literacy problems since arriving at his new school.

I have been advised that, failing a satisfactory answer to this letter, I should consult a solicitor. I hope that this will not be necessary, and look forward to your reply.

Yours,

Case 36

If that doesn't work

You should see a solicitor. One of the support organisations listed in part 8 of this book should be able to recommend one who knows about education law.

What the law says

The Education (Special Education Needs) Regulations 2001 say:

'(1) This regulation applies where a child in respect of whom a statement is maintained moves from the area of the authority which maintains the statement ('the old authority') into that of another ('the new authority').

(2) The old authority shall transfer the statement to the new authority.

(3) From the date of the transfer –

(a) the statement shall be treated for the purposes of the new authority's duties and functions under Part IV of the Act and these Regulations as if it had been made by the new authority on the date on which it was made by the old authority, and

(b) where the new authority make an assessment and the old authority have supplied the new authority with advice obtained in pursuance of a previous assessment regulations 7(5) shall apply as if the new authority had obtained the advice on the date on which the old authority obtained it.

(4) The new authority shall within 6 weeks of the date of the transfer serve a notice on the child's parent informing him –

(a) that the statement has been transferred
(b) whether they propose to make an assessment, and
(c) when they propose to review the statement in accordance with paragraph (5).

(5) The new authority shall review the statement under section 328(5)(b) before the expiry of whichever of the following two periods expires later –

(a) the period of twelve months beginning with the making of the statement, or as the case may be, with the previous review, or
(b) the period of three months beginning with the date of the transfer.

(6) Where by virtue of the transfer the new authority come under a duty to arrange the child's attendance at a school specified in the statement but in light of the child's move that attendance is no longer practicable the new authority may arrange for the child's attendance at another school appropriate for the child until such time as it is possible to amend the statement in accordance with the procedure set out in Schedule 27.'

(Regulation 23)

'The authority need not seek the advice referred to in paragraph (1)(b), (c), (d), (e) or (f) if –

(a) the authority have obtained advice under paragraph (1)(b), (c), (d), (e) or (f) respectively within the preceding 12 months, and

(b) the authority, the person from whom the advice was obtained and the child's parent are satisfied that the existing advice is sufficient for the purpose of arriving at a satisfactory assessment.'

(Regulation 7(5))

2

Case 36

PostScript

The new authority must review a statement within 12 months of the date it was issued, or last reviewed, by the old LEA, or within three months of the date of transfer whichever is the later date.

If it is practicable for a child to continue attending the same school, after moving home, then she should do so. If it is not practicable, e.g. because the school is now too far away, the new LEA must arrange for the child to attend another 'appropriate' school.

If your new LEA assess your child, they may use advice collected by the old LEA, provided it is not more than 12 months old, and provided you, as parents, agree.

Case 37

66 This is the start of our daughter's last year in primary school and we are getting worried about her transfer to secondary school. Sarah has Down's Syndrome and we have been led to believe that she will have to transfer to a special school once she reaches secondary school age – which is next September. We want her to transfer to mainstream secondary school with her friends and be supported there. Also, we are a Catholic family, and the mainstream school we want happens to be a Catholic school. Is there anything we can do to increase the chance of getting what we want for her? 99

The first step

LEAs have a duty under the Code of Practice to amend statements by February 15th in the year before a child transfers from one phase of schooling to another i.e.

(a) from primary to secondary school
(b) from primary to middle school
(c) from middle to secondary school
(d) from secondary to LEA maintained 6th form college.

From January 1st, 2003, this duty will arise under the SEN Regulations. (See *What the law says.*)

In order for statements to be amended by February 15th, discussions about school transfer need to begin early in the autumn term of the year before transfer. The best way to ensure that this happens is to request a review in this term (many LEAs do this as a matter of course).

Case 38 gives advice on influencing statement reviews and you may also find it useful to speak to someone from one of the support organisations listed in part 8. You should write to your LEA no later than December, reminding them of the duty to amend the statement by February 15th. Tell them which school you want to be named in Part 4, but if they cannot agree to this, urge them to amend the statement anyway, naming the school of their choice. This is important because appeals to the Tribunal can take up to 4 months and you cannot begin the process until the LEA have amended the statement.

2

Case 37

Remember that if you are asking for a maintained school, the LEA have a duty to agree to your request unless they can show that the school cannot meet your child's needs, or that the education of other children or the efficient use of resources would be prejudiced.

If you are seeking a mainstream school and the LEA turn you down, they must offer another mainstream school, unless other children's education would be prejudiced and there is nothing which could reasonably be done to prevent this.

But, also, remember that you can appeal for the school of your original choice even if the LEA have offered you another mainstream school (see case 18).

The LEA should take your request for the school on religious grounds seriously, but there is, in any case, a strong duty on them to give you the school of your preference for Sarah.

If that doesn't work

If the LEA refuse to amend the statement by the February 15th deadline, you will need advice from one of the organisations listed in part 8. If the delay becomes too protracted you may need to seek the help of a solicitor.

If the LEA amend the statement but without naming the school you want on transfer, you will need to appeal to the Tribunal (see part 3).

What the law says

Regulation 19 of The Education (Special Educational Needs) Regulations 2001 says:

'(1) This Regulation applies where –

(a) a statement is maintained for a child, and
(b) the child is within twelve calendar months of a transfer between phases of his schooling.

(2) In this Regulation a transfer between phases of schooling means a transfer from –

(a) primary school to middle school;
(b) primary school to secondary school;
(c) middle school to secondary school, or
(d) secondary school to an institution specified in section 2(2A) of the Act.

(3) Where this Regulation applies an authority must ensure that the child's statement is amended so that before 15th February in the calendar year of the child's transfer the statement names the school or other institution which the child will be attending following that transfer.'

Note: with effect from January 1st, 2003.

What the Code of Practice says

Thus, for all children transferring between phases, except from early education settings, a provisional recommendation should be made in the year previous to transfer so that parents can consider options at the same time as other parents. The child's statement *must* then be amended by February 15th of the year of transfer in the light of the recommendations of the annual review, the parents' views and preferences and the response to consultation by the LEA with the school or schools concerned. There will be no need to require the annual review for such children to be brought forward, since the information from the previous review can be used. All the arrangements for a child's placement should therefore be completed no later than the beginning of March before transfer. It is important for placements to be finalised as early as possible in order for any advance arrangements relating to that placement to be made and to ensure that parents and children feel confident and secure about the arrangements in question.

(Paragraph 5:72)

The LEA should consider very carefully a preference stated by parents for a denominational mainstream maintained school and representations made by parents for a denominational non-maintained special school or independent school. Denominational considerations cannot override the requirements of section 316 of the Education Act 1996.

(Paragraph 8:65)

Post Script

Parents' organisations should be pressing local councillors to get their LEA to adopt, as a policy, a strict timetable for making decisions with regard to the transfer of school for children with statements of special educational needs. This could include as a matter of policy, all parents of statemented children coming up to transfer to be written to one year before the transfer is due, with clear information on how and when the decision about their child's next school will be made.

Often, parents of children with statements are sent by mistake the same information on school transfer as parents whose children do not have statements. This can be very confusing. If this happens to you, ring one of the support organisations listed in part 8 without delay.

**Case
37**

When you are seeking a place in a school partly for religious reasons, you should seek to enlist the support of the church concerned. In some cases, diocesan boards have policies on welcoming children with special educational needs in their schools, and you may find that the school you want will, in turn, be particularly positive about accepting your child. If so, this might influence the LEA in your favour.

Case 38

66 I have concerns about my son's statement and provision. There is an annual review coming up. How can I best influence this? 99

The first step

The first step is to find out how the basic review procedure works (there are variations for children who are not at school and children having their first review after commencing their 10th year of schooling).

The LEA have a duty to review a statement, and do this in practice by considering a report sent to them by the headteacher of the child's school.

Before writing this report, the headteacher must get first written reports on the child from the parents, from anyone the LEA tell him to get advice from and from anyone the head himself or herself considers appropriate.

These reports must refer to:

(1) the child's progress;
(2) the application of the National Curriculum and substitutions for the National Curriculum;
(3) the transition plan, where one exists (i.e. for older students);
(4) whether the statement is still appropriate, or needs to be amended or dropped.

The head must invite the following people to a meeting (and send them, beforehand, copies of all reports received):

● a representative of the LEA, if asked to do so by the LEA;

- any teacher who teaches the child or is responsible for the child's provision, and anyone else in the school the head thinks appropriate;
- anyone else who the LEA or the headteacher thinks is appropriate.

Case 38

The meeting will consider points 1 to 4 above. If there are disagreements, individuals present will be able to report their own views to the LEA. When the headteacher sends the report on the meeting, he or she must indicate any lack of agreement between their report and the views of others at the meeting.

Copies of the headteacher's report to the LEA are sent to everyone who has been involved, including the parents, and the LEA's final recommendations are also copied to everyone as the last stage of the review.

As a parent you can influence your child's reviews in the following ways:

- By making your own report for the review as full and detailed as possible, arguing for what you want for your child and providing as much evidence as possible to back up your view.
- By getting the child to put his/her own views forward for the review, in whatever way is most appropriate. The Code of Practice emphasises the importance of the young person's contributions to statement reviews.
- By asking the headteacher to write for advice to any independent professional who knows your child and shares your views. If the head agrees, then this person should automatically be invited to the review meeting and have the opportunity, later, to write directly to the LEA if they disagree with the report produced by the headteacher after the meeting.
- When you receive copies of the other professionals' reports, study them carefully and try to find out who

agrees with you and who disagrees with you. Work out questions for the people who have written the reports you disagree with.

- If you disagree with the head's account of recommendations made at the meeting, which will be set out in the Annual Review Report, send your own report on the meeting to the LEA. Ask other professionals involved who share your view to do the same.

Case 38

You might find it useful to discuss how best to present your views at a review of a statement with someone from one of the support organisations listed in part 8 of this guide.

If that doesn't work

If, following the review, the LEA propose an amendment to the statement which you are not happy with, see case 33 for advice.

If you are disappointed because the LEA refuse to amend the statement in the way you wanted following a review, you might consider asking for a fresh assessment of your child's needs (see case 11 for an example of a letter you could write). Or, if you decide to ask for a change of the school named on the statement, see case 35.

What the law says

Regulation 20 of the Education (Special Educational Needs) Regulations 1994 sets out the procedure for review of a statement for a child who attends a school, other than a child in the tenth year of compulsory education. (See page 341 for the procedures in detail.)

Regulation 21 sets out the procedure for review of a statement for a child who attends a school who is in the tenth year of compulsory education. (See page 344.)

Regulation 22 sets out the procedure for review of a statement for a child who does not attend a school. (See page 348.)

2

What the Code of Practice says

Case

38

The whole of chapter 9 of the Code of Practice deals with reviews. See part 8 for advice on getting hold of the Code.

PostScript

It is always important to get professional support for your views on your child's needs whenever possible. As part of your preparation for a review, try to find out who, amongst the professionals who have worked with your child, agrees with you. Ask the headteacher and the LEA to invite a report from them for the purposes of the review. This will ensure that they are also invited to the review meeting.

Case 39

❝ I am trying to be as positive about this as possible. It's not just that I don't believe the LEA schools can meet my daughter's needs. It's not that I'm ungrateful for their offer of a place in an expensive private school – though to take it up she'd have to go residential (and I think 7 is a bit young to leave home, don't you?). The thing is, I honestly believe that I could educate Janine better than anyone else could, with a bit of support, at home. But I've been told that, as Janine has a statement, the LEA are unlikely to agree to this. What, exactly, are my rights? ❞

The first step

Section 7 of the Education Act 1966 places a duty on every parent of a child of school age to ensure that they receive efficient full time education suitable to their age, ability and aptitude, and to any special educational needs they may have. However, parents can fulfil this duty either by sending their children to school or, 'otherwise' – which, includes parents educating their own children at home.

Local Education Authorities have the power to take legal action against parents who fail to ensure that their children are educated when, for example, children do not attend school regularly (or at all) and when parents make inadequate (or no) arrangements for their education at home.

But if you, as a parent, are willing and able to provide education for your child at home, then the fact that there is a statement of special educational needs should make no difference. In fact, section 319 of the 1996 Education Act gives LEAs the power to arrange for special educational provision to be made otherwise than in a school.

The first step, then, is to write to the LEA and ask them to amend Janine's statement in part 4 in order to record that she is being educated at home. At the same time, you may want to think about any kind of support which would be helpful to you when providing for Janine. For example, a weekly visit by a specialist teacher, or a therapist?

Case 39

The letter you could write might start off like this:

Dear Chief Education Officer,

I am writing as the parent of Janine Walker, who has a statement of special educational needs maintained by your Authority. I wish to inform you that I intend to exercise my right under section 7 of 1996 education to educate Janine at home. I believe that I can do this in a way which is appropriate to her age ability and aptitude and her special educational needs, and I will be happy to provide you with information on the programme and curriculum which I intend to arrange for Janine.

I believe that, in this situation, it is appropriate for you to amend Janine's statement in part 4 to reflect the new arrangement, and I request that you now do this as soon as possible. At the same time, I would like to request amendments to part 3 of the statement in the form of the following additional points:

'The Authority's Advisory Teacher for the Hearing Impaired to visit Ms Walker on a termly basis to advise on the home education programme and offer advice on approaches and aids.'

'Weekly speech therapy, delivered by a Speech and Language therapist in weekly sessions of no less than half an hour duration.'

I look forward to your reply ...

If this does not work

If your LEA refuse to amend Part 3 of the statement, you can still educate Janine at home. However, you will not be entitled to the support for her which you would have had if Part 3 had been amended. Many LEAs more or less ignore children who are being educated at home by their parents. And this suits many parents. However, if you felt strongly about the additional support which an amended statement might give, you could ask for a fresh statutory assessment (see case 2).

Your LEA may amend the statement, but not exactly as you requested. For example, they may be happy to refer to the home education arrangement in Part 4 but not want to commit themselves to providing any help under Part 3. In this situation you will be able to appeal to the Special Educational Needs Tribunal (see case 27, and part 3 of this book).

Finally, LEAs have a duty to prosecute parents when they believe that they are failing to ensure that their children are receiving an appropriate education. It is unlikely to happen, but if you are threatened with prosecution you will need legal advice from a solicitor. The support organisations listed in part 8 will be able to suggest a solicitor you can get help from.

2

**Case
39**

What the law says

The 1996 Education Act says:

'The parent of every child of compulsory school age shall cause him to receive efficient full-time education suitable –

(a) to his age, ability and aptitude, and
(b) to any special educational needs he may have,
    either by regular attendance at school or otherwise.'

(Section 7)

'(1) Where a local education authority are satisfied that it would be inappropriate for –

2

Case

39

(a) the special educational provision which a learning difficulty of a child in their area calls for, or

(b) any part of any such provision,

to be made in a school, they may arrange for the provision (or, as the case may be, for that part of it) to be made otherwise than in a school.

(2) Before making an arrangement under this section, a local education authority shall consult the child's parent.'

(Section 319)

What the Code of Practice says

Section 7 of the Education Act 1996 recognises parents' right to choose to educate their child at home. Such arrangements are described as 'education otherwise than at school.' In such cases, if the child has a statement of special educational needs, it remains the LEA's duty to ensure that the child's needs are met. The statement must remain in force and the LEA must ensure that parents can make suitable provision, including provision for the child's special educational needs. If the parent's arrangements are suitable the LEA are relieved of their duty to arrange the provision specified in the statement. If, however, the parents' attempt to educate the child at home results in provision which falls short of meeting the child's needs, then the parents are not making 'suitable arrangements' and the LEA could not conclude that they were absolved of their responsibility to arrange the provision in the statement. Even if the LEA is satisfied, the LEA remains under a duty to maintain the child's statement and to review it annually, following the procedures set out in Chapter Nine.

(Paragraph 8:95)

In such situations section 324 (4A) of the Education Act 1996 does not require the *name* of a school to be specified in part 4 of the statement. Part 4 should state the type of school the LEA consider appropriate but go on to say that: '*parents have made their own arrangements under section 7 of the Education Act 1996.*' The statement can also specify any provision that the LEA have agreed to make under section 319 to help parents provide suitable education for their child at home.

(Paragraph 8:96)

PostScript

Many local educational authorities are supportive of parents who educate their children at home, and will advise on curriculum, out-of-home activities, record-keeping, etc. Do not feel that you need to secretive about what you are doing, and if you can think of some way in which the LEA can support you, then ask them.

On the other hand, if you come across professionals or officers who seem intent on making you feel inadequate and perhaps even guilty, contact one of the support organisations listed in part 8. Home education of children with special educational needs is becoming increasingly common, and you will find details of a support group for parents who are home-educating in part 8.

It is important for parents to keep a careful record of the work they do. Remember, although you do not legally have to send your child to school, you do legally have to ensure that they receive an appropriate education. By keeping a careful record of all the work you do with your child you will always be in a position to prove that you are fulfilling your legal duty as a parent.

Case 40

66 We've just had the annual review of our son's statement. He will be 16 this school year and the officer at the review meeting informed us that he would have to leave school in the summer and that his statement would then cease to exist. We have spent a long time arguing with the LEA to get this statement right for Richard. We do not believe that he will cope in a college and want him to continue his education in a school environment. Is it true that he will just lose his statement and that we will not be able to do anything about it? 99

The first step

Your first step must be to get some advice immediately from one of the support organisations listed in part 8 of this guide. This is because the law is not clear with regard to special educational provision beyond the age of 16 and judges in two court rulings have disagreed over an LEA's duty with regard to maintaining statements.

In 1994, in a case involving Dorset County Council, the High Court ruled that a statement could not simply cease to exist just because a young person reached the age of 16; an LEA would have to go through the proper process of ceasing to maintain the statement, which now includes giving parents the right to appeal.

However, in 1997, in a case involving Oxfordshire, the Court of Appeal (which is a higher court) ruled that, once a child was beyond the age of 16 and not on the roll of a school, an LEA were not responsible for them, nor for maintaining their statement, and that it was not necessary for an LEA to go through the process of ceasing to maintain a statement (or giving parents the right of appeal).

This apparent contradiction between judgements may only

be cleared up by a further court case or by the Government amending the law to clarify it.

With regard to Richard, if you believe that he should attend a school beyond the age of 16, but your LEA has a policy of all children leaving schools at 16, you will need to get an appeal in to the Tribunal early in Richard's last year at school in the hope of persuading the Tribunal to order a different school to be named in Part 4 of his statement. This may have to be a school in a neighbouring LEA (where children attend beyond 16) or an independent school.

2

Case 40

It is vital that you take action as early as possible in the school year. This is because it can take four to five months to get to a Tribunal hearing stage and, once Richard has reached 16 and left school, the Tribunal will have no power to order the LEA to change the statement or continue to maintain it.

You will need advice not only on how to get an appeal to the Tribunal, but also on how to get to a hearing quickly.

If that doesn't work

If Richard reaches his 16th birthday and leaves school, he may no longer be the responsibility of the LEA. You will need to consider how his education can best continue at a college. Many colleges make excellent provision for students with special educational needs. If you need advice on Richard's continuing educational career, you should contact SKILL, which supports students with disabilities and their parents (see part 8).

What the courts have said

In the judgement known as *R vs Dorset County Council and Further Education Funding Council ex parte M [1995] ELR 109*, the judge ruled:

'... a local education authority cannot divest itself of

Case

40

responsibility for a pupil's schooling when he reaches 16 by wrongfully failing to specify it, either by silence or express exclusion, in his statement and by refusing to provide it when he reaches 16 so that he cannot then satisfy the condition of the authority's continuing responsibility under Section 4(2)(a) of the 1981 Education Act, namely by being a registered pupil at a school appropriate to his needs …

Dorset's duty under Section 7(1) and (2) of the Education Act 1981 to maintain the 1992 statement of Mark's special educational needs and to arrange for him the special educational provision specified in it continues until Dorset amends or ceases to maintain the statement in accordance with the procedures set out in paragraphs 6 and 7 of schedule 1 to, and section 8 of, the 1981 Act.'

In the judgement known as *R vs Oxfordshire County Council ex parte B [1997] ELR 90* the judge ruled:

'… insofar as Auld J (the judge in the Dorset case, above) was suggesting that there remained a duty upon all LEAs to continue to maintain a statement until it was amended or ceased to be maintained on a proper proposal by the authority, that proposition is expressed in my view far too widely … In my judgement the responsibility for the registered child ends upon the child ceasing to be registered and the maintenance of the statement … would cease with the cessation of that responsibility and registration …'

Post Script

Following a judgement known as *S v Essex County Council and the Special Educational Needs Tribunal* (unreported) a parent can appeal to the tribunal even though by the time of the hearing the child concerned is no longer the LEA's responsibility (i.e. is over 16 and not on the roll of a school). The key issue, the judge decided, was that the child was the responsibility of the LEA when the decision to cease to maintain his statement was made. See page 268 for more information on this case.

The law on special education changes regularly as a result of rulings in the High Court. A book such as this can therefore be out of date in some respects before it even reaches the bookshop. This is all the more reason for contacting the support organisations listed in part 8 for advice if you are having a problem getting the special educational provision your child needs.

2

Case 40

Part 3

Appealing to the Special Educational Needs Tribunal

Appealing to the Special Educational Needs Tribunal

If your negotiations with the LEA do not achieve what you want for your child, you may need to appeal to the Special Educational Needs Tribunal.

When can I appeal?

The law provides a right of appeal in the following situations:

When your child does not have a statement ...

When your child does not have a statement, and the LEA refuse to do an assessment under the 1996 Education Act (see cases 2, 9 and 10)

When your child does not have a statement, and the LEA do an assessment under the 1996 Education Act but refuse to issue a statement (see case 16)

When the LEA finalise a first statement ...

When the LEA first send you a final statement, you can appeal if:

● you disagree with the description of your child's needs in Part 2 of the statement (see case 27);
● you disagree with special educational provision in Part 3 of the statement (see case 27);
● you are unhappy with the school named in Part 4 of the statement (see cases 29 and 37);
● there is no school named in Part 4 and you are unhappy about this.

When your child has a statement ...

When your child has a statement and the LEA refuse to carry out a further assessment under the 1996 Education Act.

When your child has a statement and the LEA do an

assessment under the 1996 Education Act but refuse to amend the existing statement. If this happens, you can appeal if:

- you disagree with the description of your child's needs in Part 2;
- you disagree with special educational provision in Part 3;
- you are unhappy with the school named in Part 4;
- there is no school named in Part 4 and you are unhappy about this.

When your child has a statement, and the LEA do an assessment under the 1996 Education Act and amend the existing statement. If this happens, you can appeal if:

- you disagree with the description of your child's needs in Part 2;
- you disagree with special educational provision in Part 3;
- you are unhappy with the school named in Part 4;
- there is no school named in Part 4 and you are unhappy about this.

Note: You are not limited to appealing against the specific amendment made.

When the LEA amend your child's statement without doing an assessment, you can appeal if:

- you disagree with the description of your child's needs in Part 2;
- you disagree with special educational provision in Part 3;
- you are unhappy with the school named in Part 4;
- there is no school named in Part 4 and you are unhappy about this.

Note: You are not limited to appealing against the specific amendment made.

When the LEA ceases to maintain your child's statement (see case 40).

When the LEA refuses to change the name of the school on your child's statement (see case 35).

How do I appeal?

Your LEA should let you know of your right to appeal when they inform you of their decision. You should also receive a booklet called *Special Educational Needs Tribunal – How to appeal*. If you have not been sent this, ask the LEA to send you one or telephone the Tribunal office (01325 392 555) and you'll be posted a copy free of charge. The booklet is easy to understand and contains much of the information about appeals that you will need. The staff at the Tribunal office are also able to answer queries.

At the back of the booklet you will find a form to fill in and send to the Tribunal. This form is called the *Notice of Appeal*, and you must make sure you provide all the information it asks for. It must arrive at the Tribunal within two months of your LEA telling you of your right to appeal.

You will need to set out your reasons for appeal. You can use a separate sheet for these, but try to keep them brief and to the point. There is no need to set out your full argument; just let the Tribunal know the main issues that you are unhappy with. Concentrate on what are now the main issues of the case and what you are asking for, rather than dwelling on what has gone wrong in the past.

Can I succeed against the LEA?

It is not possible to know for sure if any case will be successful. The Special Educational Needs Tribunal is independent of the LEA, though, and many parents are successful in their appeals. A high proportion of cases do not reach a hearing – usually because the LEA back down or a reasonable solution is found with which all concerned are happy. Many LEAs begin to negotiate once an appeal is started.

Do I need a solicitor?

Legal help in the form of funding is not available for representation by a solicitor or barrister at the Special Educational Needs Tribunal. If you are receiving income support, job-seekers allowance or have very low income, you will be entitled to free legal advice which could help with preparing your case but will not cover representation at the hearing. Most cases are likely to be decided on the facts rather than on points of law, however, and most parents should be able to represent themselves in the informal setting of the Tribunal. If you do decide to pay for a solicitor, make sure it is one of the few who have experience of special education law.

Where might I go wrong?

It is important to remember that the Tribunal rules have to be strictly followed. For example, the Notice of Appeal must be sent to the Tribunal within two months from the day you received the letter telling you of your right to appeal. This applies even if you are negotiating with the LEA and hope to manage without an appeal.

You need to get your written evidence ready as soon as possible as this must be sent in by the deadline the Tribunal give you for your 'Statement of Case.' This will be at least 30 working days from when you are told.

The case will be decided on the evidence before the tribunal on the day. You are unlikely to succeed without relevant evidence. If the LEA are disputing the nature and extent of your child's learning difficulties, you will need professional evidence from someone suitably qualified who knows or has met your child. This could be a teacher, for example, and may be someone who has already provided advice that the

LEA have ignored. The professional evidence should specify and quantify the provision your child needs if this is in dispute. The tribunal will be unwilling to name a school unless they have evidence from someone who knows about what it can offer. If the LEA's case turns on what the school can reasonably provide from within its resources, you will need someone who knows about the school budget to give evidence.

Remember, too, that the tribunal will look at the whole statement, even though you may want only to change part of it. In general, when you are appealing against the school named in Part 4, it is best to appeal against Parts 2 and 3 as well.

What if I don't succeed?

If you do not succeed in your appeal, there is a possibility of a further appeal to the High Court, but only on a point of law. You will need legal advice to decide whether you have an appeal in law, and then, if you do appeal, legal representation in the High Court. Unless you are on a low income which brings you within the legal help bracket, you are likely to face difficulties in taking an appeal. Legal costs are likely to be large and, even if you can afford to pay your own solicitors, you run the risk of being made to pay the LEA's costs if you are unsuccessful.

The decision of the tribunal can sometimes be reviewed if, for example, there has been a procedural error or fraud discovered after the decision. An application to review the decision must be made in writing not later than ten working days after the decision was sent.

Part 4

Discrimination against disabled children in schools

Discrimination against disabled children in schools

4

Introduction

From the early 1980s, there was growing pressure by disabled people and their organisations for legislation to begin to address the discrimination that disabled people face. This pressure grew through increasing awareness that the disadvantaged situation of disabled people was overwhelmingly as a result of the way that society deals with and provides for disabled people, rather than as a result of the individual's medical condition. Around fourteen attempts at anti-discrimination legislation were made, principally by backbench MPs bringing private member's bills, all of which were unsuccessful.

However, in 1995, the then Government of the day passed the Disability Discrimination Act (the DDA). That act introduced, for the first time in British law, some anti-discrimination protection for some disabled people in respect of some discrimination. However, critically, the DDA excluded education from those services to which disabled people had new rights, so that no disabled child or student had any new or different rights arising from that act, in respect of their entitlement to education.

After the General Election in 1997, the new Government came to power on the back of a manifesto committing themselves to extending rights for disabled people through enhancing and strengthening anti-discrimination legislation. They established a Ministerial Task Force which reported in December 1999. The Task Force made a number of recommendations, including extending anti-discrimination legislation for disabled people into the field of education.

The Special Educational Needs and Disability Act

Then, on May 11th 2001, the Special Educational Needs and Disability Act (the SENADA) received Royal Assent and was passed into law.

The SENADA deals with two areas of law –

- amendments to Special Educational Needs Law; primarily in Part 4 of the Education Act 1996 (which is covered elsewhere in this book), and
- amendments to the DDA to extend it into education.

This chapter will look at the new arrangements that will cover disabled children in schools, as a result of the amendments to the DDA brought about by the SENADA. Those amendments come into force in September 2002. Accordingly they will only cover incidents of discrimination on or after that date.

Who is a disabled person ?

Unusually, the DDA gives a definition of disability which is different to that contained in other legislation. In particular, the definition of disability – in effect, who is covered by the DDA – is not the same as the definition given to children with Special Educational Needs in Part 4 of the Education Act 1996. As a result, there are certainly some disabled children (who are protected by the DDA) who are not deemed to have Special Educational Needs and, conversely, there are some children with Special Educational Needs, even with statements, who are not deemed to be disabled for the purposes of the DDA.

The DDA defines a person as having a disability if: 'They have a physical or mental impairment which has a substantial and long-term adverse affect on their ability to carry out normal day to day activities.'

Physical impairment is not defined (although it certainly includes those with sensory impairments). Mental impairment is defined as including both people with learning difficulties and also those with a mental illness. However, for those with a mental illness, it only 'counts' (so that the person is covered by the DDA) if that illness is 'clinically well recognised.'

It is not sufficient for the person simply to have a physical or mental illness. In addition, that impairment must have 'a substantial and long-term adverse affect on the person's ability to carry out normal day to day activities.'

Substantial is defined as lasting for at least twelve months. This does not mean that the individual must have already had the impairment for at least twelve months but, rather, that they either have had it or, if it is 'newly acquired', it is anticipated to last for at least twelve months.

Finally, the definition of a 'substantial adverse affect on a day to day activity' is a reference to eight day-to-day activities defined in legislation:

- mobility,
- manual dexterity,
- physical co-ordination,
- continence,
- ability to lift, carry or otherwise move everyday objects,
- speech, hearing or eyesight,
- memory or ability to concentrate, learn or understand, and
- perception of the risk of physical danger.

In other words, at least one of those so-called day-to-day activities must be adversely affected in a substantial way, in order for the disabled person to be covered by the DDA. None of this is straightforward! The Government has produced guidance on the meaning of the definition of disability which expands further.

What are the new obligations towards disabled children in education?

The DDA is amended to require that schools and others:

- do not treat disabled children less favourably, for a reason relating to their disability, and
- make reasonable adjustments to avoid putting disabled children at a substantial disadvantage, as compared with non-disabled children.

This second obligation, the duty to make a reasonable adjustment, does not, however, cover –

- auxiliary aids and services, which remains the responsibility of the statementing process, and
- alterations to the physical features of the school, which are the subject of separate duties on schools and Local Education Authorities who are required to produce Accessibility Strategies and Plans.

What is covered by education?

Every aspect of school life is covered by the new duties. In particular, schools and other education providers must not discriminate in –

1. Admissions

This includes the arrangements made for determining the admission of pupils to a school, including the criteria for deciding who will be admitted to the school when it is over subscribed and the operation of that criteria, the terms on which the school or Local Education Authority offers pupils admissions to the school and by refusing or deliberately omitting to accept an application for admission to the school from someone who is disabled.

2.   Education and Associated Services

This is meant to cover all aspects of school life including –

- preparation for entry to the school,
- the curriculum,
- teaching and learning,
- classroom organisation,
- timetabling,
- grouping of pupils,
- homework,
- access to school facilities,
- activities to supplement the curriculum (such as a drama group visiting a school),
- school sports,
- school policies,
- breaks and lunchtimes,
- school meals,
- interaction with peers,
- assessment and exam arrangements,
- school discipline and sanctions,
- school clubs and activities,
- school trips,
- school arrangements for working with other agencies,
- preparation for pupils for the next phase of education.

3.   Exclusions

Finally the duties cover exclusions from schools so as to make it unlawful to exclude a disabled pupil for a reason relating to the pupil's disability.

What is discrimination?

Discrimination is defined as –

- treating a disabled pupil or prospective pupil less favourably for a reason relating to his or her disability than someone to whom that reason does not apply, without justification, or

- failing to make a reasonable adjustment to admission arrangements and to education and associated services to ensure that disabled pupils or prospective pupils are not placed at a substantial disadvantage in comparison with their non-disabled peers, without justification.

However, because of the words 'without justification', the law expressly allows discrimination in two situations –

- where it can be justified as the result of a permitted form of selection, or
- where the reason for the discrimination is both material to the circumstances of the particular case and substantial.

For it to be 'material and substantial' there has to be a clear connection between the reason that the responsible body gives and the circumstances of the particular case. The reason also has to be a substantial reason; i.e. one that is more than minor or trivial.

Some factors which may inform whether or not discrimination is 'material and substantial', and therefore lawful, include –

- the need to maintain academic, musical, sporting and other standards,
- the financial resources available to the responsible body,
- the cost of taking the step,
- the extent to which it is practicable to take a step,
- the extent to which aids and services might be provided through a statement of special educational needs,
- health and safety requirements,
- the interest of other pupils and persons who may be admitted to the school as pupils.

Who has duties towards disabled children?

Bodies who are required to ensure non-discrimination include not only the governing bodies of maintained (state) schools (including both mainstream and special schools) but also nurseries, independent schools, pupil referral units, the provision of Local Authority portage services etc.

What happens if unlawful discrimination arises?

Most claims of discrimination in schools are dealt with by the new, expanded role given to the Special Educational Needs Tribunal, which is re-named the Special Educational Needs and Disability Tribunal. However, in respect of claims of discrimination in the admission of disabled applicants to maintained schools, or the permanent exclusion from maintained schools, those claims and cases are dealt with by the expanded roles given to the Local Education Authority and governing body Independent Appeal Panels for admissions and exclusions.

Remedies available to a disabled pupil who has been discriminated against do not include financial compensation. However, they might include –

- disability training for staff,
- the preparation of guidance for staff on combating disability discrimination,
- meetings between a Local Education Authority Equal Opportunity Officer, parents, the pupil and the school to review what reasonable adjustments (aside from those to physical premises or which would otherwise be covered by statements) might be required,
- the review or alteration of school of Local Education Authority policies,

- additional tuition to compensate for missed lessons,
- the relocation of facilities (short of requiring an adjustment to physical premises),
- the admission of a disabled pupil to an independent school or the admission on the same terms as pupils who are not disabled,
- additional tuition for a temporarily excluded pupil to enable him/her to catch up,
- a formal written apology.

In addition, Independent Appeal Panels can, of course, order the admission of a pupil or overturn the permanent exclusion of a pupil.

Claims of discrimination normally have to be brought within 6 months, although there are conciliation arrangements, operated by the Disability Rights Commission, which might extend this period.

Further information

The Disability Rights Commission has also produced guidance specifically concerned with discrimination in schools, which provides further helpful advice. However, it will be sometime before we know exactly how affective this legislation is and the extent to which disabled children will be able to benefit from the new law. For details contact the DRC on 08457 622 633.

Part 5

Judicial review and public funding for cases

Judicial review and legal aid

This part of the guide has five sections:

1. What is judicial review?
2. The principles of administrative law
3. What can the court do for your child?
4. Judicial review procedure
5. Costs and legal aid

What is judicial review?

Judicial review is a special type of legal action in which the High Court looks at an action, decision or omission of a public body to see whether it is within the law.

In the field of special educational needs, the public body (the 'respondent' in legal jargon) may be either:

- the local education authority;
- the Secretary of State for Education and Skills and, in Wales, the National Assembly for Wales;
- the president of the Special Educational Needs Tribunal;
- the governing body of a particular school.

However, judicial review is not restricted to the area of education. Most decisions of public bodies such as central and local government which affect the public are subject to the control of the courts in this way. For example, the High Court regularly looks at decisions on subjects such as immigration, homelessness and community care using the judicial review procedure.

In the course of reviewing all these different types of decision, the Court has developed a set of rules which apply generally to the activities of people and institutions carrying out statutory duties. Lawyers call these rules the principles of *administrative law.*

Administrative law has two important features. The first is that its rules apply irrespective of what the public body's decision is about. So, for example, a decision by the High Court on the powers of one local authority to license a cinema may be relevant to the question of whether a different authority can legally adopt a policy of never placing a child with special educational needs in a school outside its area.

The second important feature of administrative law is that its rules are not written down anywhere in a convenient and definitive form. They are not like the rules in the Act or the Regulations (see part 9) which are set out in black and white. Although it is possible to summarise them, they ultimately depend upon *precedent* – that is, what judges have said in previous cases. And, of course, different lawyers will interpret this in different ways.

This aspect of administrative law causes a lot of confusion both for parents and for administrators. It is difficult enough to get to grips with the detailed rules in the Act and the Regulations, and many people are completely unaware that – in addition to those rules – their rights and obligations are affected by general legal principles which are not written down.

This part of the book explains:

- the rules which the High Court applies when it is reviewing decisions about the education of children with special educational needs;
- what happens in an application for judicial review.

We hope this will give parents a better idea of when and how to use judicial review to protect the legal rights of their children.

In the next section we summarise *the principle rules of administrative law* which everyone making decisions about a child's education must follow. Then, we look at what the court can do for your child. Following this, we explain the

205

stages in an application for judicial review. Finally, as expense is a major worry for people who have to retain lawyers, we describe the help which may be available through the Legal Help Scheme.

The principles of administrative law

To succeed in an application for judicial review about special educational needs, you must show either:

- that the LEA (or other public body) do not have the legal power to make the decision or to take the action which you object to; or
- that the LEA (etc.) are under a legal duty to act or make a decision in a certain way and are refusing or failing to do so.

Lawyers refer to such a decision, action or failure to act as being *ultra vires*. This is a Latin phrase which, in English, literally means 'beyond the powers.'

Ultra vires is a difficult legal concept. The basic idea is that, in the United Kingdom, Parliament is a sovereign body. This means that, in contrast with the governments of countries like the USA, which have written constitutions and built-in protections for minority rights, the UK Parliament can legally do whatever it wishes.

It follows that:

- no other person or public body in the United Kingdom can have sovereign powers;
- every other person or institution which has public powers has them only because Parliament has given those powers to them. They only have the limited powers which Parliament has permitted and no more.

The constitutional basis of judicial review is that the court (acting on behalf of the Crown) is supervising the exercise of the powers delegated by Parliament and ensuring that those powers have not been exceeded.

This is reflected in the names of judicial review cases which always take the form: *The Queen on the application of A v B County Council.* This means that the Crown, on behalf of B, is calling on A County Council to account for the way it has used the powers which have been entrusted to it.

There is no definitive list of the ways in which the people and institutions which govern us can exceed the powers which Parliament has given them. However, the cases in which the courts have decided that public bodies have acted *ultra vires* can be divided into a number of broad categories:

Excess of power: cases where (whether deliberately or because they have misunderstood what their powers are) public bodies have done something which, legally, they simply cannot do.

Error of law: cases where public bodies have made an error of law in reaching their decision.

Improper exercise of discretion: cases involving the improper exercise of discretionary powers by public bodies.

Irrationality: cases in which the decision is completely unreasonable (or *irrational* or *Wednesbury unreasonable* to use the legal jargon).

Procedural errors: cases in which the procedures which public bodies have adopted have not followed the rules laid down by Parliament or have otherwise been unfair.

Breach of the Human Rights Act: since October 2000, public bodies must, in addition, act in accordance with the Human

Rights Act. The Act establishes a series of key principles (or 'Articles') and it might be possible for a public body to be held to have acted unlawfully if one of those Articles is breached.

Excess of power

The first ground upon which a judge can say that an LEA, the Secretary of State or the Tribunal have acted *ultra vires* is that they have done something which they simply have no power to do.

This is comparatively rare, because public bodies normally have a fairly good idea of what their powers are and take advice from their lawyers if they are not sure. But the point can be illustrated with two made-up examples:

- an LEA name speech therapy in Part 3 of a child's statement and insist that the parents must pay the therapist's fees;
- an LEA insist on parents paying for transport when the school is the nearest one at which the disabled child's needs can be met.

In both of these cases the public body would have no power to act in this way and, on an application for judicial review, the High Court could intervene and nullify the decision.

Examples of this type of *ultra vires* do occur from time to time in real life. For example, it is not unknown for LEAs to fail to arrange for the special educational provision which is required by a statement. For further discussion of this problem see case 32.

Error of law

A public body does not have to be exceeding its powers deliberately in order to be acting *ultra vires*. What it is legally allowed to do can be a difficult question.

208

For example:

> An LEA make a statement which lists 'weekly counselling' under Part 6 as 'non-educational provision.' When the counselling does not materialise, the parents raise the matter with the LEA, who reply: 'because this is listed under Part 6 of the statement as 'non-educational provision', the law does not allow us, as an LEA, to make the arrangements for it.'

5

This is an error in law, in that although the law does not insist on an LEA arranging non-educational provision, it does not actually prohibit it.

Judicial review for error of law is possible because the court assumes that Parliament does not intend the public bodies to which it has delegated powers to apply the wrong law when reaching decisions. The court has therefore decided that no public body has any power to make an error of law upon which the outcome of a decision depends. A decision based on an error of law is therefore *ultra vires*.

'Error of law' can be justified as a ground of judicial review on the basis that if an LEA, etc. misinterpret the law, they cannot be doing what Parliament wanted them to do and must instead be doing something which Parliament has not given them powers to do.

The error must be a legal one. You cannot win an application for judicial review by proving an error of *fact*.

It is often difficult to tell a legal error from a factual one. Perhaps the easiest way for someone who is not a lawyer to understand the distinction is to think of the difference between asking the wrong question and giving the wrong answer.

For example, if an LEA looks at the wrong issues (perhaps its own policy of reducing out-county placements rather than a child's individual needs), it is asking the wrong question ('Can we afford this?' rather than 'What does this child need?') and making a legal error.

However, if two experts disagree on whether your daughter *needs* an out-of-county placement and the LEA or Tribunal decides that she does not, that is, at most, simply giving the wrong answer to the right question ('What does this child need?'). This, if it is an error at all, is an error of fact and the court cannot interfere with the decision (but see the section on 'Irrationality').

Judicial review is not about whether a decision is *right* but whether it is *legal* in the sense of being within the powers of the person or body which made it.

For example:

> Following an annual review meeting at a school, the headteacher completes the annual review report and sends it to the LEA. The report strongly recommends an increase in the amount of help the child is receiving under the statement and recommends an amendment to Part 3 so that 'three hours of support per week' is replaced by 'five hours of support per week.' The report refers to the fact that all of the professionals who were present at the review meeting believed this increase to be necessary.

> After considering the review report, the LEA decides to make no amendments to the statement and they write informing the parents of this decision.

The LEA officers have made no legal error in these circumstances. Although they have to await the review report before reviewing the statement, and although they have to make their decision 'in the light of' the report, they are not under a legal duty to follow the recommendations in the report and, therefore, are not making an error in law by choosing not to do so.

Improper exercise of discretion

Parliament often confers powers on public bodies which they do not have to use in every case, but may use when they consider it appropriate.

5

An example occurs in section 320(1) of the Education Act 1996 which reads:

'A local education authority may make such arrangements as they think fit to enable a child for whom they maintain a statement ... to attend an institution outside England and Wales which specialises in providing for children with special needs.'

Reading that section, an LEA might think that, as Parliament has said 'may' and not 'shall', they can do whatever they like.

But that would not be correct – discretionary powers must be exercised in accordance with the general principles of administrative law.

Like the other rules of administrative law, the principles which apply to the use of discretionary powers can only be found by reading the reported decisions of the court. The following is a summary, but applying the principles to particular cases can be difficult and (unless there is a right of appeal to the Tribunal against the decision) it may be worth contacting one of the Helpline organisations for advice (see part 8).

The basic principles are that discretionary powers must be exercised by the person or body to whom they were given and not by someone else.

For example:

> Your daughter has Down's Syndrome. You want her to be educated in your local mainstream school and the law says that this is what should happen unless:

- the provision she needs cannot be made in that school;
- the education of other children would be harmed; or
- there would be an inefficient use of resources.

The LEA's educational psychologist agrees with you that none of these present any problem in your daughter's case, but the headteacher and governing body of the school are unwilling to admit her. When the statement is finalised, it says that your daughter should attend a mainstream school twenty miles away and, when you complain about this, the LEA write back to say that it is not their policy to force schools to admit children with special educational needs against their wishes.

This is not a proper exercise of the LEA's discretion to decide on your daughter's placement. They must consult the school, but it must make the final decision themselves. In this case, the effect of their policy is that the decision on your daughter's placement has been made by the school, not by the LEA. Although you will have to appeal to the Tribunal, you may also be able to bring a judicial review against the LEA if it has a policy of *never* ordering a school to admit a child with special educational needs.

This example also shows that discretionary powers must be exercised on an individual basis, not on the basis of a policy which is applied inflexibly whatever the personal circumstances of the people affected by the decision. These powers must also be exercised in good faith and to promote the purposes for which the power has been given (in this case to promote the education of children with special needs).

For example:

Your son is now 14 and has been recognised as being autistic since he was five. There has been a long history of trouble between you and the LEA over the special educational provision which he needs.

212

Three years ago, you successfully appealed to the Special Educational Needs Tribunal to increase the provision in your son's statement. More recently, relations with the education officer in charge of your son's case have deteriorated still further and you complained to the Ombudsman. Last week the Ombudsman reported in your favour, heavily criticising the way in which your son's case had been handled and awarding you £3,000 compensation. Today you received a letter from the education officer proposing an amendment which would halve the help your son is receiving in school. Your son's statement is not due for a review and nothing suggests that his condition has improved recently.

You should see a solicitor about applying for judicial review immediately. There seems to be a strong case for saying that the education officer has made his decision in order to 'punish' you for complaining. That is not allowed. He must exercise the LEA's powers in good faith and not for non-educational purposes.

When discretionary powers are exercised, they must take into account all relevant circumstances and no irrelevant ones.

For example:

Your GP recently raised concerns with you about your six-year-old's development and arranged a referral for an examination by an occupational therapist. The therapist's report suggested that your daughter was experiencing problems with fine motor control of a kind which would impact on her classroom work. However, when the school was asked to read the report and to consider whether your daughter should be entered on the special needs register, the answer was 'no', on the grounds that because the referral to the therapist came from your GP, this was a medical not an educational report. The head and the governing body repeated this decision and reasoning.

Although it is true that the governing body ultimately has discretion over which children are placed on the school's special needs register, in this case they are basing their decision on an irrelevant factor. Whether a child has special educational needs or not depends on whether she has a learning difficulty or a disability which calls for additional or different provision to that normally available in schools. The fact that it was a medical professional (a GP), not an educational professional (such as a teacher or an educational psychologist), who first picked up on the child's needs is irrelevant. Also, by failing even to consider the occupational therapist's report, the governors are failing to take account of information which is clearly relevant to their decision.

Taken cumulatively, these principles mean that, far from having a free hand when an Act of Parliament says that they 'may' do something, LEAs and the Secretary of State are in fact operating under heavy restrictions and can only use their discretionary powers in a way and for a purpose which the courts recognise as proper.

Irrationality

Generally, the High Court will not use their powers of judicial review to interfere with a decision just because they disagree with it or because they think that the LEA, etc. got their facts wrong. It is usually necessary to prove that some sort of legal or procedural error has occurred.

But there is a residue of cases where the decision is so bizarre that the High Court has been prepared to say that it was so utterly unreasonable that it could not be allowed to stand. Almost by definition, decisions like this will be very rare: one Law Lord has described the test as being that the decision must be so unreasonable that 'the decision maker must have taken leave of his senses' before the court will strike it down.

Lawyers refer to decisions that are challenged on this ground as *irrational* or *Wednesbury unreasonable*. This is a reference to the decision of the court of appeal in *Associated Provincial Picture Houses Limited vs Wednesbury Corporation*[1] in which it was said that the court could set aside a decision which was 'so absurd that no sensible person could ever dream that it lay within the powers of the authority.'

Nowadays, the courts usually describe an irrational decision as being one 'which no reasonable authority, acting in good faith and properly directing itself as to the applicable law, could have reached.'

For example:

An example of Wednesbury unreasonableness can be found in a recent case[2]:

The applicant was a 16-year-old boy with severe language difficulties. He had previously attended a special school outside the county which was suitable but which did not take pupils over 16. The local authority suggested that he should attend the local College of Further Education even though it had no facilities whatsoever to meet his language needs. The background to the case indicated that the reason for this suggestion was to force the Further Education Funding Council to assume responsibility for, and pay for, his education.

The judge found that the LEA were wrong and that they were still responsible for the applicant's education even though he was over 16. He therefore did not have to decide about the suggestion that the applicant should attend the local college but added that if he had had to make a decision on that point he would have found that it was Wednesbury unreasonable.

---

[1] [1947] 2 ALL ER 680
[2] *R vs Dorset CC ex parte Goddard* [1995] ELR 109

Wednesbury cases are a very limited exception to the rule that judicial review is about whether a decision is legal and not about whether the court agrees with it or whether it is factually correct. It is rare for a case which relies solely on this ground to succeed.

Procedural errors

Procedural errors can lead to judicial reviews in two ways. Most obviously, there may be a breach of a written rule in the Regulations about how the assessment or appeal processes must be conducted. But even if there is not, the procedure taken as a whole must not be unfair by being biased against one side or by failing to take account of what both sides have to say.

Although you should always take proper legal advice before starting a judicial review, it is particularly important to do so if you are going to rely on mistakes of procedure. This is because the judge may refuse to make the order you want even if he agrees with you that a procedural mistake has been made. You will probably have to convince him in addition that the error is more than trivial and has influenced the eventual decision or prejudiced you in some other way.

You should also remember that, even if you win a judicial review on procedural grounds, the LEA, etc. will then have to go through the process again and may lawfully reach exactly the same decision as long as it complies with the proper procedures.

The Regulations
The Special Educational Needs Regulations contain detailed rules about the steps which an LEA must follow when assessing educational needs as special or reviewing a statement. Similarly, the Tribunal Regulations govern what happens at hearings of the Tribunal and give parents rights to call witnesses and to ask questions of the witnesses who are called by the LEA.

These rules are designed to ensure that parents have a maximum opportunity to consider the views of other people – and to put their own views – at each stage. A failure to follow the procedure set down will be an error of law and may be subject to judicial review.

Normally such a judicial review would be for an order to nullify the resulting decision but, if you are quick enough, it might be possible to get an order to prevent the assessment process from going any further until the error has been corrected.

The duty to act fairly
The duty to act fairly is also sometimes referred to as the rules of 'natural justice' which often leads to misunderstandings.

A decision is not contrary to natural justice just because you think it is unfair.

As explained above, Parliament is a sovereign body and legally can be as unfair as it likes. Provided an unfair law is unambiguous, public bodies such as LEAs must obey it and courts and tribunals must enforce it. It may therefore be that the LEA, the Secretary of State and the Tribunal not only can, but must, make a decision which you think is unfair.

One reason for this is that unfairness is in the eye of the beholder. Parents of children who do not have special educational needs may think it is extremely unfair that the provision for your child is protected because s/he has a statement while the provision for their children can be cut. The point here is not who is right, but that this sort of disagreement about unfairness is economic and political rather than legal. Courts and tribunals simply cannot make that sort of decision: they have to go by the letter of the law.

So, what do lawyers mean when they talk about 'natural justice' or the 'duty to act fairly'? The answer is that those concepts are about *procedural fairness* – that is to say, the way in which decisions are made and not the content of those decisions.

217

There are two basic rules. The first is that decision-makers should not be biased. The second is that decision-makers should hear what everyone involved has to say in an even-handed way.

The rule against bias
Some parents feel that the whole system of assessing the educational needs of their children – and in particular the fact that the assessment is carried out by the same LEA which will then have to find the resources from a limited budget to make any provision which is assessed as being necessary – is biased against them. But that type of bias is not sufficient for judicial review.

What you need to prove is the sort of bias which occurs when the person making the decision has a direct financial interest in the outcome or is a relative, friend or associate of one of those affected.

Proving that there has been actual bias against you would be very difficult. Fortunately that is not necessary. To succeed, you only have to show that there is a real danger that the decision may have been influenced by bias.

For example:

> Your son attends a school for children with severe learning difficulties which has been selected for closure from the two SLD schools maintained by the LEA. Naturally, all of the parents at your son's school are unhappy. But you are also confused, for the school which is to be retained, and to which your child must transfer, is an older building, in need of extensive repairs, whereas your son's school is modern and was purpose-built only nine years ago. The Secretary of State has yet to give his approval for the closure, although the decision as to which one to recommend has been made by the County Council.

> You discover that the Special Needs Officer wrote the report presented to the councillors by the Chief Education Officer, and that his wife is the headteacher of the school to remain open.

There is a real danger that the report prepared by the Special Educational Needs Officer, and its recommendation, has been influenced by a desire to protect his wife's position. This danger in itself may be sufficient for the court to accept an application for judicial review.

A fair hearing

The requirement of a fair hearing means that there should be an equal opportunity for both sides to put their case. What is necessary in any given case depends upon the nature of the decision which is being made. In the context of special educational needs, the standards which the courts might have insisted upon have largely been pre-empted by the procedures which Parliament and the Secretary of State have laid down in the Act and the Regulations.

However, there may still be occasions where, say, a tribunal falls below the standards which normally apply and fails to give a parent (or possibly an LEA) even-handed treatment, without actually breaking any written rule.

For example:

> Three days before the date of your Special Educational Needs Tribunal hearing, an elderly relative falls gravely ill and you have to go to take care of them. The tribunal refuses an application for an adjournment of the hearing and goes ahead without you being present. Your representative turns up in your place, but it is clear that the members of the tribunal panel are irritated by your absence and you believe that this colours their judgement of the case, which you lose.

The court may consider that the tribunal has denied you a fair hearing by refusing to fix a new date for the hearing.

Because there are so many possible ways in which public bodies might fall short of fairness, it is hard to be dogmatic about what would or would not be a breach of the duty to act fairly. As a general rule, if you feel you have not been given an opportunity to put your case in your own way, or that the LEA have adopted an unfair procedure or have been given 'an extra crack of the whip' by the Tribunal or the Secretary of State, and if the Act does not allow an appeal against the decision, then you should contact one of the support organisations listed in part 8 of this guide for further advice and, if appropriate, a referral to a solicitor.

The Human Rights Act

The Human Rights Act 1998 requires public bodies, such as local education authorities and schools, to act generally in accordance with the principles established in the Act. There are a number of principles but the key ones which may effect the provision of education are:

— The right to a fair hearing (Article 6)

— The right to respect for private and family life (Article 8)

— The right for protection of the Human Right Act to be given without discrimination (Article 14)

— The right not to be denied an education (Article 2 to the First Protocol).

The way in which the Human Rights Act may affect education law is very complicated but, for example, it may be used where a disabled child is required, against his wishes and those of his parents, to attend a residential school if he is to be provided with education. Although it is by no means clear, this may arguably be a breach of Article 8 (the right to family and private life).

What can the court do for your child?

First of all, what do you want the court to do?

Obviously this will depend upon which of the problems described in part 2 of this book you are encountering. In general terms however there are four types of problems which can arise:

- Something has been done that you disagree with and you want it to be undone – for example, the LEA have changed the person providing support for your child from a teaching assistant to a non-teaching assistant.
- Something has not been done which should have been done and you want to ensure that it is done. For example, having made a statement of your son's special educational needs, the LEA then fail to 'arrange' the provision which the statement calls for.[1]
- The LEA are threatening to do something which you feel is not in your child's interests and which you think is contrary to the Act, the Regulations or the Code of Practice. For example, your son has been placed in an independent special school. Your LEA is now threatening to stop paying the independent school because they say one of their own special schools can meet his needs just as well. They are basing their argument on the advice of their own special school headteacher, who does not know your child. You suspect that the LEA are simply trying to save money and you want the court to stop them in their tracks.
- The LEA have already fallen short of what is required of them and you think that your child has been harmed as a result. For example, your daughter has been sent to an assessment centre, but after two years no steps have been taken to carry out an assessment. In the meantime, she has been diagnosed as autistic. An educational psychologist tells you that if she had had proper help years ago she

---

[1] Contrary to the Education Act 1996, section 324(5)(a)

would not now be as far behind her age group as she is, and would probably not have developed the behavioural difficulties which she is now displaying. You want compensation for her.

A judge hearing a judicial review application has powers to deal with all of these situations. There are six different orders which he can make if he decides in favour of a child or his or her parents (or the 'applicant', to use the legal jargon). These are:

- A quashing order
- A mandatory order
- A prohibiting order
- An injunction
- A declaration
- Damages.

Each of these is dealt with below.

A quashing order

The most important order the court can make is a quashing order. This order deals with the first type of situation described above by depriving the decision which is being challenged of all legal effect. From a legal point of view, the decision does not exist once a quashing order has been made. Lawyers call this 'quashing' the decision.

For example:

The LEA has produced a statement for your son without obtaining up-to-date advice from his school. Instead, they have simply annexed copies of his old school reports to the statement.

222

The LEA has acted *ultra vires*. They must take fresh advice from all the relevant professionals listed in the Regulations. The court may grant a quashing order to quash the statement.

A mandatory order

The second order which the judge can make is called a mandatory order. It tells the LEA or other public body to perform its legal duties if they are refusing or failing to do so.

For example:

Your daughter's statement says that she is to receive ten hours of teaching support each week. When it arrives, there is a covering letter from the LEA saying that they do not have enough money in their budget at present to pay for another teacher, but your daughter's name will be placed on a waiting list and she will receive the extra help 'as soon as resources permit, possibly in the next financial year'.

The LEA cannot do this, and have a legal duty to arrange the educational provision specified in Part 3 of the statement. They must find the necessary resources now and the court may issue a mandatory order to compel them to do so.

A prohibiting order

A prohibiting order is like a quashing order but operates at an earlier stage – i.e. before the decision which is being challenged is actually made. If an LEA or other public body is threatening to make an illegal decision – i.e. one which could be quashed by a quashing order, if it had been made – the court may make a prohibiting order to stop it.

For example:

> Case 40 provides an example of a situation in which prohibition might help. In that case, the LEA are threatening to cease to make the provision in your son's statement as soon as he reaches 16 and for no reason other than his age. Following the Goddard case (see above and part 5) it is clear that this would be illegal. Applying for a prohibiting order now may ensure that the position is sorted out before your son's 16th birthday.

The same effect could also be achieved by an interim injunction and, perhaps as a result of this overlap, prohibition is quite a rare order in practice.

An injunction

An injunction is an order from the Court telling an LEA, the Secretary of State or the Tribunal either to do something or not to do it.

In either case, disobedience or failure to comply is a contempt of court and can be punished by a fine, imprisonment or by sequestration (confiscation of assets) – or in the case of the Secretary of State, by parliamentary censure.

There are two types of injunction – interim (temporary) and final (permanent). Final injunctions are made at the end of a case, after a full hearing, and govern the relationships of the parties for the indefinite future.

For example:

> Your son has cerebral palsy and needs to be taken the six miles to his special school by car. The LEA refuse to arrange and pay for transport on the grounds that you – his father – are registered as unemployed and are therefore available to take and collect your son from school yourself.

However, you are also registered disabled, following an industrial accident, and it is impossible for you to drive. An injunction can compel the LEA to provide transport for your son at their own expense.

Interim injunctions deal with the period between the start of the case and the final hearing and, sometimes, the whole case depends on whether or not you manage to get one.

For historical reasons there is a large overlap between injunctions and the other orders. For example, if you want to compel an LEA to make the provision set out in your child's statement, you could do it either by obtaining a mandatory order or by getting a mandatory injunction. If you want the LEA not to go ahead with a reassessment of your child's needs you could ask for a prohibiting order or for an injunction ordering them not to do so.

A declaration

As its name suggests, a declaration declares the legal rights and obligations of the parties or the legal status of a decision or act. Unlike an injunction, it does not tell anyone to do or not to do something, nor does it threaten them with punishment if they disobey.

However, there are occasions when parents need an authoritative and binding statement of their or their child's legal rights. It is then that the declaration comes into its own.

For example:

A good example of the use of a declaration can be found in *ex parte M*, the 'Lancashire' case on speech therapy (see part 6). M's parents obtained a declaration from the court that speech therapy could amount to 'educational provision.' It followed from this that Lancashire were correct to have included it in M's Statement and were obliged to arrange and pay for the therapy.

5

Similarly in the Goddard case (above and part 6), the judge made a declaration that Dorset's duty to maintain the applicant's statement continued after his 16th birthday and that Dorset were in breach of it.

Again, there is considerable overlap with other remedies. For example, if you disagree with a ruling of the Secretary of State, you could either ask the court to quash it by a quashing order or to declare that it is legally incorrect.

Damages

If you are in the fourth situation – that is you feel your child has been harmed by something illegal which has been done in the past – you can also use the judicial review procedure to claim damages. However, there are a number of restrictive rules which make this difficult in practice.

First of all, you are only allowed to claim damages in a judicial review application if you could have claimed them in an ordinary court action started at the same time. In other words, your child will not automatically get compensation just because you have won the judicial review. You have to prove what lawyers call a 'tort' as well as at least one of the grounds for judicial review. A tort is a civil wrong in private law such as negligence, breach of statutory duty or misfeasance in a public office.

The need to prove one of these leads to a second difficulty which is specific to the law on education, namely that not all the duties imposed in Acts of Parliament are the same. Some duties certainly give rise to a claim for damages, but others do not.

The House of Lords has decided that a local education authority cannot be held liable to pay damages to someone because of the way that it has carried out its legal duties. However, in some cases, local education authorities and others have separate (what are known as 'common law') duties quite apart from those set out in law and although these duties may look identical to the duties given to them by Parliament, they may result in claims for compensation. This is a complicated area of law upon which specialist legal advice should be sought. In any event, there have been cases where individuals have been able to sue local education authorities and others because of the negligent provision of education by individuals.

Judicial review procedure

Parents who decide to start a judicial review are strongly advised to instruct a solicitor to handle the case. If you do not know of a solicitor with experience of judicial review and the law governing special educational needs, you should contact one of the support organisations listed in part 8, who will be able to refer you to one. Your child may be entitled to public funding to pay for the legal costs.

What follows is a brief outline of the various stages in a judicial review and is designed to help parents understand the advice and information which they will receive from their lawyers. It is not a do-it-yourself guide for litigants in person; we strongly advise you not to start a judicial review without legal advice.

It is also important to remember that every case is different and that what follows is only general advice. If your lawyers advise you to do something which goes against what is said in this section or to do something which is not mentioned, it is likely that there are good reasons for this.

There are two stages to an application for judicial review. The first is the application for permission. If permission is granted then there is a second stage which involves a full hearing of the application. Finally there is the hearing.

The application for permission

Unlike other types of legal action, before you can start an application for judicial review, you first have to get permission from the court.

Time limits

The time limit for applying for permission is very short. You must apply promptly and in any event within three months from the date of the decision you are challenging. This means that the application should be made as soon as possible; there have been cases in which parents who have applied outside the three months period have not been allowed to go ahead because they were too late.

If you think you may need to apply for judicial review, you should therefore approach a solicitor as soon as possible. He or she will then be able to tell you how quickly an application should be made in practice, given your particular problem.

The court does have the power to extend the time limit if there is a good reason for the delay, but it does not have to do so. One common cause of delay is getting public funding (particularly if you have to appeal). The court will usually extend the time limit if this has been a problem in your case, but only if you have not contributed to the delay in any way. It is therefore important for your solicitor to keep careful records of all communications with the Legal Services Commission.

The documents

Once public funding has been granted, your solicitor needs two formal legal documents to make the application for permission. He/she will probably send the papers on the case to a barrister, who will draft these documents.

The first document is called a *Claim Form* and is a statement of the decision which you want to challenge, the facts of your case and the reasons why you say the decision is unlawful.

228

The second document is a witness statement. This will confirm the truth of the facts set out in your *Claim Form* and will contain a written statement of your evidence. Copies of all the documents which are relevant to your case (e.g., the statement of special educational needs and the reports of the teachers and educational psychologists, etc.) will be *exhibited* to the witness statement. This means that they will be put into separate marked bundles and referred to in the main text of the witness statement.

Ideally, a witness statement should be signed by someone who has first-hand knowledge of what is stated in it. This means that one of the parents will probably have to sign the witness statements, and it also means that in a complex case there may be two or more such statements.

Persons applying for judicial review are required to put all relevant information before the Court. This means that it may be that a witness statement which your solicitor asks you to sign may contain things which you would prefer not to tell the Court.

It is extremely important that you should read the witness statement before you sign it and that everything you say in it is correct. This is for two reasons:

- if you sign something that you either know is untrue, or you do not believe to be true, you can be prosecuted for perjury and possibly sent to prison;
- although in most judicial reviews all the evidence is given by witness statement so that no-one has to go into the witness box, the court does have the power to order you to attend the hearing and be cross-examined. This would mean that you would have to go into the witness box, where the respondents' barrister would ask you questions about what you have said in the statement. Such orders are very rare in practice, but one of the occasions on which they may be made is when there is a reason for thinking that what is said in the witness statement is not the truth.

So, you should not assume that the witness statement is correct just because your solicitor or barrister has drafted it for you. Check for yourself and ask your solicitor to have it changed if it is wrong.

Because children under 18 cannot usually bring court actions in their own name, one or both of the parents (or some other appropriate adult) has to put their name on the papers as the child's *litigation friend*. Your solicitor will be able to explain the legal implications of this in more detail, but what it means in practice is that you will have to sign a consent form, agreeing to act as litigation friend. Your solicitor will also have to sign a certificate saying that there is no conflict of interest between you and your child.

Making the application for permission
Before lodging an application for permission, your solicitor will have served what is known as a 'letter before action' on the other side, giving them notice of your intention to bring a judicial review and asking them to take certain steps within a specified period of time. It is important to do this in order to give the other side a final opportunity to do what it is that they should be doing.

When the documents are ready, your solicitor will file them at the Administrative Court Office in the High Court in London or in Cardiff. Once them have been filed there, copies must be sent to the other side (the Defendant); for example, the Local Education Authority, and, sometimes to another interested party (such as the Secretary of State). Your solicitor will have to also file a document known as a Certificate of Service, confirming that he/she has served the papers on the other side.

The other side will then have 21 days in which to put such information as they wish, before the court. Sometimes, if the matter is very urgent, the court can make orders shortening this timescale but they will only do so in exceptional circumstances.

Once the other side has had an opportunity to lodge their information, all of the papers will be put before a judicial review. Usually, this consideration is done privately, without a formal hearing and this is known as consideration of the application for permission to bring a judicial review 'on the papers'. However, it is possible to ask for a formal hearing to deal with permission and this might happen if the matter is especially urgent, if an injunction is required, and can also happen if permission is initially refused.

If the judge refuses permission, both on the papers and, subsequently, at any oral hearing (at which you may be represented by a barrister) it may be possible to make a further, final application for permission to bring judicial review to the Court of Appeal.

After permission is granted

If you are successful in obtaining permission, the court may make further orders; for example allowing for the exchange of further documents. There may also be discussion with a view to trying to settle the matter, without the need for a further hearing.

However, if a settlement does not arise, the matter is then likely to proceed to a full hearing.

The hearing

The hearing takes place before a High Court judge or, occasionally, before a *divisional court* of two judges. The hearing is in public and the media may be in court, but it is possible to ask the court for an order that your child should not be identified in any publicity about the case.

Unless one of the solicitors involved in the case is one of the very few who have the right to speak in the High Court, both sides will be represented by a barrister (or, occasionally, more than one).

The barristers on each side will have prepared a *skeleton argument*, a written outline of the points which they will be making to the court. The applicant's barrister will begin by explaining the background to the case to the judge and will then make legal submissions. The respondents' barrister then puts his or her case and the applicant's barrister has the right to reply. The hearing will normally take a day or so.

By this time the whole process is in the hands of the lawyers. It is very unusual for parents to have to give oral evidence, and unless they have been ordered to do this there is no need for them even to be in court (although they will usually want to be present).

Although the judge may give his decision at the end of the argument, it is more usual for him to *reserve judgement*. This means that he will take time to think about the case and give a longer, reasoned judgement. If this happens, there will be a further short hearing at the court when the judge reads out his decision and then deals with questions of costs and permission to appeal.

Appeals

Either side can appeal to the court of appeal against the judge's decision, but they first have to get permission to appeal. This can be, and usually is, requested from the judge immediately after he has announced his decision (although it is possible to make the application later).

If permission is refused, you can make another application to the court of appeal. The application will be considered by a single court of appeal judge (known as a Lord Justice of Appeal). If he or she also refuses permission, that is the end of the case.

If permission is granted, there will be a further hearing before the court of appeal, probably about a year later (although sooner in urgent cases). In most cases, the court of

appeal's decision will be final. It is possible
further appeal (again with permission) to tʰ
but in education cases this is very rare inᶜ

The timescale

At the moment, a routine application for judicial review
usually takes about 4 to 9 months from the application for
permission to judgement. This is not necessarily because of
delay on the part of the lawyers. The bulk of the time is spent
sitting in the queue (or the 'list', as it is called) waiting for an
appointment with the judge.

It may well be that a delay of up to 9 months would be
particularly damaging for a child with special needs, if the
matter concerns a failure to provide appropriate education.
You should therefore discuss with your lawyers what can be
done to speed things up.

For example, it may be possible to persuade the judge who
grants permission that the case is urgent and should be
expedited. Expedition is a polite way of describing queue-
jumping and, as all the cases in the queue are likely to be
important, some judges may be reluctant to agree to this.
Other judges, however, may agree that a case about a child's
education is particularly urgent, so an application for
expedition is always worth considering.

If you are asking for expedition, you should also consider
asking for the time limits to be abridged (i.e. shortened). For
example, the defendants normally have 5 days in which to
prepare any further evidence, after permission has been
granted. The judge may be prepared to reduce this to 21 days
or possibly even less.

Alternatively, you may be able to protect your child's position
by applying for an interim injunction to cover the period

tween the application for permission and the hearing. These are discussed in more detail earlier in the section on injunctions on page 224.

Statutory appeals against decisions of the Special Educational Needs Tribunal

On occasion, if a decision of the Special Educational Needs Tribunal is considered to be wrong in law, it may be appealed to the High Court. First of all, the courts make an important distinction between arguments of fact and arguments of law. Arguments of fact are broadly not appealable and so if it is the case that you do not like the decision, even if you may have good grounds for doing so, this may not be appealable. However, if you can show that the Tribunal has made some mistake in law, you may be able to take the matter further. Usually, you will need to get the advice of a specialist lawyer. The method of bringing a statutory appeal to the High Court is like a more simplified version of a judicial review.

First of all, it is very important to note that any statutory appeal must be lodged within 28 days of the Tribunal's decision. Although it is possible to bring an appeal after this, the courts will only do so in exceptional circumstances.

An appeal will be lodged by the person lodging a Notice of Appeal and support documentation but, unlike a judicial review, there is no preliminary, permission stage. Once the documents have been lodged, the other side will have an opportunity of lodging evidence and the matter will then proceed to a hearing.

The other side will usually be both the Tribunal and the local education authority.

It is also possible to get orders such as expedition to have an urgent hearing, as part of the proceedings.

Costs and Public funding

Costs

Unfortunately, like most legal actions, judicial review is potentially expensive. Although the precise costs will depend upon the circumstances of the particular case, it is safe to say that most ordinary people could not afford to start judicial review proceedings without public funding.

If you do not qualify for public funding, it is vital that you obtain a quote before any legal action is taken.

The costs risk is increased by the rule that *costs follow the event*. This means that if you win your judicial review, the LEA etc. will have to pay most, but not all, of your legal costs; but if you lose, you will have to pay most, but not all, of theirs.

Even if you are advised that you have a very strong case (and therefore that your opponent will probably end up paying your costs), there are still a number of problems:

- Lawyers can only predict the result of cases based on what they know about the facts and on their previous experience of similar cases. No lawyer can guarantee the outcome of a case so, however strong your advisers think your case may be, there is always a risk that you will lose and have to pay your own costs and those of your opponents.
- Even if you win, your opponent will only pay your costs at the end of the case, and possibly only after the amount they have to pay has been assessed (or 'taxed', as lawyers call it) by the court. Unless you have particularly under-standing lawyers, they will want to be paid more often than this – probably every three months or so. This means that you will have to find the money for your lawyers fees long before you have any chance of getting it back.
- If you win, the other side will probably not have to pay all your legal costs. Even so, you will still be liable to pay all your legal bills in full.

- If the case is settled before conclusion it may be difficult to get costs.

It is now possible for lawyers to take cases in a whole range of areas, on a 'no win, no fee' basis. This means that the lawyer will take the view that because of the prospects of success, he or she will agree to take the case for the client for free, on the basis that if and when the case is successful, the other side will meet his or her costs. However, in the case of judicial review, it is still relatively rare for lawyers to agree to take on cases on a 'no win, no fee' basis; partly because of the difficulties in guaranteeing success but also because many judicial reviews tend to settle very early on, before the other side may become liable to meet costs, so that the lawyer may not get paid at all. In addition, most 'no win, no fee' agreements are backed up by insurance policies and it is still relatively difficult to get appropriate insurance for judicial review cases. However, public funding may be available in the child's name.

Public funding

There are two types of public funding which may be relevant in cases involving special educational needs – legal help (previously know as claim 10 assistance or green form assistance) and legal representation (previously known as legal aid).

Legal help
Because of recent changes in public funding, the Legal Services Commission (the body which has replaced the Legal Aid Board) has now entered into agreement with a number of providers of legal services (including law firms) for the provision of services. This means that, by and large, solicitors will only have 'contracts' to provide advice and assistance if they have shown to the Legal Services Commission that they have the necessary expertise and skill to do so (although there are a number of exceptions to this rule). Accordingly, the first thing to do is to find a firm of solicitors or other provider who has a contract in education law.

A solicitor who has a contract to provide education law will be permitted to do a limited amount of work advising or helping a client on legal issues. The scheme is often used to do the preliminary work needed for a full application for legal representation but it can also be used to help prepare an appeal to the Special Educational Needs Tribunal. However, it does not allow a solicitor to be paid for representing a client, either at a Tribunal or in Court. (Unusually, the Legal Help Scheme may allow for a solicitor to attend at a Tribunal to assist a parent under a system known as a 'Mackenzie Friend' but, strictly speaking, the solicitor is not allowed to actually represent – i.e. speak on behalf of – the individual.

The legal help form asks for the details of the income and savings of the client and his or her partner and the solicitor will then undertake a simple means test to determine whether the individual is eligible. Unfortunately, individuals under the age of 16 must usually apply for legal help through their parents and it is their parents' means which are taken into account.

If the individual qualifies for legal help, the solicitor can do up to £500 worth of work under the scheme but after that, it is necessary to apply for further time/funding from the Legal Services Commission. In addition, it may be possible, on occasion, to use the legal help scheme to obtain expert's reports; for example for the purposes of bringing an appeal to the Special educational Needs Tribunal.

Individuals are automatically entitled to legal help if they:

- are on Income Support or certain levels of Working Families Tax Credit or Disabled Persons Tax Credit, or with an income below a certain level (which changes from year to year).
- have savings of less than £1,000 (with certain additional amounts allowed, depending on the number of dependants).

- save in exceptional circumstances, have not received help under the Legal Help Scheme on the same matter within the last six months, from another solicitor or legal services provider.

Legal Representation

If it is necessary or appropriate to go to Court (for example in the case of a judicial review of a statutory appeal against a decision of the Special Educational Needs Tribunal) then your solicitor may apply for Legal Representation.

For those solicitors and legal services providers who have education law contracts, in certain situations, they have what are known as 'devolved powers' from the Legal Services Commission to grant emergency legal representation, themselves, without having to wait for a decision from the legal Services Commission. However, in all cases, forms must be lodged with the Legal Services Commission.

In order to obtain legal representation, there are two broad test applied:

- A means test, and
- A merits test.

The means test assesses an individual's financial circumstances. However in many (although not all) cases going to Court, children may themselves have their means tested, rather than having to rely on their parents' means, so that many children will be eligible for legal representation, even though their parents may not be eligible for legal help. (However, note that in some cases, for example, a statutory appeal to the High Court against a decision of the Special Educational Needs Tribunal, it remains the parent, and not the child, who must bring the case and who therefore would apply for legal representation if appropriate.)

If legal representation is granted, the Legal Services Commission will meet the legal costs and there is some protection against the individual so that if the case is lost, the other side will not usually be able to get their costs paid by the individual concerned.

The merits test is much more complicated and takes into accounts a nuber of factors including, in particular, the likely prospects of success and the cost of the case as against the prospective benefit to the individual concerned. In addition, there are special rules governing cases which are deemed to have a 'significant wider public interest' and your solicitor will be able to deal with this, if necessary.

If the case is being brought in order to recover money or property, then the Legal Services Commission operates what is known as the statutory charge. This permits the Legal Services Commission to have 'first call' and the solicitor should explain this further to you.

In addition, if legal representation is granted and the individual has some money (although not very much) it may be that the Legal Services Commission will require the individual to make a contribution towards the cost of the case.

Part 6

Case law

Case law

'Case law' is the law which is developed by the courts as they make their judgements on how the law is to be interpreted.

Not all judgements have implications for all children in all schools in all LEAs. The ones summarised below do, however, and we have referred to most of these cases in our advice to parents.

R vs The Secretary of State for Education and Science, ex parte E [1992] 1 ELR 377

E was a 13-year-old boy with literacy and numeracy problems. His statement referred to both of these as special educational needs in Part 2, but only specified provision to meet the literacy problems in Part 3. The LEA's explanation was that as the numeracy difficulties were not serious enough for them to have to make any provision (i.e. they could be met from the school's own resources), they did not have to specify this provision in Part 3. The parents disagreed and appealed to the Secretary of State and then applied for judicial review. The court upheld their application.

The Secretary of State appealed to the court of appeal, and lost.

The final judgement included these rulings:

'A child has special educational needs if he has a learning difficulty which requires special educational provision. Of course a child may have more than one learning difficulty. If the special educational provision which the child requires for all his needs can be determined, and provided, by his ordinary school, then no statement is necessary. But once the local education authority have decided that they are required to determine that some special educational provision is provided for him, they have to maintain a statement for him under section 7 in respect of that child, not in respect of any particular learning difficulty that he may have. Then the statement must specify in Part 2 the authority's assessment of the special educational needs of the child ... and in Part 3 the special educational provision to be made for the purpose of meeting those needs ...

The local education authority is obliged to determine the special educational provision that should be made for the child in respect of each and every educational need identified in the statement ...

... the duty of the authority is then to arrange that the special educational provision specified in the statement is made for the child. It may be that in some cases, or in relation to some particular needs, it will not be possible for the authority to fulfil that duty without themselves providing the requisite special educational provision. But where the authority take the view that the school is able to provide some part of the special educational provision which the child requires, then they will fulfil their duty by arranging that the school do so provide that part of the special educational provision.'

The *ex parte E* judgement means that Part 2 of a statement should not be worded vaguely, like this: 'Jenny has a variety of special educational needs, as revealed by her assessment.'

Also, Part 3 of a statement should not be written like this: 'Jenny should receive the help appropriate to her needs.'

If your child's statement does not spell out each of her special educational needs in Part 2, or if it doesn't describe provision to meet each of those needs in Part 3, you should challenge it on the grounds that it is contrary to the judgement in *ex parte E*.

(See cases 21, 22, 24, 27 and 29)

L vs Clarke and Somerset County Council [1998] ELR 129

The parents of a boy with dyslexia appealed to the Tribunal against Parts 3 and 4 of his statement. Their concern with Part 3 was that it failed to set out the number of hours of help the boy should receive under the statement. The Tribunal refused to order that the statement be made more specific by the help being quantified and the parents appealed to the High Court on this point, which they considered to be an error in law.

The judge ruled:

> 'A requirement that the help to be given should be specified in the statement in terms of hours per week was not an absolute and universal precondition of the legality of a statement ... however ... in very many cases it will not be possible to fulfil the requirement to specify the special educational provision considered appropriate to meet the child's needs, including specification of staffing arrangements and curriculum, unless hours per week are set out. The real question, as it seems to me, in relation to any particular statement is whether it is so specific and so clear as to leave no room for doubt as to what has been decided is necessary in the individual case.'

(See cases 22, 28 and 29)

R vs Hereford and Worcester County Council, ex parte P [1992] 2 ELR 732

This was a challenge to the arrangements made for transporting a boy with Down's Syndrome to a special school. The parents believed that the journey would take so long that their son would arrive at school in no fit state to learn anything.

The judge ruled as follows:

> 'It is implicit in section 55(1) of the Education Act 1944 that the LEA is under a duty to make such arrangements as it considers necessary for a child to reach school without

undue stress, strain or difficulty such as would prevent him from benefiting from the education the school has to offer ... it follows that where a child with special educational needs requires transport to get him to school the transport which the LEA proposes to make available must therefore be non-stressful transport ... '

(See case 28)

R vs Surrey County Council Education Committee ex parte H [1985] 83 LGR 219

In this case, the High Court ruled:

'There is no question of Parliament having placed the local education authority under an obligation to provide a child with the best possible education ... or to educate him or her to his or her maximum potential.'

This is an important judgement to bear in mind if you are arguing for a place in a specialist independent school for your child. You must not rest your case only on proving how good the school is or how well it will meet your child's needs. Both the LEA and the Tribunal may agree with you that the independent school is the best possible option for your child, but they may still decide that one of the LEA's schools can meet his needs.

So, your task is to present as much evidence as you can which shows that the school the LEA are offering, or any other school they could offer, cannot meet your child's needs as these are described in the statement. It helps if you have a full and detailed Part 2.

(See cases 23 and 29)

R vs Lancashire County Council ex parte M [1989] 2 ELR 279

In this case, known as 'the Lancashire judgement', M had a statement which specified speech therapy provision under Part 3 as 'special educational provision'. When that provision was not made, the LEA claimed that they had made a clerical

6

error when writing the statement and that speech therapy must always be 'non-educational provision' on the grounds that speech therapists are employed by health authorities.

M's parents challenged this interpretation of the law by seeking judicial review and were successful, in that the court ruled that speech therapy could be either a medical provision or an educational provision, depending on the nature of the child's needs for the therapy; and, that the question of who employed the therapists was irrelevant to this decision.

The LEA appealed against this judgement, but it was upheld by the court of appeal.

The judgement included this comment, which is useful as guidance as to whether a child's need for any kind of therapy is 'medical' or 'educational':

'To teach an adult who has lost his larynx because of cancer might be considered as treatment rather than education. But to teach a child who has never been able to communicate by language, whether because of some chromosomal disorder … or because of social cause … seems to us just as much educational provision as to teach a child to communicate in writing.'

Many LEAs still tell parents that speech therapy always belongs under the heading 'non-educational provision' (i.e. Part 6 of a statement, where no-one has a strict legal duty to provide it). They still tell parents that this is because speech therapists are employed by health authorities. However, the Lancashire judgement specifically rejected this argument. It is the child's need for therapy which is of key importance. The main task for parents is to argue that their child's need for speech therapy is 'educational' rather than 'medical'.

All you have to go on is the judge's example, drawing the distinction between a need for speech therapy following surgery on your larynx (medical) and the need for speech therapy due to chromosomal disorder (educational).

Obviously, under this distinction, the majority of children with special educational needs have speech therapy needs which are 'educational' and which therefore should be set out in Part 2 of a statement. All Down's Syndrome children, for example, have an 'educational' not 'medical' need for speech therapy, according to the distinction made in the Lancashire judgement.

Many LEAs openly disregard the Lancashire judgement. Why? Because once the need for speech therapy is accepted as 'educational', it must be set out under Part 2 of the statement as one of the child's 'special educational needs.' And, once the need is set out under Part 2, then according to *ex parte E,* the speech therapy provision *must* be specified under Part 3, so that the ultimate responsibility for making the provision then rests with the LEA. They may *ask* the health service to provide the therapists but, if that isn't possible, the LEA themselves must make the arrangements needed and cover the cost.

The message for parents is: 'Get your child's need for speech therapy written into Part 2, as a special educational need, and the rest should follow.'

(See case 25)

For a case which considered whether occupational therapy and physiotherapy could be 'educational provision', see *Bromley London Borough Council v Special Educational Needs Tribunal and Other* (page 259).

R vs London Borough of Harrow ex parte M [1997] ELR 62

M was a six-year-old girl with cerebral palsy who had a statement of special educational needs. Part 3 of the statement specified occupational therapy, physiotherapy and speech therapy, but these provisions had only ever been partially arranged, and for a period M had had no therapies at all. The LEA argued that, because they had made a formal request of the Health Authority to provide these therapies, they were themselves relieved of any further duty to 'arrange' these provisions. The court disagreed and ruled:

'In clear terms the obligation upon a LEA under s 168 (5) 1993 (now s 324 (5) EA 1996. ed) is simply expressed and subject to no qualification whether express or implied. The construction of the section for which the respondents contended would have involved writing words into the statute which not only are not there, but, more importantly, would manifestly fail to serve the child for whose benefit this part of the 1993 (now 1996) Act exists.'

(See case 32)

C vs Lancashire County Council [1997] ELR 377

The parents in this case appealed to the High Court when they lost a Tribunal appeal to have their child placed in a mainstream school. The judge dismissed the appeal but, in a comment on the issue of efficient use of resources, set out how LEAs and Tribunals must address this issue in future.

In summary, the judge ruled that a two-stage process was required in reaching a decision. First, an LEA or Tribunal must establish whether one alternative was in fact more expensive than another. Then, if so, they must make the decision as to whether the additional expenditure involved in meeting the parent's preference was justified:

'... one has to look at the figures, decide whether there is an additional cost, and then do a balancing exercise weighing the additional cost against the parents' preference ... it is partly a factual exercise and partly a balancing exercise.'

(See case 28)

R vs Oxfordshire County Council ex parte P [1996] ELR 153

Sam Pittick attended his local mainstream school, with a statement which provided him with 20 hours of learning support. His parents were happy with the level of support and with his placement, believing that Sam, like other children with Down's Syndrome, could have his needs best met in a mainstream school.

Then his parents heard from other parents that the LEA, Oxfordshire, were informing schools that they would, in future, have to meet the cost of the first five hours of a child's statemented provision. It seemed to Sam's parents that this would jeopardise his chances of being accepted by a mainstream secondary school come the time for transfer as, in doing so, the school would be also accepting responsibility for meeting the cost of five hours of his learning support. Also, Sam's parents were unhappy at his present school having suddenly to find extra money for Sam from their special needs budget, and particularly concerned that this should not result in provision being reduced for other pupils at the school who also had special educational needs but who did not have the protection of statements.

Sam's mother, Ann Pittick, advised and supported by IPSEA, approached a solicitor in order to apply for judicial review of the LEA's actions. It took over a year for the case to be heard.

The judge ruled that it was not unlawful for the LEA to obtain agreement from a school, after a statement had been finalised, that part of the cost of the special educational provision set out on the statement should be met from the school's own budget. The judge said:

> 'So far as can be gleaned from the papers, it was in about mid-1992 that the (LEA) began to explore the possibility that the school might pay out of its own budget for five hours of the ancillary support; and this was in the context of a wider initiative by which the cost of special provision

6

being made for children with statements who were being educated in mainstream schools might, in part, be funded by the school, rather than in its entirety by the authority out of its central budget ...

The (LEA's) decision ... could, of course, only be put into effect with the concurrence of the school ...

In the ordinary course of things, before the advent of the Education Reform Act 1988, it was no doubt factually inherent in the day-to-day administration of section 7(2) of the 1981 Education Act (which places on LEAs the duty to arrange the special educational provision set out in a statement) that the local authority would be bound to pay for the provision. Under the system of delegated budgets provided for by the Act of 1988, local authority schools ... have the power, within the limits of their budget, to decide how the money allocated to them shall be spent ... if in a particular case the school agrees to deploy some of its budget resources towards the cost of special educational provision for one of its children, there is no conceivable breach of section 7(2) ...

But if ... the school were suddenly to turn round and say that they were no longer prepared to apply any part of their budget to the cost of the 20 hours extra support, it is undoubted that the (LEA) would immediately have to meet the full cost. The provision would in any event be secure.'

This judgement was supported the following year by the judgement in *R vs Hillingdon Borough Council ex parte the Governing Body of Queensmead School* (see page 254).

(See Case 33)

R vs Cumbria County Council ex parte P [1995] COD 267

P's statement referred to speech therapy under Part 3 but in such vague terms that his father did not have a clear idea of how much help to expect for his son. The speech therapist's advice recommended three hours a week. P received one hour per week.

The statement did seem to be specific, however, about the money that would be spent on P's provision: 'P's needs entitle him to extra funding at Band Level 3. This is now £6,000 a year.'

P's father obtained professional advice that three hours of speech therapy a week could not be obtained for the annual sum of £6,000. He therefore concluded that the reason why his son could not have the therapy he needed was that the figure of £6,000 acted as a ceiling on the spending that could be made on his son's special educational provision. He therefore sought judicial review in order to challenge the legality of the LEA's banding policy, in that it seemed to place a fetter on the LEA's ability to give P the provision which his needs called for.

The application failed, but the judge's comments on the situation provide useful guidance to other parents facing a similar problem. This is an extract from the judgement:

'... the County has a policy of allocating pupils with special educational needs into various bands or categories. All but one of these of these have a cash figure against them. Pupils are categorised according to the degree of impairment as assessed by the authority into 12 categories set out in a document entitled the Cumbria Scheme for Local Management of Schools ...

I am not persuaded that it is illegal. The scheme does not indicate any unwillingness by the authority to have regard to the need for securing that special education provision is made for pupils who have special educational needs ...

Nor does the scheme as such fetter the authority's discretion as to what is contained in the statements of any of its statemented pupils...

I am not persuaded that the authority regarded itself in any way as being fettered by the figure of £6,000 ... There is, in my judgement, no need to specify such a figure in the statement. I am told, and can well believe, that many parents are pleased to know the amount of extra money which their offspring received compared with the generality of pupils. If in the present case nothing other than a sentence on the lines of '£6,000 is allocated to pay for all P's needs' has appeared in Part 3 of the statement I would have regarded this as not complying with the requirements of specificity contained in the statute and regulations. The reason for that is that the appeal process becomes impossible to operate if the parent, and indeed the Secretary of State, does not know what the nature of the provision is which the authority intends to make. However, that is not this case ...

Failure to have appropriate material in the statement and appendices: I have already touched on part of this and found room for criticism. There are other matters in respect of which there seems further such room ... I understand and sympathise with the uncertainty in which the parents found themselves following the way in which their son's statement has been dealt with ...

The statement is unsatisfactory in several respects and the authority ought to produce a new statement as soon as is compatible with their duties of consultation and consideration and the authority ought to produce it in such a form as makes it clear to P's parents what the authority consider their son ought to receive by way of special educational provision and non-educational provision for his profound communication difficulties. Then the parents will be in a position to appeal if they wish to.'

(See case 27)

R vs Dorset County Council and Further Education Funding Council ex parte M [1995] ELR 109

This was a challenge to an LEA's attempt to argue that it had no responsibility for a pupil with a statement once he had reached the age of 16. This is what the judge decided:

> ' ... a local education authority cannot divest itself of responsibility for a pupil's schooling when he reaches 16 by wrongfully failing to specify it, either by silence or express exclusion, in his statement and by refusing to provide it when he reaches 16 so that he cannot then satisfy the condition of the authority's continuing responsibility under Section 4(2)(a) of the 1981 Education Act, namely by being a registered pupil at a school appropriate to his needs ...

> Dorset's duty under Section 7(1) and (2) of the Education Act 1981 to maintain the 1992 statement of Mark's special educational needs and to arrange for him the special educational provision specified in it continues until Dorset amends or ceases to maintain the statement in accordance with the procedures set out in paragraphs 6 and 7 of schedule 1 to, and section 8 of, the 1981 Act.'

(See case 40)

R vs Oxfordshire County Council ex parte B, Court Of Appeal [1997] ELR 90

B was a boy with autism and severe learning difficulties. His LEA operated a policy of all children leaving school at the age of 16 and continuing their education at local colleges. B's mother was not sure that the college could meet B's needs and, when the LEA ceased to maintain his statement, she challenged the LEA via judicial review on the grounds that they should have followed the appropriate procedure for ceasing to maintain a statement.

The judge made reference to the earlier Dorset judgement, made by Auld J (see above) but distinguished his opinion from it by ruling:

'... insofar as Auld J (the judge in the Dorset case, above) was suggesting that there remained a duty upon all LEAs to continue to maintain a statement until it was amended or ceased to be maintained on a proper proposal by the authority, that proposition is expressed in my view far too widely ... In my judgement the responsibility for the registered child ends upon the child ceasing to be registered and the maintenance of the statement... would cease with the cessation of that responsibility and registration...'

(See case 40)

P vs Hillingdon London Borough Council [1998] ELR 38

Ms Phelps, as an adult, sued her LEA for failing to diagnose her dyslexia. The judge ruled that an educational psychologist had been negligent in failing to detect dyslexia and awarded damages.

This case was appealed and although the Court of Appeal reversed the High Court Judgement, the House of Lords reinstated the judgement.

R vs Hillingdon London Borough Council ex parte the Governing Body of Queensmead School [1997] ELR 331

This case supported the *Oxfordshire ex parte P* (see page 249) and arose from a dispute between a school governing body and an LEA.

The Governors of Queensmead School applied for judicial review when the LEA changed their formula for delegating funds to schools for statemented pupils, with the effect that the amount the school received for such pupils was cut from £77,250 to £30,068. The Governors argued that the cut was unlawful because it would leave the school unable to make the special educational provision specified in pupils' Statements.

The High Court agreed with the Governors, commenting:

'... if the formula produces a sufficient sum, the school cannot complain. But if the formula does not in fact produce a sum sufficient to meet the special educational provision set out in the statements, the LEA must give more. It cannot require the school to make up the balance.'

(See case 33)

City of Bradford Metropolitan Council vs A [1997] ELR 417

This case examined whether nursing provision could ever be 'special educational provision', and be specified in Part 3 of a Statement. It arose from an LEA appeal against a Special Educational Needs Tribunal Order that Part 3 of a 6 year old child's Statement should include: '... *the presence of a nurse at all times at a school when A (the child) is present.*'

The High Court upheld the LEA's appeal, and the judge's decision included the following explanation:

'It seems to me that what I have to do ... is to explore where the border lies between the 'special educational provision' which is set out in Part 3 ... which must by definition be 'educational' and the 'non-educational needs' to be provided for in Parts 6 and 5 of the Statement, which are the needs of the child for which the Authority consider that provision is appropriate if a child is to properly benefit from the special educational provision. In my judgement, nursing care falls fairly and squarely into the latter category, even in a case of this kind where on the evidence before the court, A unhappily has fits which lead to injury and distraction from her teaching on a scale which is described in the reports in the Statement before me.

This, in my judgement, is not 'educational provision' according to the meaning of those words as approved by the Court of Appeal, but 'non-educational provision': provision which is appropriate if a child is to benefit properly from the special educational provision.'

Referring the matter back to the Tribunal, the judge commented:

'I have no doubt that the appropriate course for me to take is to remit this matter to the special educational needs tribunal. They were concerned with the central issue as to whether Lister School was an appropriate school to meet the needs and objectives set out in the Statement. I have held as a matter of law that they were not entitled to require that school to have 100% nursing cover. Accordingly, it seems to me that the only just and fair way to deal with the matter is to send the matter back to the tribunal for reconsideration of their decision with the benefit of this judgement. Whether they come to a different decision on the central issue, or whether they decide to leave the matter alone and simply delete the reference to nursing care in Part 3 of the statement is a matter very much for them . . . There is nothing, in my judgement, which should in any way preclude the tribunal from making whatever order it thinks fit by way of amendment to the statement and, if necessary, amending part of the order that they made earlier, when they determine the just order to make on this appeal in the light of my judgement.'

R vs East Sussex County Council ex parte T [1998] ELR 251

This House of Lords appeal ruled that when an LEA make provision at home for a child who cannot attend school, under Section 19 of the Education Act 1996, they must provide what is necessary, not just what they feel they can afford.

Although the girl involved in this case did not have a Statement of Special Educational Needs the judgement is potentially useful in situations where children with Statements are excluded or are out of school because of a dispute between their parents and the LEA.

The girl, T, suffered from ME and found it at times impossible to attend school. From 1992 onwards the LEA provided 5 hours a week Home Tuition. Then, in 1996, the LEA decided to cut all Home Tuition to a maximum of 3 hours a week. This decision was taken purely because of the Authority's difficulties with identifying resources, not because they had reason to believe that T, or any other child affected, needed less help. The parents applied for judicial review and as a result the LEA's decision was quashed. The LEA appealed and the decision was overturned. Finally, the parents appealed to the House of Lords, who re-instated the original ruling against the LEA.

Section 19(1) of the Education Act 1996 says:

'Each local education authority shall make arrangements for the provision of suitable full-time or part-time education at school or otherwise than at school for those children of compulsory school age who, by reason of illness, exclusion or otherwise, may not for any period receive suitable education unless such arrangements are made for them.'

Section 19(7) explains:

'In this section "suitable education", in relation to the child or young person, means efficient education suitable to his age, ability and aptitude and to any special educational needs he may have.'

In the final judgement the House of Lords ruled:

'There is nothing in the Act to suggest that resource considerations are relevant to the question of what is "suitable education". On their face those words connote a standard to be determined purely by educational considerations. This view is much strengthened by the definition of "suitable education" in section 298(7) (now section 19(7) EA 1996) which spells out expressly the factors which are relevant to the determination of suitability, viz. the education must be "efficient" and "suitable to his age, ability and aptitude" and also suitable "to any special educational needs he may have". All these express factors relate to educational considerations and nothing else. There is nothing to indicate that the resources available are relevant . . .

The argument is not one of insufficient resources to discharge the duty but of a preference for using the money for other purposes. To permit a local authority to avoid performing a statutory duty on the grounds that it prefers to spend the money in other ways is to downgrade a statutory duty to a discretionary power . . . Parliament has chosen to impose a statutory duty as opposed to a power, requiring the local authority to do certain things. In my judgement the courts should be slow to downgrade such duties into what are, in effect, mere discretions over which the court would have very little real control. If Parliament wishes to reduce public expenditure on meeting the needs of sick children then it is up to Parliament so to provide. It is not for the courts to adjust the order of priorities as between statutory duties and statutory discretions.'

(See case 35)

R vs London Borough of Barnet ex parte G [1998] ELR 281

This case confirmed that amendments made to a Statement as a result of a Tribunal Order do not have a retrospective effect. For example, parents could not argue that, having won their case at Tribunal for additional help, this would place a duty on the LEA to 'make up' the missing provision caused by the original decision. Nor that parents could be reimbursed if the Tribunal ordered a placement in a private school for which the parents, hitherto, had been paying the fees.

In this case, the LEA issued a Statement for the boy concerned, naming one of its own schools. The boy's father did not believe that the LEA's choice of school could meet his son's needs and so he placed him in a private school at his own expense, and appealed to the Tribunal. The appeal was

258

successful, and the Tribunal ordered the LEA to name the private school in the Statement. The father then wrote to the LEA seeking reimbursement of the fees he had paid to the private school, on the grounds that the Tribunal decision had shown that this was indeed the correct school for his son and that the LEA had 'got it wrong.' The LEA refused and the parent applied for judicial review of this refusal.

The father's attempt to obtain reimbursement via judicial review failed. He appealed to the Court of Appeal, but again failed, with the judge identifying the main legal point as follows:

'... nowhere in the statute is there anything to indicate that an amendment to a statement is to have effect in monetary terms, let alone any express indication that if, on appeal, it is shown that the local education authority should have made provision they are liable to make recompense in those cases where the parents themselves have incurred relevant expense. If that had been the intention of Parliament I would expect to find some express provision to that effect in the Act.'

This case clarified the position whereby a Statement is valid from the point that it is made, not following the conclusion of an appeal.

Hackney London Borough Council vs Silyadin [1998] ELR 571, Hereford and Worcester County Council v Lane [1998] ELR 319 and Bromley vs Special Educational Needs Tribunal and Others, QBD and CA [1999] ELR 260

These cases generally confirm that where a parent is appealing to the Tribunal for a place in a more expensive school than the LEA school named on a statement (for example, a specialist residential school), and the tribunal agree with the parents that the school named by the LEA cannot meet the child's needs, the tribunal must not automatically order that the school of the parent's choice is written into Part 4. Because LEAs have a responsibility to use their resources efficiently, the tribunal must be prepared to consider proposals put forward by an LEA to make the provision specified in Part 3 as an alternative to automatic placement at the (more expensive) school of the parent's choice.

However, the final judgement in the latest of these three cases, *Bromley vs SENT, Court of Appeal,* places responsibility for bringing forward alternatives for consideration by the tribunal on the LEA:

> 'Two consequences, both criticised by Mr Straker, were spelt out by the tribunal. The first was that Part 4 be amended to substitute C school for R school. This conclusion has caused the LEA understandable anxiety on account of its very high cost. But Mr Straker's criticism of the tribunal for failing to afford the LEA a further opportunity to canvass alternatives to C school is in my view misplaced. While proceedings before the tribunal are not expected to mimic litigation, a SENT is in the ordinary way entitled to expect each side to bring its full case forward, at least to the extent of putting down the necessary markers. No such marker was put down by the LEA.'

C vs Special Educational Needs Tribunal and London Borough of Greenwich [1999] ELR 5

The boy in this case had emotional and behavioural difficulties and was 16 years old. His Statement referred to a Pupil Referral Unit, and his father had appealed to the Tribunal for a special school to be named, instead of the PRU. A further ground of appeal concerned the content of Part 3 of the Statement.

The Tribunal dismissed the appeal against placement in the PRU, but included in the Order: '*He needs now to have an assessment of the extent of (sic) which he can properly be expected, given his lack of formal schooling over the last two years, to follow the national curriculum.*'

On appeal to the High Court, the decision of the tribunal with regard to attendance at the Pupil Referral Unit was held to be appropriate, but the judge was critical of the tribunal's leaving it to another body to make a decision on whether modifications were needed to the National Curriculum. It had been open to the tribunal to adjourn the hearing if they believed there was a need for further evidence, and this is what they should have done, rather than refering to the need for a further assessment and then leaving it to some other body. The judgement included the following comment:

'The tribunal failed ... to determine whether it was in fact appropriate for C to follow the whole curriculum ... Instead, it provided for an assessment to be made by someone else (without even specifying by whom) and left the whole issue up in the air. It thereby put in place an extra-statutory assessment process by which there would be no right of appeal. In the event, the PRU has carried out the assessment, forming its own view of what C is capable of doing; and C's parents disagree with the outcome of the assessment. The matter, it is submitted, is one which should have been resolved by the tribunal at the time of its decision rather than being left open in this highly unsatisfactory way ... I have serious doubts whether it is open to a tribunal to make a provision for a future assessment of this kind – an assessment calculated to determine the extent of a child's curriculum needs. It is the tribunal's responsibility on appeal to determine what the needs are and what provision is required for them. It is far from clear to me that it can, in effect, delegate that kind of responsibility to someone else, thereby creating just the kind of problem that has arisen here where the outcome is disputed but there is no avenue of appeal.'

London Borough of Bromley and Special Educational Needs Tribunal and Others, QBD and CA [1999] ELR 260

This judgement confirmed that a child's need for occupational therapy, physiotherapy and speech therapy could be a 'special educational need' and that the therapies to meet these needs could be specified in Part 3 of a Statement as 'special educational provision.' Although the status of these therapies had been considered by earlier judgements (in the case of speech therapy, in the Lancashire judgement, see page 245; in the case of occupational and speech therapy in *B vs Isle of Wight Council [1997] ELR 279* the Bromley judgement is important because of the detail of the discussion.

The child, S, was 12 at the time of the judgement. He had quadriplegic cerebral palsy and impaired vision. He was unable to walk, sit up or stand and was totally reliant on adults for all his mobility needs apart from head movements. He was unable to wash, dress, toilet or feed himself. He was able to understand only a small number of words in contexts which were familiar to him and was considered to be functioning overall below the level of a one-year-old.

The Special Educational Needs Tribunal ordered that S's needs for occupational, physiotherapy and speech therapy were 'educational' and the therapies were 'special educational provision' for S. The LEA appealed against this decision to the High Court.

The judgement at Queen's Bench Division took as a starting point the definition of 'education' in the Shorter Oxford English Dictionary, one part of which is: '*the process of nourishing or rearing; the process of bringing-up; the systematic instruction, schooling or training given to the young … in preparation for the work of life.*'

The Court considered evidence provided by an educational psychologist who was supporting the parents at the tribunal '*that the purpose of education for S was to maximise his control over his own environment and that education for S involved a series of over-learning the basic functions of his day: eating, drinking, toileting, dressing, etc and co-operating about them.'*

The LEA's appeal hinged on the argument that the tribunal had been wrong to regard these as educational needs and provisions. The parents argued that education for S would not be to teach him Modern languages or Physics but *'to teach him so that he may be prepared for the very limited work of his life.'*

The High Court was supportive of the parents' and the tribunal's interpretation:

> 'If, as is undoubtedly clear, S needs to learn eating and drinking skills then, as it seems to me, to assist him in learning those skills will be an educational provision for him.'

A further ground on which the LEA appealed was that the tribunal in its Order had not quantified the amounts of therapy to be specified in the amended Statement. Their argument was that if the tribunal had made clear how much therapy was needed, they could possibly have demonstrated their ability to provide the required level from within their own provisions. The judge considered *'L and Clarke vs Somerset County Council'* (see page 244), and in the light of this earlier judgement made the following decision:

> 'At first sight the appellants (the LEA) seemed to have a good point in complaining that the number of hours should have been specified. However, Mr Gordon, in reliance on *L and Clarke vs Somerset County Council* (1999) ELR 129, argues that it will not always be possible to specify the number of hours and that, he says, is the case here. *L and Clarke vs Somerset County Council* was a decision of Laws J. He held that whilst there could be some cases where flexibility should be retained it was plain that statute required a very high degree of specificity. It is clear that very often specification of hours a week will be necessary

and there will then be a need for that amount of therapy to be provided. However, the real question in relation to any particular statement is whether it is so specific and clear as to leave no room for doubt as to what has been decided in the individual case.

I start with the fact that Part 3 of the current statement does not attempt to specify any number of hours. It would not be possible to do that. The tribunal's decision was that the therapy should be provided as an integral part of S's day and throughout his waking day. Thus when S is awake there will need to be available language therapy and the other therapies, not of course constantly but as required so that the lessons may be constantly impressed upon him. In the circumstances, I reject this complaint.'

This aspect of the case is unique in two ways: it features an LEA appealing on the ground that special educational provision should be quantified in a Statement (as opposed to defending the position that quantification is not required). Also, it contains the only actual example in case law of a child who does not require their Statemented provision to be quantified: as such, the very exceptional nature of S's needs, provisions and placement give an indication of how rare non-quantification should be.

(See case 25)

R vs Chair of Governors and Headteacher of A and S School ex parte T [2000] ELR 274

This case confirmed that where a school is named by an LEA in a child's Statement of Special Educational Needs, that school must admit the child. It upheld the judgement in *R vs Manchester City Council ex parte S [1999] ELR 414.*

The boy's mother had expressed a preference for a school maintained by the neighbouring LEA. Following consultation with the neighbouring LEA and the school, the responsible LEA issued a Statement naming the school of the parent's preference. Despite their clear duty under section 324(5)(b)

Education Act 1996, the governors of the school refused to admit the boy. Judicial review was sought in order to quash the decision of the governors and the court made clear that governors' duty to admit the boy was absolute, as their school was named on his Statement.

The judgement included this comment:

'Hopefully, the consultation process required by Schedule 27 will in most cases prevent schools having foisted upon them from elsewhere, pupils subject to statements of special educational needs with whom they cannot cope. However, if this does happen, the remedy lies in the hands of the school. The school must, in good time, refer the matter to the Secretary of State and operate the procedure under ss 495 and 496 of the Act. The very existence of this procedure means that the construction of s 324(5)(b) for which the applicant contends is perfectly workable... I express the hope that in future when disputes arise between local education authorities and schools, all parties will co-operate in bringing such disputes to an early resolution. It is quite unacceptable that a 12 year old boy should be deprived of education for half a term because two public bodies cannot agree about the interpretation of a statute.'

(See case 18)

B vs Harrow London Borough Council and the Special Educational Needs Tribunal [2000] ELR 110

This was an important case that went to the House of Lords. It concerned a parent who expressed preference for a special school in a neighbouring borough, but was turned down by her LEA, on the grounds of it being an inefficient use of resources. The LEA named one of their special schools. The parent appealed to the Tribunal, but lost. The LEA's case was that it would cost an additional £11,000 to £12,000 to send him to the neighbouring LEA's school and that this would be an inefficient use of resources.

The parent appealed against the tribunal decision to the High Court, arguing that the tribunal had made an error in calculating solely the cost to the responsible LEA, Harrow, rather than taking both LEAs' resources into account. She lost this appeal, the High Court ruling that the resources which had to be considered were those of the Authority which maintained the statement, and no other Authority.

The mother then appealed to the Court of Appeal, which overturned the High Court's judgement by ruling that both the 'sending' LEA's and the 'receiving' LEA's resources must be taken into account when calculating if there was 'inefficiency.'

The 'sending' Authority, Harrow, appealed to the House of Lords, whose judgement finally settled the dispute by confirming the tribunal's and the High Court's verdict: the resources to be taken into account in such a situation were those of the 'sending' Authority only.

In order to understand the argument in *B vs Harrow*, it is necessary to bear in mind that the law on school admissions and school 'choice' is different for non-statemented children and that this give rise not only to different procedures, but also to difference in the rights enjoyed by parents whose children do not have statements as compared to parents whose children do have statements.

Section 411 of the Education Act 1996 gives parents of children without statements (i.e. the overwhelming majority of parents) the right to express a preference for a school, and it gives LEAs the duty to comply with this preference unless certain conditions obtain – one of these being the inefficient use of resources. S 411 refers to an LEA's duty to comply, equally, with an expression of preference for a school made by parents living outside the Authority's own area.

In short, if a parent whose child does not have a statement is seeking a place in a school in a neighbouring LEA, they direct their request (and express their preference) to that school – not to their own LEA. If parents are denied the school of their preference, their right to appeal is to an Independent Appeal Panel which sits in the neighbouring Authority.

However, when the parent of a child with a statement expresses a preference for a school, they do so, not under s 411 but under Schedule 27 of the Act, which sets out arrangements for children with statements. Rather than making the request to the school in the neighbouring LEA, parents whose children have statements address it to their own LEA (which must consult the school and the neighbouring LEA before making the ultimate decision). The parent's right of appeal, should they be turned down, is not to the Independent Appeal Panel of their LEA or of the neighbouring LEA, but to the Special Educational Needs Tribunal. When the reason for turning a parent down is 'inefficient use of resources', only the resources of the parent's own LEA are taken into account.

The House of Lords' judgement explained the reasoning behind their decision by reference to the wording of Schedule 27 and the Code of Practice:

'It seems to me also relevant in considering the question as to whose resources are referred to in Schedule 27, para 3(3) to bear in mind that the scheme for special educational needs provision is for children for whom the local education authority is "responsible". Those are children, inter alia, who are "in their area" (s 321(3)). It is on the parents of such children that the notice of intended assessment and the statement of special educational needs are to be served and for such children that provision is to be made. This points in my view to the resources concerned being those of the responsible local education authority. Such a result is reflected in the Code of Practice issued by the Secretary of State under s 313 of the Act, to which both the local education authority and the tribunal on an appeal must "have regard". That code in para 4:41 states three considerations governing the naming of a school in a statement, one of which is that the placement is compatible with "the efficient use of **the LEA's** resources" (emphasis added). "The LEA" is the authority making the statement ... What it means is that the resources concerned are those of the authority whose resources will be used, i.e. the authority which pays.'

S vs Essex County Council and the Special Educational Needs Tribunal, 19 April 2000 (unreported at time of going to press)

This important case concerned a young person who was over the age of statutory schooling and who had been taken off the roll of the school by the time his parents' appeal reached the Special Educational Needs Tribunal. The case considered the issue of when an LEA ceased to be 'responsible' in terms of having a duty to respond to an appeal to the Tribunal. The High Court decided that the critical issue was whether the young person was of statutory school age at the time when the LEA made the decision which his parents were appealing against; not, as the LEA had argued, whether he was above statutory school age at the time of the hearing.

Part 7

Complaining

If you are unhappy about the way your LEA is acting, you could consider making a complaint, either to the Secretary of State for Education or to the Local Government Ombudsman. This part of the guide will help you decide who to complain to, and how to do it. However, before you write your complaint, it is a good idea to discuss the options with one of the support organisations listed in part 8.

Complaining to the Secretary of State

There are two situations in which you can make a formal complaint to the Secretary of State against your LEA or the governors of your child's school: when they are failing to fulfil a legal duty and when they are acting unreasonably.

Failing to fulfil a legal duty

When you write a letter complaining that your LEA or your child's school are failing to fulfil a legal duty, you must:

- say that you are making the complaint under *Section 497 of the 1996 Education Act;*
- quote the specific legal duty which your LEA or school have failed to fulfil;
- give the evidence, including copies of any letters which you have received which show what has happened.

Case 12, where an LEA is not fulfilling its legal duty to keep to the time limits set out in the Regulations, is an example of a situation in which a parent would be able to make a complaint under section 497 of the 1996 Education Act. The letter of complaint might look something like this:

Secretary of State for Education
Department for Education
Sanctuary Buildings
Great Smith Street
London
SW1P 3BT

Dear Secretary of State,

I am writing to make a formal complaint under Section 497 of the 1996 Education Act against ... local education authority on the grounds that they have failed to fulfil their legal duty to complete my child's assessment of special educational needs in the period set out in the 1994 Regulations.

I received a letter on October 7th telling me that the assessment was due to begin. It is now May, and I have heard nothing further from the LEA, despite having written six times to ask what was happening. So far as I know, the LEA has no reasonable excuse not to have kept to the time limits and completed the statement within ten weeks, which is what the Regulations require.

I enclose copies of all correspondence relating to this complaint ...

Case 5 describes a situation in which you might want to complain that the governors of your child's school are failing to fulfil their legal duty. Your letter of complaint could start like this:

Secretary of State for Education
Department for Education
Sanctuary Buildings
Great Smith Street
London
SW1P 3BT

Dear Secretary of State,

I am writing to make a formal complaint under Section 497 of the 1996 Education Act against the governors of ... school on the grounds that they have failed to fulfil their legal duty under Section 317 of the 1996 Education Act to 'use their best endeavours' to ensure that my daughter's special educational needs are provided for.

For the past eight weeks, Shirley has not been getting the support which she is supposed to receive under her individual education plan. I have raised this matter with the headteacher and the chair of the governing body, but without any satisfaction and I enclose copies of correspondence between myself and the school on this issue...

If you believe that you have grounds for a complaint under Section 497 of the 1996 Education Act, you should get advice on wording your complaint from one of the support organisations listed in part 8.

Acting 'unreasonably'

Complaints against an LEA or a school acting unreasonably are less easy to make than complaints on the grounds that they have failed to fulfil a legal duty. That is because there is not a clear definition in law of what 'unreasonable' means.

As a general rule, if you can make a complaint under Section 497 of the 1996 Act ('failure to fulfil a legal duty') then do that rather than complaining of unreasonableness. However, in some cases, the complaint of unreasonableness is the only option. For example, in **case 7,** the LEA is acting legally in proposing to assess Lloyd. There is no appeal to the Tribunal either, in this situation. The only option Lloyd's parents have is to try making a complaint of unreasonableness against the LEA to the Secretary of State. The letter could start off like this:

Secretary of State for Education
Department for Education
Sanctuary Buildings
Great Smith Street
London
SW1P 3BT

Dear Secretary of State,

I am writing to make a formal complaint under Section 496 of the 1996 Education Act against ... local education authority on the grounds that they are acting unreasonably by proposing to assess my son under Section 323 of the 1996 Education Act when there is no evidence that he has special educational needs, nor have any professionals who know Lloyd said that he has special needs, apart from the headteacher of his school. And, when I asked the headteacher to provide evidence for his opinion, he was unable to do so.

I have complained both to Lloyd's school about them referring Lloyd for assessment and to the Chief Education Officer. Copies of the correspondence are enclosed for your information ...

Time

It is difficult to judge how long it will take the Department for Education to investigate a formal complaint. It may be months; it may be a year or more. However, swift action at a local level can follow a formal complaint, and it is always worthwhile copying your complaint to your local councillor and asking him/her to take the matter up directly with the Chief Education Officer.

For further advice and information on making a complaint to the Secretary of State for Education, contact one of the support organisations listed in part 8.

Complaining to the Ombudsman

The official name for the Ombudsman is the Local Commissioner for Administration. You can make a complaint about your local authority to the Ombudsman if you believe that they have caused you (or your child) injustice because of maladministration.

What is maladministration?

Basically, maladministration is the term used when a council either does something wrong, or fails to do something which it should have done. Here are some examples:

- delay, with no good cause;
- failure to follow the council's agreed policies;
- acting with bias or malice;
- failure to take account of matters which they should have considered;
- failure to tell people of their rights.

The most common complaint which parents of children with special educational needs make to the Ombudsman is over their LEA's delay in making the proper provision to meet their child's needs.

What is injustice?

The Ombudsman cannot investigate a complaint of maladministration unless you can also show that it has caused injustice. You can't complain just because the council has done something wrong. You must also explain the bad effect that this has had on you and your family. Some examples of injustice are:

- that your child has missed out on his/her education (e.g. by not being allowed to attend school, or by not receiving the special help needed);
- that you have suffered financial loss;
- that you and your family have suffered stress.

The three months rule

Normally the Ombudsman will not investigate a complaint about maladministration unless it has happened within the preceding three months.

If you think that you might have grounds for complaint to the Ombudsman, you should discuss the situation with one of the support organisations (part 8) before putting your complaint in writing. Or, you can ring the Ombudsman's office direct and they will send you a free booklet explaining how to complain, plus a form. The booklet is also available from libraries.

If you live in England, send your complaint to:

The Commission for Local Administration in England
21 Queen Anne's Gate
London
SW1H 9BU.
Tel: 0207-915 3210
If you live in Wales, send your complaint to:

The Commission for Local Administration in Wales
Derwen House
Court Road
Bridgend
CF31 1BN
Tel: 01656-661 325

You do not need the Ombudsman's form to make a complaint. Instead, you can write a letter along these lines:

Dear Sir or Madam,

I am writing to make a complaint of maladministration leading to injustice against ... local education authority.

The maladministration

The maladministration was the failure of the LEA to respond to repeated requests from my daughter's school and from me that she be examined by an educational psychologist. I have a number of letters showing how often the requests were made and copies of LEA acknowledgements and 'promises'. However, despite the fact that both the school and I believed that the advice of a psychologist was needed, no response was made for 18 months, and I believe that this delay was maladministration on the part of the LEA.

The history of my problems with the LEA, and of their maladministration, is set out below.

October 12th 1998: I wrote to the LEA asking to be sent information on special education provision in the county for children under 5 years old.

November 22nd 1998: I telephoned to find out why my letter in October had not been replied to. I spoke to Mr Simmons, the officer with responsibility for special needs, and was told to ring back and ask for a Miss Jenkins, as she was responsible for all under-5s provision.

November 22nd to December 24th: I made ten phone calls to the Education Department, leaving a message each time asking Miss Jenkins to return my call. She was always 'out of the office' and never did ring me back.

... etc.

The injustice

As a result of the maladministration, I was unaware of the existence in the area of two special needs 'opportunity playgroups'. I placed my daughter in the nearest private nursery, and at my own expense paid an occupational therapist and a speech therapist to visit for weekly sessions with her. Although I was happy with the efforts made by the nursery, the staff did not have the training nor the experience of the staff at the LEA's own opportunity playgroups. Therefore:

1. My daughter was deprived of specialist provision which was available to her.

2. The LEA failed to inform me of my rights as a parent of a child with special needs.

3. I was put to unnecessary expense paying for the therapies when I believe now that an assessment would have shown them to be necessary provision for my daughter.

4. For 18 months, my whole family suffered from the stress involved in trying (in vain) to get the LEA to fulfil their proper duties towards my daughter.

... etc.

Time

A complaint to the Ombudsman can take up to a year to be investigated. However, swift action at a local level can follow a formal complaint, and it is always worthwhile copying your complaint to your local councillor and asking her or him to take the matter up directly with the Chief Education Officer.

The Ombudsman publicises his findings and can recommend that LEAs pay parents compensation. These sums are never huge, but LEAs generally award the amount recommended by the Ombudsman.

For further advice and information on making a complaint to the Ombudsman, contact one of the support organisations listed in part 8 or ring the Ombudsman direct (see above for the numbers).

Complaining to the Local Authority Monitoring Officer

Under the Local Government and Housing Act 1989, every local authority must appoint a Monitoring Officer with responsibility for reporting on any act taken or decision made by the Authority which either breaches the law, or may breach the law.

In most local authorities, the role of Monitoring Officer is given to the Chief Executive, or the head of the Legal Department. You could write to the Monitoring Officer if you thought that your LEA were acting in breach of the law with regard to meeting your child's needs, or if the LEA were proposing to bring in a policy which would, when enacted, mean they were breaching the law with regard to meeting all children's special educational needs in your area.

You could start your letter like this:

The Monitoring Officer
Town Hall
Etc . . .

Dear Sir or Madam,

I am writing to request that you use your powers under s5 of the Local Government and Housing Act 1989 to investigate and report on the policy which is being proposed with regard to provision in schools for children with statements of special educational needs. I have attached a letter which all parents of children at ... received from the Headteacher last week. It informed us that the authority was proposing to reduce LEA support for children with statements, and to require schools to increase their contribution to meeting the costs of statemented provision. Our Headteacher says this is not possible, so after half term non-teaching assistant hours are being cut for all pupils with statements.

As a parent, I believe that the LEA will be acting illegally if it creates a situation in which it is failing to provide the special educational provision specified on my child's statement. This is because the LEA will be in breach of s324 of the Education Act 1994. I ask you to investigate and report on this policy as a matter of urgency ...

7

If the Monitoring Officer accepts your argument that there is a breach of law, or a likely breach of law, he or she will investigate the situation and produce a report which must be circulated to all the elected members of the Authority (the councillors).

If the Monitoring Officer refuses to investigate your complaint, or reports that there is no breach of law likely, you should contact one of the support organisations (see part 8) for the name of a solicitor who will give advice on whether there are further steps you can take.

Part 8

Support organisations and further reading

Support organisations and further reading

Support organisations

If you work for an organisation which advises parents of children with special educational needs, but which is not listed here, please let IPSEA know.

Organisations which will advise parents of children with special educational needs, regardless of the specific nature of the child's disability:

Advisory Centre for Education (ACE)
Telephone helpline: 0808 800 5793
Exclusion advice line: 0808 8000 327
Weekdays 2.00pm to 5.00pm

Children's Legal Centre
Telephone helpline: 01206 872 466
Weekdays 9.00am to 5.00pm

Contact a Family
Telephone helpline: 0207 608 8700
Weekdays 9.00am to 5.00pm
Free Parent Line: 0808 808 3555
Weekdays 10.00am to 4.00pm

Education Otherwise (home education)
Telephone helpline: 0870 730 0074

Independent Panel For Special Education Advice (IPSEA)
Telephone helpline: 0800 018 4016
Tribunal support service: 01394 384711

National Association for Special Educational Needs
Telephone helpline: 01827 311500
Weekdays 9.00am to 5.00pm

Network 81
Telephone helpline: 01279 647 415
Weekdays 10.00am to 2.00pm

Norfolk Network 81
Telephone helpline: 01603 614 647
Weekdays 9.00am to 7.00pm

Parents for Inclusion
Telephone helpline: 0207 582 5008
Tuesday, Wednesday, Thursday 10.00am to 12.00pm/
1.00pm to 3.00pm

The Rathbone Society
Telephone helpline: 0800 917 6790
Weekdays 10.00am to 4.00pm

SKILL: National Bureau for Students with Disabilities
Telephone helpline: 0207 450 0620 (Main office)
Free information line: 0800 328 5050
Weekdays 1.30pm to 4.30pm

*Organisations which advise parents of children with
specific disabilities:*

Association for All Speech Impaired Children (AFASIC)
Telephone helpline 08453 555577
Monday to Wednesday 10.00am to 4.00pm
Thursday 11.00am to 2.00pm

Association for Spina Bifida and Hydrocephalus (ASBAH)
Telephone helpline: 01733 555 988
Weekdays 9.00am to 5.00pm

British Dyslexia Association
Telephone helpline: 0118 966 8271
Weekdays 10.00am to 12.45pm; 2.00pm to 4.45pm

British Epilepsy Association
Telephone helpline: 0808 800 5050
Monday to Thursday 9.00am to 4.30pm (Friday 4.00pm)

8

Child Growth Foundation
Telephone helpline: 0208 995 0275 or 020 8994 7625
Weekdays 9.00am to 4.00pm

Cystic Fibrosis Trust
Telephone helpline: 0208 464 7211
Weekdays 9.00am to 5.00pm

Down's Syndrome Association
Telephone helpline: 0208 682 4001
Weekdays 9.00am to 5.00pm

Hyperactive Children's Support Group
Telephone helpline: 01243 551 313
Weekdays 10.00am to 1.00pm

The Multiple Sclerosis Society
Telephone helpline: 0808 800 8000
Weekdays 9.00am to 9.00pm

National Autistic Society
Education Advocacy Line: 0800 358 8667
Telephone helpline: 0870 600 8585
Tribunal support: 0800 358 8668
Weekdays 10.00am to 4.00pm

Royal National Institute for the Blind
Telephone helpline: 08457 669999
Weekdays 9.00am to 5.00pm

SCOPE – for people with cerebral palsy
Telephone helpline: 0808 800 3333
Weekdays 9.00am to 9.00pm
Sat/Sun 2.00pm to 6.00pm
Main Office: 0207 619 7100
Weekdays 8.00am to 5.30pm

Tuberous Sclerosis Association
Telephone helpline: 0199 3881238

Other publications you should have

● *Special Educational Needs – a Parents' Guide: Parents' Charter* (Copies are available in Bengali, Chinese, Greek, Gujarati, Hindi, Punjabi, Turkish, Urdu, Vietnamese and Welsh)

● *Special Educational Needs Code of Practice*

● *Special Educational Needs Tribunal – How to Appeal*

All of the above are free publications on special educational needs which are available from the Department for Education and Skills, telephone 0845 602 2260.

● *Sent Ahead* by Sally Capper. IPSEA's guide for parents appealing to the Special Educational Needs Tribunal. £9.99 from: IPSEA, 6 Carlow Mews, Woodbridge IP12 1EA.

● *ACE's Special Education Handbook.* This is not free, but it is probably the most popular guide to the law on special education written from the parents' perspective. Available from: ACE, 18 Aberdeen Studios, 22 Highbury Grove, London N5 2EA. Ring 0808 800 5793 for price.

● *Children with Special Needs. Assessment, Law and Practice – Caught in the Acts* by John Friel (Jessica Kingsley Publishers, 1995). This is not so easy to digest as the ACE book, but it is an important source book, particularly for information on important case law judgements.

● *Education, Law and Practice* by David Ruebain, John Ford and Mary Hughes (Legal Action Group 1999).

Part 9

The law

Education Act 1996

9

(Sections 312 to 336A, Schedule 26 and Schedule 27)

Introductory

Meaning of
'special
educational
needs' and
'special
educational
provision' etc.

Section 312

(1) A child has 'special educational needs' for the purposes of this Act if he has a learning difficulty which calls for special educational provision to be made for him.

(2) Subject to subsection (3) (and except for the purposes of section 15A or 15B a child has a 'learning difficulty' for the purposes of this Act if –

(a) he has a significantly greater difficulty in learning than the majority of children of his age,

(b) he has a disability which either prevents or hinders him from making use of educational facilities of a kind generally provided for children of his age in schools within the area of the local education authority, or

(c) he is under compulsory school age and is, or would be, if special educational provision were not made for him, likely to fall within paragraph (a) or (b) when of that age.

(3) A child is not to be taken as having a learning difficulty solely because the language (or form of the language) in which he is, or will be, taught is different from a language (or form of a language) which has at any time been spoken in his home.

(4) In this Act 'special educational provision' means –

(a) in relation to a child who has attained the age of two, educational provision which is additional to, or otherwise different from, the educational provision made generally for children of his age in schools maintained by the local education authority (other than special schools) and

(b) in relation to a child under that age, educational provision of any kind.

(5) In this Part –

'child' includes any person who has not attained the age of 19 and is a registered pupil at a school;
'maintained school' means any community, foundation or voluntary school or any special school not established in a hospital.

Code of Practice

Section 313

(1) The Secretary of State shall issue, and may from time to time revise, a code of practice giving practical guidance in respect of the discharge by local education authorities and the governing bodies of maintained schools, of their functions under this Part.

(2) It shall be the duty of –

Code of Practice

(a) local education authorities, and such governing bodies, exercising functions under this Part, and

(b) any other person exercising any function for the purpose of the discharge by local education authorities, and such governing bodies, of functions under this Part

– to have regard to the provisions of the code.

(3) On any appeal under this Part to the Tribunal, the Tribunal shall have regard to any provision of the code which appears to the Tribunal to be relevant to any question arising on the appeal.

(4) The Secretary of State shall publish the code as for the time being in force.

(5) In this Part 'the Tribunal' means the Special Educational Needs Tribunal.

Section 314

Making and approval of code

(1) Where the Secretary of State proposes to issue or revise a code of practice, he shall prepare a draft of the code (or revised code).

(2) The Secretary of State shall consult such persons about the draft as he thinks fit and shall consider any representations made by them.

(3) If he determines to proceed with the draft (either in its original form or with such modifications as he thinks fit) he shall lay it before both Houses of Parliament.

(4) If the draft is approved by resolution of each House, the Secretary of State shall issue the code in the form of the draft, and the code shall come into effect on such day as the Secretary of State may by order appoint.

Note: The functions of the Secretary of State in sections 313 and 314 are exercised in Wales by the National Assembly for Wales.

Special educational provision: general

Section 315

Review of arrangements

(1) A local education authority shall keep under review the arrangements made by them for special educational provision.

289

(2) In doing so the authority shall, to the extent that it appears necessary or desirable for the purpose of co-ordinating provision for children with special educational needs, consult the governing bodies of community, foundation and voluntary schools and community, foundation and special schools in their area.

Section 316

(1) This section applies to a child with special educational needs who should be educated in a school.

(2) If no statement is maintained under section 324 for the child, he must be educated in a mainstream school.

(3) If a statement is maintained under section 324 for the child, he must be educated in a mainstream school unless that is incompatible with –

(a) the wishes of his parent, or
(b) the provision of efficient education for the other children.

(4) In this section and section 316A 'mainstream school' means any school other than –

(a) a special school, or
(b) an independent school which is not –

(i) a city technology college,
(ii) a city college for the technology of the arts, or
(iii) a city academy.

Section 316A

(1) Section 316 does not prevent a child from being educated in –

(a) an independent school which is not a mainstream school, or
(b) a school approved under section 342,

if the cost met otherwise than by a local education authority.

(2) Section 316(2) does not require a child to be educated in a mainstream school during any period which in which –

(a) he is admitted to a special school for the purposes of an assessment under section 323 of his educational needs and his admission to that school is with the agreement of –

(i) the local education authority,
(ii) the head teacher of the school or, if the school is in Wales, its governing body,
(iii) his parent, and

(iv) any person whose advice is advice is to be sought in accordance with regulations made under paragraph 2 of Schedule 26;

(b) he remains admitted to a special school, in prescribed circumstances, following an assessment under section 323 at that school;

(c) he is admitted to a special school, following a change in his circumstances, with the agreement of –

(i) the local education authority,

(ii) the head teacher of the school or, if the school is in Wales, its governing body, and

(iii) his parent;

(d) he is admitted to a community or foundation special school which is established in a hospital.

(3) Section 316 does not affect the operation of –

(a) section 348, or

(b) paragraph 3 of Schedule 27.

(4) If a local education authority decide –

(a) to make a statement for a child under section 324, but

(b) not to name in the statement the school for which a parent has expressed a preference under paragraph 3 of Schedule 27, they shall, in making the statement, comply with section 316(3).

(5) A local education authority may, in relation to their mainstream schools taken as a whole, rely on the exception in section 316(3)(b) only if they show that there are no reasonable steps that they could take to prevent the incompatibility.

(6) An authority in relation to a particular mainstream school may rely on the exception in section 316(3)(b) only if it shows that there are no reasonable steps that it or another authority in relation to the school could take to prevent the incompatibility.

(7) The exception in section 316(3)(b) does not permit a governing body to fail to comply with the duty imposed by section 324(5)(b).

(8) An authority must have regard to guidance about section 316 and this section issued –

(a) for England, by the secretary of State,

(b) for Wales, by the National assembly for Wales.

(9) That guidance shall, in particular, relate to steps which may, or may not, be regarded as reasonable for the purposes of subsections (5) and (6).

(10) 'Prescribed', in relation to Wales, means prescribed in regulations made by the National Assembly for Wales.

(11) 'Authority' –

   (a) in relation to a maintained school, means each of the following –

   (i)   the local education authority,
   (ii) the schools governing body, and

   (b) in relation to maintained nursery school or a school or a pupil referral unit, means the local education authority.

Duties of governing body or LEA in relation to pupils with special educational needs

Section 317

(1) The governing body, in the case of a community, foundation or voluntary school, and the local education authority, in the case of a maintained nursery school, shall –

   (a) use their best endeavours, in exercising their functions in relation to the school, to secure that, if any registered pupil has special educational needs, the special educational provision which his learning difficulty calls for is made,
   (b) secure that, where the responsible person has been informed by the local education authority that a registered pupil has special educational needs, those needs are made known to all who are likely to teach him, and
   (c) secure that the teachers in the school are aware of the importance of identifying, and providing for, those registered pupils who have special educational needs.

(2) In subsection (1)(b) 'the responsible person' means –

   (a) in the case of a community, foundation or voluntary school, the head teacher or the appropriate governor (that is, the chairman of the governing body or, where the governing body have designated another governor for the purposes of this paragraph, that other governor), and
   (b) in the case of a nursery school, the head teacher.

(3) To the extent that it appears necessary or desirable for the purpose of co-ordinating provision for children with special educational needs –

   (a) the governing bodies of community, foundation or voluntary schools shall, in exercising functions relating to the provision for such children, consult the local education authority, and the governing bodies of other such schools, and
   (b) in relation to maintained nursery schools, the local education authority shall, in exercising those functions, consult the funding authority and the governing bodies of community, foundation or voluntary schools.

(4) Where a child who has special educational needs is being educated in a community, foundation or voluntary school or a maintained nursery school, those concerned with making special educational provision for the child shall secure, so far as is reasonably practicable and is compatible with –

(a) the child receiving the special educational provision which his learning difficulty calls for,

(b) the provision of efficient education for the children with whom he will be educated, and

(c) the efficient use of resources,

that the child engages in the activities of the school together with children who do not have special educational needs.

(5) Each Governors' report shall include a report containing such information as may be prescribed about the implementation of the governing body's policy for pupils with special educational needs.

(6) The annual report for each community, foundation or voluntary or grant-maintained school shall also include a report containing information as to –

(a) the arrangements for the admission of disabled pupils;

(b) the steps taken to prevent disabled pupils from being treated less favourably than other pupils; and

(c) the facilities provided to assist access to the school by disabled pupils;

– and for this purpose 'disabled pupils' means pupils who are disabled persons for the purposes of the Disability Discrimination Act 1995.

(7) In this section 'annual report' means the report prepared under section 42 of the Schools Standards and Framework Act 1998.

1995 c. 50

Section 317A

(1) This section applies if –

Duty to inform parent where special educational provision made

(a) a child for whom no statement is maintained under section 324 is a registered pupil at –

(i) a community, foundation or voluntary school, or

(ii) a pupil referral unit,

(b) special educational provision is made for him at the school because it is considered that he has special educational needs, and

(c) his parent has not previously been informed under this section of special educational provision made for him at the school.

(2) If the school is a pupil referral unit, the local education authority must secure that the head teacher informs the child's parent that special educational provision is being made for him at the school because it is considered that he has special educational needs.

(3) In any other case, the governing body must inform the child's parent that special educational provision is considered and that he has special educational needs.

Section 318

Provision of goods and services in connection with special educational needs

(1) A local education authority may, for the purpose only of assisting –

   (a) the governing bodies of community, foundation or voluntary schools (in their or any other area) in the performance of the governing bodies' duties under section 317(1)(a), or

   (b) the governing bodies of community or foundation special schools (in their or any other area) in the performance of the governing bodies' duties,

– supply goods or services to those bodies.

(2) The terms on which goods or services are supplied by local education authorities under this section to the governing bodies of community, foundation or voluntary schools or community or foundation special schools in any other area may, in such circumstances as may be prescribed, include such terms as to payment as may be prescribed.

(3) A local education authority may supply goods or services to any authority or other person (other than a governing body within subsection (1)) for the purpose only of assisting them in making for any child to whom subsection (3A) applies any special educational provision which any learning difficulty of the child calls for.

(3A) This subsection applies to any child –

   (a) who is receiving relevant nursery education within the meaning of section 123 of the School Standards and Framework Act 1998, or

   (b) in respect of whose education grants are (or are to be) made under section 1 of the Nursery Education and Grant-Maintained Schools Act 1996.]

(4) This section is without prejudice to the generality of any other power of local education authorities to supply goods or services.

Section 319

(1) Where a local education authority are satisfied that it would be inappropriate for –

(a) the special educational provision which a learning difficulty of a child in their area calls for, or

(b) any part of any such provision, to be made in a school,

– they may arrange for the provision (or, as the case may be, for that part of it) to be made otherwise than in a school.

(2) Before making an arrangement under this section, a local education authority shall consult the child's parent.

Section 320

(1) A local education authority may make such arrangements as they think fit to enable a child for whom they maintain a statement under section 324 to attend an institution outside England and Wales which specialises in providing for children with special needs.

(2) In subsection (1) 'children with special needs' means children who have particular needs which would be special educational needs if those children were in England and Wales.

(3) Where a local education authority make arrangements under this section in respect of a child, those arrangements may in particular include contributing to or paying –

(a) fees charged by the institution,

(b) expenses reasonably incurred in maintaining him while he is at the institution or travelling to or from it,

(c) his travelling expenses, and

(d) expenses reasonably incurred by any person accompanying him while he is travelling or staying at the institution.

(4) This section is without prejudice to any other powers of a local education authority.

Special educational provision otherwise than in schools

Provision outside England and Wales for certain children

Identification and assessment of children with special educational needs

Section 321

(1) A local education authority shall exercise their powers with a view to securing that, of the children for whom they are responsible, they identify those to whom subsection (2) below applies.

(2) This subsection applies to a child if –

(a) he has special educational needs, and

(b) it is necessary for the authority to determine the special educational provision which any learning difficulty he may have calls for.

General duty of local education authority towards children for whom they are responsible

(3) For the purposes of this Part a local education authority are responsible for a child if he is in their area and –

    (a) he is a registered pupil at a maintained school,

    (b) education is provided for him at a school which is not a maintained school but is so provided at the expense of the authority or the funding authority,

    (c) he does not come within paragraph (a) or (b) above but is a registered pupil at a school and has been brought to the authority's attention as having (or probably having) special educational needs, or

    (d) he is not a registered pupil at a school but is not under the age of two or over compulsory school age and has been brought to their attention as having (or probably having) special educational needs.

Duty of Health Authority or local authority to help local education authority

Section 322

(1) Where it appears to a local education authority that any Health Authority or Primary Care Trust or local authority could, by taking any specified action, help in the exercise of any of their functions under this Part, they may request the help of the authority or trust, specifying the action in question.

(2) An authority or a trust whose help is so requested shall comply with the request unless –

    (a) they consider that the help requested is not necessary for the purpose of the exercise by the local education authority of those functions, or

    (b) subsection (3) applies.

(3) This subsection applies –

    (a) in the case of a Health Authority or Primary Care Trust, if that authority or trust consider that, having regard to the resources available to them for the purpose of the exercise of their functions under the National Health Service Act 1977, it is not reasonable for them to comply with the request, or

    (b) in the case of a local authority, if that authority consider that the request is not compatible with their own statutory or other duties and obligations or unduly prejudices the discharge of any of their functions.

1977 c. 49.

(4) Regulations may provide that, where an authority or trust are under a duty by virtue of subsection (2) to comply with a request to help a local education authority in the making of an assessment under section 323 or a statement under section 324 of this Act, they must, subject to prescribed exceptions, comply with the request within the prescribed period.

(5) In this section 'local authority' means a county council, a county borough council, a district council (other than one for an area for which there is a county council), a London borough council or the Common Council of the City of London.

Section 323

(1) Where a local education authority are of the opinion that a child for whom they are responsible falls, or probably falls, within subsection (2), they shall serve a notice on the child's parent informing him –

9

Assessment of educational needs

(a) that they are considering whether to make an assessment of the child's educational needs,

(b) of the procedure to be followed in making the assessment,

(c) of the name of the officer of the authority from whom further information may be obtained, and

(d) of the parent's right to make representations, and submit written evidence, to the authority within such period (which must not be less than 29 days beginning with the date on which the notice is served) as may be specified in the notice.

(2) A child falls within this subsection if –

(a) he has special educational needs, and

(b) it is necessary for the authority to determine the special educational provision which any learning difficulty he may have calls for.

(3) Where –

(a) a local education authority have served a notice under subsection (1) and the period specified in the notice in accordance with subsection (1)(d) has expired, and

(b) the authority remain of the opinion, after taking into account any representations made and any evidence submitted to them in response to the notice, that the child falls, or probably falls, within subsection (2),

– they shall make an assessment of his educational needs.

(4) Where a local education authority decide to make an assessment under this section, they shall give notice in writing to the child's parent of that decision and of their reasons for making it.

(5) Schedule 26 has effect in relation to the making of assessments under this section.

(6) Where, at any time after serving a notice under subsection (1), a local education authority decide not to assess the educational needs of the child concerned they shall give notice in writing to the child's parent of their decision.

Section 324

(1) If, in the light of an assessment under section 323 of any child's educational needs and of any representations made by the child's parent in pursuance of Schedule 27, it is necessary for the local education authority to determine the special educational provision which any learning difficulty he may have calls for, the authority shall make and maintain a statement of his special educational needs.

9

(2) The statement shall be in such form and contain such information as may be prescribed.

Statement of special educational needs

(3) In particular, the statement shall –

(a) give details of the authority's assessment of the child's special educational needs, and

(b) specify the special educational provision to be made for the purpose of meeting those needs, including the particulars required by subsection (4).

(4) The statement shall –

(a) specify the type of school or other institution which the local education authority consider would be appropriate for the child,

(b) if they are not required under Schedule 27 to specify the name of any school in the statement, specify the name of any school or institution (whether in the United Kingdom or elsewhere) which they consider would be appropriate for the child and should be specified in the statement, and

(c) specify any provision for the child for which they make arrangements under section 319 and which they consider should be specified in the statement.

(4A) Subsection (4)(b) does not require the name of a school or institution to be specified if the child's parent has made suitable arrangements for the special educational provision specified in the statement to be made for the child.

(5) Where a local education authority maintain a statement under this section, then –

(a) unless the child's parent has made suitable arrangements, the authority –

(i) shall arrange that the special educational provision specified in the statement is made for the child, and

(ii) may arrange that any non-educational provision specified in the statement is made for him in such manner as they consider appropriate, and

298

(b) if the name of a maintained school is specified in the statement, the governing body of the school shall admit the child to the school.

(5A) Subsection (5)(b) has effect regardless of any duty imposed on the governing body of a school by section 1(6) of the School Standards and Framework Act 1998.

(6) Subsection (5)(b) does not affect any power to exclude from a school a pupil who is already a registered pupil there.

(7) Schedule 27 has effect in relation to the making and maintenance of statements under this section.

Section 325
(1) If, after making an assessment under section 323 of the educational needs of any child for whom no statement is maintained under section 324, the local education authority do not propose to make such a statement, they shall give notice in writing of their decision.

(2) In such a case, the child's parent may appeal to the Tribunal against the decision.

(2A) A notice under subsection (1) must inform the parent of the right of appeal under subsection (2) and contain such other information as may be prescribed.

(2B) Regulations may provide that where a local education authority are under a duty under this section to serve any notice, the duty must be performed within the prescribed period.

(3) On an appeal under this section, the Tribunal may –

(a) dismiss the appeal,
(b) order the local education authority to make and maintain such a statement, or
(c) remit the case to the authority for them to reconsider whether, having regard to any observations made by the Tribunal, it is necessary for the authority to determine the special educational provision which any learning difficulty the child may have calls for.

Section 326
(1) The parent of a child for whom a local education authority maintain a statement under section 324 may –

(a) when the statement is first made
(b) if an amendment is made to the statement, or
(c) if, after conducting an assessment under section 323, the local education authority determine not to amend the statement,

9

– appeal to the Tribunal against the description in the statement of the authority's assessment of the child's special educational needs, the special educational provision specified in the statement or, if no school is named in the statement, that fact.

(1A) An appeal under this section may be against any of the following –

(a) the description in the statement of the local education authority's assessment of the child's special educational needs,
(b) the special educational provision specified in the statement (including the name of a school so specified),
(c) if no school is specified in the statement, that fact.

Appeal against contents of statement

(2) Subsection (1)(b) does not apply where the amendment is made in pursuance of –

(a) paragraph 8 (change of named school) or 11(3)(b) (amendment ordered by Tribunal) of Schedule 27, or
(b) directions under section 442 (revocation of school attendance order);

– and subsection (1)(c) does not apply to a determination made following the service of notice under paragraph 2A (amendment by LEA) of Schedule 27 of a proposal to amend the statement.

(3) On an appeal under this section, the Tribunal may –

(a) dismiss the appeal,
(b) order the authority to amend the statement, so far as it describes the authority's assessment of the child's special educational needs or specifies the special educational provision, and make such other consequential amendments to the statement as the Tribunal think fit, or
(c) order the authority to cease to maintain the statement.

(4) On an appeal under this section the Tribunal shall not order the local education authority to specify the name of any school in the statement (either in substitution for an existing name or in a case where no school is named) unless –

(a) the parent has expressed a preference for the school in pursuance of arrangements under paragraph 3 (choice of school) of Schedule 27, or
(b) in the proceedings the parent, the local education authority, or both have proposed the school.

(5) Before determining any appeal under this section the Tribunal may, with the agreement of the parties, correct any deficiency in the statement.

Section 326A

(1) This section applies if –

(a) the parent of a child has appealed to the Tribunal under section 325, 328, 329 or 329A or paragraph 8(3) of Schedule 27 against a decision of a local education authority, and

(b) the authority notifies the Tribunal that they have determined that they will not, or will no longer, oppose the appeal.

Unopposed appeals

(2) The appeal is to be treated as having been determined in favour of the appellant.

(3) If an appeal is treated as determined in favour of the appellant as a result of subsection (2), the Tribunal is not required to make any order.

(4) Before the end of the prescribed period, the authority must –

(a) in the case of an appeal under section 325, make a statement under section 324 of the child's educational needs,

(b) in the case of an appeal under section 328, 329, or 329A, make an assesment of the child's educational needs,

(c) in the case of an appeal under paragraph 8(3) of Schedule 27 against a determination of the authority not to comply with the parent's request, comply with the request.

(5) An authority required by subsection (4)(a) to make a statement under section 324 must maintain the statement under that section.

(6) Regulations under this section, so far as they relate to Wales, require the agreement of the National Assembly for Wales.

Section 327

(1) This section applies where –

Access for local education authority to certain schools

(a) a local education authority maintain a statement for a child under section 324, and

(b) in pursuance of the statement education is provided for the child at a school maintained by another local education authority.

(2) Any person authorised by the local education authority shall be entitled to have access at any reasonable time to the premises of any such school for the purpose of monitoring the special educational provision made in pursuance of the statement for the child at the school.

Section 328

Reviews of educational needs

(1) Regulations may prescribe the frequency with which assessments under section 323 are to be repeated in respect of children for whom statements are maintained under section 324.

(2) Where –

(a) the parent of a child for whom a statement is maintained under section 324 asks the local education authority to arrange for an assessment to be made in respect of the child under section 323,

(b) no such assessment has been made within the period of six months ending with the date on which the request is made, and

(c) it is necessary for the authority to make a further assessment under section 323,

Reviews of
educational
needs

– the authority shall comply with the request.

(3) If in any case where subsection (2)(a) and (b) applies the authority determine not to comply with the request –

(a) they shall give notice in writing of that fact to the child's parent, and

(b) the parent may appeal to the Tribunal against the determination.

(3A) A notice under subsection (3)(a) must inform the parent of the right of appeal under subsection (3)(b) and contain such other information as may be prescribed.

(3B) Regulations may provide that where a local education authority are under this section to serve any notice, the duty must be performed within the prescribed period.

(4) On an appeal under subsection (3) the Tribunal may –

(a) dismiss the appeal, or

(b) order the authority to arrange for an assessment to be made in respect of the child under section 323.

(5) A statement under section 324 shall be reviewed by the local education authority –

(a) on the making of an assessment in respect of the child concerned under section 323, and

(b) in any event, within the period of 12 months beginning with the making of the statement or, as the case may be, with the previous review.

(6) Regulations may make provision –

(a) as to the manner in which reviews of such statements are to be conducted,

(b) as to the participation in such reviews of such persons as may be prescribed, and

(c) in connection with such other matters relating to such reviews as the Secretary of State, or in Wales, the National Assembly for Wales considers appropriate.

Section 329

(1) Where –

(a) the parent of a child for whom a local education authority are responsible but for whom no statement is maintained under section 324 asks the authority to arrange for an assessment to be made in respect of the child under section 323,

(b) no such assessment has been made within the period of six months ending with the date on which the request is made, and

(c) it is necessary for the authority to make an assessment under that section,

– the authority shall comply with the request.

Assessment of educational needs at request of child's parent

(2) If in any case where subsection (1)(a) and (b) applies the authority determine not to comply with the request –

(a) they shall give notice in writing of that fact to the child's parent, and

(b) the parent may appeal to the Tribunal against the determination.

(2A) A notice under subsection (2)(a) must inform the parent of the right of appeal under subsection (2)(b) and contain such other information as may be prescribed.

(3) On an appeal under subsection (2) the Tribunal may –

(a) dismiss the appeal, or

(b) order the authority to arrange for an assessment to be made in respect of the child under section 323.

Section 329A

(1) This section applies if –

(a) a child is a registered pupil at a relevant school (whether or not he is a child in respect of whom a statement is maintained under section 324),

(b) the responsible body asks the local education authority to arrange for an assessment to be made in respect of him under section 323, and

(c) no such assessment has been made within the period of six months ending with the date on which the request is made.

Review or assessment of educational needs at request of responsible body

(2) If it is necessary for the authority to make an assessment or further assessment under section 323, they must comply with the request.

(3) Before deciding whether to comply with the request, the authority must serve on the child's parent a notice informing him –

    (a) that they are considering whether to make an assessment of the child's educational needs,

    (b) of the procedure to be followed in making the assessment,

    (c) of the name of their officer from whom further information may be obtained, and

    (d) of the parent's right to make representations, and submit written evidence, to them before the end of the period specified in the notice ('the specified period').

(4) The specified period must not be less than 29 days beginning with the date on which the notice is served.

(5) The authority may not decide whether to comply with the request until the specified period has expired.

(6) The authority must take into account any representations made, and any evidence submitted, to them in response to the notice.

(7) If, as a result of this section, a local education authority decide to make an assessment under section 323, they must give written notice to the child's parent and to the responsible body which made the request, of the decision and of their reason for making it.

(8) If, after serving a notice under subsection (3), the authority decide not to assess the educational needs of the child –

    (a) they must give written notice of the decision and of their reasons for making it to his parent and to the responsible body which made the request, and

    (b) the parent may appeal to the Tribunal against the decision.

(9) A notice given under subsection (8)(a) to the child's parent must –

    (a) inform the parent of his right to appeal, and

    (b) contain such other information (if any) as may be prescribed.

(10) On an appeal under subsection (8) the Tribunal may –

    (a) dismiss it, or

    (b) order the authority to arrange for an assessment to be made in respect of the child under section 323.

(11) This section applies to a child for whom relevant nursery education is provided as it applies to a child who is a registered pupil at a relevant school.

(12) 'Relevant school' means –

    (a) a maintained school,
    (b) a maintained nursery school,
    (c) a pupil referral unit,
    (d) an independent school,
    (e) a school approved under section 342.

(13) 'The responsible body' means –

    (a) in relation to a maintained nursery school or a pupil referral unit, the head teacher,
    (b) in relation to any other relevant school, the proprietor or head teacher, and
    (c) in relation to a provider of relevant nursery education, the person or body of persons responsible for the management of the provision of that nursery education.

(14) 'Relevant nursery education' has the same meaning as in section 123 of the School Standards and Framework Act 1998, except that it does not include nursery education provided by a local education authority at a maintained nursery school.

(15) 'Prescribed', in relation to Wales, means prescribed in regulations made by the National Assembly for Wales.

Section 331

Assessment of educational needs of children under two

(1) Where a local education authority are of the opinion that a child in their area who is under the age of two falls, or probably falls, within subsection (2) –

    (a) they may, with the consent of his parent, make an assessment of the child's educational needs, and
    (b) they shall make such an assessment if requested to do so by his parent.

(2) A child falls within this subsection if –

    (a) he has special educational needs, and
    (b) it is necessary for the authority to determine the special educational provision which any learning difficulty he may have calls for.

(3) An assessment under this section shall be made in such manner as the authority consider appropriate.

(4) After making an assessment under this section, the authority –

    (a) may make a statement of the child's special educational needs, and

(b) may maintain that statement, in such manner as they consider appropriate.

9

Section 332

(1) This section applies where a Health Authority, a Primary Care Trust or a National Health Service trust, in the course of exercising any of their functions in relation to a child who is under compulsory school age, form the opinion that he has (or probably has) special educational needs.

Duty of Health Authority, a Primary Care Trust or National Health Service trust to notify parent etc.

(2) The Authority or trust –

(a) shall inform the child's parent of their opinion and of their duty under paragraph (b), and

(b) after giving the parent an opportunity to discuss that opinion with an officer of the Authority or trust, shall bring it to the attention of the appropriate local education authority.

(3) If the Authority or trust are of the opinion that a particular voluntary organisation is likely to be able to give the parent advice or assistance in connection with any special educational needs that the child may have, they shall inform the parent accordingly.

Advice and information for parents

Section 332A

(1) A local education authority must arrange for the parent of any child in their area with special educational needs to be provided with advice and information about matters relating to those needs.

(2) In making the arrangements, the authority must have regard to any guidance given –

(a) for England, by the Secretary of State,

(b) for Wales, by the National Assembly for Wales.

(3) The authority must take such steps as they consider appropriate for making the services provided under subsection (1) known to –

(a) the parents of children in their area,

(b) the head teachers and proprietors of schools in their area, and

(c) such other persons as they consider appropriate.'

Resolution of disputes

Section 332B

(1) A local education authority must make arrangements with a view to avoiding or resolving disagreements between authorities (on the one hand) and parents of children in their area (on the other) about the exercise by authorities of functions under this Part.

(2) A local education authority must also make arrangements with a view to avoiding or resolving, in each relevant school, disagreements between the parents of a relevant child and the proprietor of the school about the special educational provision made for that child.

(3) The arrangements must provide for the appointment of independent persons with the function of facilitating the avoidance or resolution of such disagreements.

(4) In making the arrangements, the authority must have regard to any guidance given –

    (a) for England, by the Secretary of State,
    (b) for Wales, by the National Assembly for Wales.

(5) The authority must take such steps as they consider appropriate for making the arrangements made under subsections (1) and (2) known to –

    (a) the parents of children in their area,
    (b) the head teachers and proprietors of schools in their area, and
    (c) such other persons as they consider appropriate.

(6) The arrangements cannot affect the entitlement of a parent to appeal to the Tribunal.

(7) In this section-

'authorities' means the governing bodies of maintained schools and the local education authority,

'relevant child' means a child who has special educational needs and is a registered pupil at a relevant school.

(8) For the purposes of this section a school is a relevant school in relation to a child if it is –

    (a) a maintained school or a maintained nursery school,
    (b) a pupil referral unit,
    (c) a city technology college, a city college for the technology of the arts or a city academy,
    (d) an independent school named in the statement maintained for the child under section 324, or
    (e) a school approved under section 342.'

Special educational needs tribunal

Section 333

Constitution of Tribunal

(1) The Tribunal shall exercise the jurisdiction conferred on it by this Part.

(2) There shall be appointed –

    (a) a President of the Tribunal (referred to in this Part as 'the President'),

    (b) a panel of persons (referred to in this Part as 'the chairmen's panel') who may serve as chairman of the Tribunal, and

    (c) a panel of persons (referred to in this Part as 'the lay panel') who may serve as the other two members of the Tribunal apart from the chairman.

(3) The President and the members of the chairmen's panel shall each be appointed by the Lord Chancellor.

(4) The members of the lay panel shall each be appointed by the Secretary of State.

(5) Regulations may –

    (a) provide for the jurisdiction of the Tribunal to be exercised by such number of tribunals as may be determined from time to time by the President, and

    (b) make such other provision in connection with the establishment and continuation of the Tribunal as the Secretary of State considers necessary or desirable.

(6) The Secretary of State may, with the consent of the Treasury, provide such staff and accommodation as the Tribunal may require.

The President and members of the panels

Section 334

(1) No person may be appointed President or member of the chairmen's panel unless he has a seven year general qualification (within the meaning of section 71 of the Courts and Legal Services Act 1990).

(2) No person may be appointed member of the lay panel unless he satisfies such requirements as may be prescribed.

(3) If, in the opinion of the Lord Chancellor, the President is unfit to continue in office or is incapable of performing his duties, the Lord Chancellor may revoke his appointment.

(4) Each member of the chairmen's panel or lay panel shall hold and vacate office under the terms of the instrument under which he is appointed.

(5) The President or a member of the chairmen's panel or lay panel –

    (a) may resign office by notice in writing to the Lord Chancellor or (as the case may be) the Secretary of State, and

    (b) is eligible for re-appointment if he ceases to hold office.

Section 335

(1) The Secretary of State may pay to the President, and to any other person in respect of his service as a member of the Tribunal, such remuneration and allowances as the Secretary of State may, with the consent of the Treasury, determine.

(2) The Secretary of State may defray the expenses of the Tribunal to such amount as he may, with the consent of the Treasury, determine.

Section 336

Remuneration and expenses

(1) Regulations may make provision about the proceedings of the Tribunal on an appeal under this Part and the initiation of such an appeal.

(2) The regulations may, in particular, include provision –

Tribunal procedure

(a) as to the period within which, and the manner in which, appeals are to be instituted,

(b) where the jurisdiction of the Tribunal is being exercised by more than one tribunal –

(i) for determining by which tribunal any appeal is to be heard, and

(ii) for the transfer of proceedings from one tribunal to another,

(c) for enabling any functions which relate to matters preliminary or incidental to an appeal to be performed by the President, or by the chairman,

(d) ...

(e) for hearings to be conducted in the absence of any member other than the chairman,

(f) as to the persons who may appear on behalf of the parties,

(g) for granting any person such disclosures or inspection of documents or right to further particulars as might be granted by a county court,

(h) requiring persons to attend to give evidence and produce documents,

(i) for authorising the administration of oaths to witnesses,

(j) for the determination of appeals without a hearing in prescribed circumstances,

(k) as to the withdrawal of appeals,

(l) for the award of costs or expenses,

(m) for taxing or otherwise settling any such costs or expenses (and, in particular, for enabling such costs to be taxed in the county court),

(n) for the registration and proof of decisions and orders, and

(o) for enabling the Tribunal to review its decisions, or revoke or vary its orders, in such circumstances as may be determined in accordance with the regulations.

(2A) Proceedings before the Tribunal shall be held in private, except in prescribed circumstances.

9

(3) The Secretary of State may pay such allowances for the purpose of or in connection with the attendance of persons at the Tribunal as he may, with the consent of the Treasury, determine.

(4) Part 1 of the Arbitration Act 1950 shall not apply to any proceedings before the Tribunal but regulations may make provision corresponding to any provision of that Part.

(4A) The regulations may make provision for an appeal under this Part to be heard, in prescribed circumstances, with a claim under Chapter 1 of Part 4 of the Disability Discrimination Act 1995.

(5) Any person who without reasonable excuse fails to comply with –

    (a) any requirement in respect of the discovery or inspection of documents imposed by the regulations by virtue of subsection (2)(g), or

    (b) any requirement imposed by the regulations by virtue of subsection (2)(h).

– is guilty of an offence.

(6) A person guilty of an offence under subsection (5) is liable on summary conviction to a fine not exceeding level 3 on the standard scale.

Compliance with orders

Section 336A

(1) If the Tribunal makes an order, the local education authority concerned must comply with the order before the end of the prescribed period beginning with the date on which it is made.

(2) Regulations under this section, so far as they relate to Wales, require the agreement of the National Assembly for Wales.

Note: The functions of the Secretary of State in sections 333, 334, 335 and 336 are exercised in Wales by the National Assembly for Wales.

Schedule 26

Making of Assessments under Section 323

Introductory

1

In this Schedule 'assessment' means an assessment of a child's educational needs under section 323.

Medical and other advice

2

(1) Regulations shall make provision as to the advice which a local education authority are to seek in making assessments.

(2) Without prejudice to the generality of sub-paragraph (1), the regulations shall require the authority, except in such circumstances as may be prescribed, to seek medical, psychological and educational advice and such other advice as may be prescribed.

Manner, and timing, of assessments, etc.

3

(1) Regulations may make provision –

   (a) as to the manner in which assessments are to be conducted,
   (b) requiring the local education authority, where, after conducting an assessment under section 323 of the educational needs of a child for whom a statement is maintained under section 324, they determine not to amend the statement, to serve on the parent of the child a notice giving the prescribed information, and
   (c) in connection with such other matters relating to the making of assessments as the Secretary of State considers appropriate.

(2) Sub-paragraph (1)(b) does not apply to a determination made following the service of notice under paragraph 10 of Schedule 27 (amendment of statement by LEA) of a proposal to amend the statement.

(3) Regulations may provide –

   (a) that where a local education authority are under a duty under section 323, 329 or 329A to serve any notice, the duty must be performed within the prescribed period,
   (b) that where a local education authority have served a notice under section 323(1) or 329A(3) on a child's parent, they must decide within the prescribed period whether or not to make an assessment of the child's educational needs,

(c) that where a request has been made to a local education authority under section 329(1), they must decide within the prescribed period whether or not to comply with the request, and

(d) that where a local education authority are under a duty to make an assessment, the duty must be performed within the prescribed period.

(4) Provision made under sub-paragraph (3) –

(a) may be subject to prescribed exceptions, and

(b) does not relieve the authority of the duty to serve a notice, or make a decision or assessment, which has not been served or made within the prescribed period.

Attendance at examinations

4

(1) Where a local education authority are considering whether to make an assessment, they may serve a notice on the parent of the child concerned requiring the child's attendance for examination in accordance with the provisions of the notice.

(2) The parent of a child examined under this paragraph may be present at the examination if he so desires.

(3) A notice under this paragraph shall –

(a) state the purpose of the examination,

(b) state the time and place at which the examination will be held,

(c) name an officer of the authority from whom further information may be obtained,

(d) inform the parent that he may submit such information to the authority as he may wish, and

(e) inform the parent of his right to be present at the examination.

Offence

5

(1) Any parent who fails without reasonable excuse to comply with any requirements of a notice served on him under paragraph 4 commits an offence if the notice relates to a child who is not over compulsory school age at the time stated in it as the time for holding the examination.

(2) A person guilty of an offence under this paragraph is liable on summary conviction to a fine not exceeding level 2 on the standard scale.

Schedule 27

Making and Maintenance of Statements under Section 324

Introductory

1

In this Schedule –

'amendment notice' has the meaning given in paragraph 2A,
'statement' means a statement under section 324,
'periodic review' means a review conducted in accordance with section 328(5)(b), and
're-assessment review' means a review conducted in accordance with section 328(5)(a).

2

(1) Before making a statement, a local education authority shall serve on the parent of the child concerned a copy of the proposed statement.

(2) But that is a subject to sub-paragraphs (3) and (4).

(3) The copy of the proposed statement shall not specify any prescribed matter.

(4) The copy of the proposed statement shall not specify any matter in pursuance of section 324(4).

Amendments to a statement

2A

(1) A local education authority shall not amend a statement except –

    (a) in compliance with an order of the Tribunal,
    (b) as directed by the Secretary of State under section 442(4), or
    (c) in accordance with the procedure laid down in this Schedule.

(2) If, following a re-assessment review, a local education authority propose to amend a statement, they shall serve on the parent of the child concerned a copy of the proposed amended statement.

(3) Sub-paragraphs (3) and (4) of paragraph 2 apply a to a copy of a proposed amended statement served under sub-paragraph (2) as they apply to a copy of a proposed statement served under paragraph 2(1).

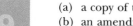

(4) If, following a periodic review, a local education authority propose to amend a statement, they shall serve on the parent of the child concerned –

    (a) a copy of the existing statement, and
    (b) an amendment notice.

(5) If, at any time, a local education authority propose to amend a statement, they shall proceed as if the proposed amendment were an amendment proposed after a periodic review.

(6) An amendment notice is a notice in writing giving details of the amendments to the statement proposed by the authority.

Provision of additional information

2B

(1) Sub-paragraph (2) applies when a local education authority serve on a parent –

    (a) a copy of a proposed statement under paragraph 2,
    (b) a copy of a proposed amended statement under paragraph 2A, or
    (c) an amendment notice under paragraph 2A.

(2) The local education authority shall also serve on the parent a written notice explaining (to the extent that they are applicable) –

    (a) the arrangements under paragraph 3,
    (b) the effect of paragraph 4, and
    (c) the right to appeal under section 326.

(3) A notice under sub-paragraph (2) must contain such other information as may be prescribed.

Choice of school

3

(1) Every local education authority shall make arrangements for enabling a parent

    (a) on whom a copy of a proposed statement has been served under paragraph 2,
    (b) on whom a copy of a proposed amended statement has been served under paragraph 2A, or
    (c) on whom an amendment notice has been served under paragraph 2A which contains a proposed amendment about –

    (i) the type or name of a school or institution, or
    (ii) the provision made for the child concerned under arrangements made under section 319,

to be specified in the statement.

to express a preference as to the community, foundation or voluntary school at which he wishes education to be provided for his child and to give reasons for his preference.

(2) Any such preference must be expressed or made within the period of 15 days beginning –

(a) with the date on which the written notice mentioned in paragraph 2B was served on the parent, or

(b) if a meeting has (or meetings have) been arranged under paragraph 4(1)(b) or (2), with the date fixed for that meeting (or the last of those meeting).

(3) Where a local education authority make a statement in a case where the parent of the child concerned has expressed a preference in pursuance of such arrangements as to the school at which he wishes education to be provided for his child, they shall specify the name of that school in the statement unless –

(a) the school is unsuitable to the child's age, ability or aptitude or to his special educational needs, or

(b) the attendance of the child at the school would be incompatible with the provision of efficient education for the children with whom he would be educated or the efficient use of resources.

Consultation on specifying name of school in statement

3A

(1) Sub-paragraph (2) applies if a local education authority are considering –

(a) specifying the name of a maintained school in a statement, or

(b) amending a statement –

(i) if no school was specified in the statement before the amendment, so that a maintained school will be specified within it,

(ii) if a school was specified in the statement before the amendment, so that a different school, which is a maintained school, will be specified in it.

(2) The local education authority shall –

(a) Serve a copy of the proposed statement or amended statement, or of the existing statement and of the amendment notice, on each affected body, and

(b) Consult each affected body.

(3) 'Affected body' means

(a) the governing body of any school which the local education authority are considering specifying; and

(b) if a school which the local education authority are considering specifying is maintained by another local education authority, that authority.

Representations

4

(1) A parent on whom a copy of a proposed statement has been served under paragraph 2, or on whom a proposed amended statement or an amendment notice has been served under paragraph 2A, may –

(a) make representations (or further representations) to the local education authority about the content of the proposed statement or the statement as it will have effect if amended in the way proposed by the authority, and

(b) require the authority to arrange a meeting between him and an officer of the authority at which the proposed statement or the statement as it will have effect if amended in the way proposed by the authority can be discussed.

(2) Where a parent, having attended a meeting arranged by a local education authority under sub-paragraph (1)(b), in relation to –

(a) a proposed statement, or

(b) an amendment proposed following a re-assessment review,

disagrees with any part of the assessment in question, he may require the authority to arrange such meeting or meetings as they consider will enable him to discuss the relevant advice with the appropriate person or person.

(3) In this paragraph –

'relevant advice' means such of the advice given to the authority in connection with the assessment as they consider to be relevant to that part of the assessment with which the parent disagrees, and

'appropriate person' means the person who gave the relevant advice or any other person who, in the opinion of the authority, is the appropriate person to discuss it with the parent.

(4) Any representations under sub-paragraph (1)(a) must be made within the period of 15 days beginning –

(a) with the date on which the written notice mentioned in paragraph 2B was served on the parent, or

(b) if a meeting has (or meetings have) been arranged under sub-paragraph (1)(b) or (2), with the date fixed for that meeting (or the last of those meetings).

(5) A requirement under sub-paragraph (1)(b) must be made within the period of 15 days beginning.

(6) A requirement under sub-paragraph (2) must be made within the period of 15 days beginning with the date fixed for that meeting arranged under sub-paragraph (1)(b).

Making the statement

5
(1) Where representations are made to a local education authority under paragraph 4(1)(a), the authority shall not make or amend the statement until they have considered the representations and the period or the last of the periods allowed by paragraph 4 for making requirements or further representations has expired.

(2) If a local education authority make a statement, it may be in the form originally proposed (except as to the matters required to be excluded from the copy of the proposed statement) or in a form modified in the light of the representations.

(2A) If a local education authority amend a statement following service of a proposed amended statement under paragraph 2A, the amended statement made may be in the form proposed or in a form modified in the light of the representations.

(2B) If the local education authority amend a statement following service of an amendment notice, the amendments may be those proposed in the notice or amendments modified in the light of the representations.

(3) Regulations may provide that, where a local education authority are under a duty (subject to compliance with the preceding requirements of this Schedule) to make a statement, the duty, or any step required to be taken for performance of the duty, must, subject to prescribed exceptions, be performed within the prescribed period.

(4) Such provision shall not relive the authority of the duty to make statement, or take any step, which has not been performed or taken within that period.

Service of statement

6

(1) Where a local education authority make or amend a statement they shall serve a copy of the statement, or the amended statement, on the parent of the child concerned.

(2) They shall, at the same time, give the parent written notice of his right to appeal under section 326(1) against –

    (a) the description in the statement of the authority's assessment of the child's special educational needs,

    (b) the special educational provision specified in the statement (including the name of a school specified in the statement),

    (c) or if no school is named in the statement, that fact.

(3) A notice under sub-paragraph (2) must contain such other information as may be prescribed.

Keeping, disclosure and transfer or statements

7

(1) Regulations may make provision as to the keeping and disclosure of statements.

(2) Regulations may make provision, where a local education authority become responsible for a child for whom a statement is maintained by another authority, for the transfer of the statement to them and for Part IV to have effect as if the duty to maintain the transferred statement were their duty.

Change of named school

8

(1) Sub-paragraph (2) applies where –

    (a) the parent of a child for whom a statement is maintained which specifies the name of a school or institution asks the local education authority to substitute for that name the name of a maintained school specified by the parent, and

    (b) the request is not made less than 12 months after –

    (i) an earlier request under this paragraph,

    (ii) the service of a copy of the statement or amended statement under paragraph 6,

(iii) if the parent has appealed to the Tribunal under Section 326 or this paragraph, the date when the appeal is concluded, whichever is the later

(2) The local education authority shall comply with the request unless –

(a) the school is unsuitable to the child's age, ability or aptitude or to his special educational needs, or
(b) the attendance of the child at the school would be incompatible with the provision of efficient education for the children with whom he would be educated or the efficient use of the resources.

(3) Where the local education authority determine not to comply with the request –

(a) they shall give notice in writing of that fact to the parent of the child, and
(b) the parent of the child may appeal to the Tribunal against the determination.

(3A) A notice under sub-paragraph (3)(a) must inform the parent of the right of appeal under sub-paragraph (3)(b) and contain such other information as may be prescribed.

(4) On the appeal the Tribunal may –

(a) dismiss the appeal, or
(b) order the local education authority to substitute for the name of the school or other institution specified in the statement the name of the school specified by the parent.

(5) Regulations may provide that, where a local education authority are under a duty to comply with a request under this paragraph, the duty must, subject to prescribed exceptions, be performed within the prescribed period.

(6) Such provision shall not relieve the authority of the duty to comply with such a request which has not been complied with within that period.

Procedure for ceasing to maintain a statement

9

(1) A local education authority may not cease to maintain a statement except in accordance with paragraph 11.

(2) Sub-paragraph (1) does not apply where the local education authority –

(a) cease to maintain a statement for a child who has ceased to be a child for whom they are responsible, or

(b) are ordered to cease to maintain a statement under section 326(3)(c),

11

(1) A local education authority may cease to maintain a statement only if it is no longer necessary to maintain it.

(2) Where the local education authority determine to cease to maintain a statement –

(a) they shall give notice in writing of that fact to the parent of the child, and
(b) the parent of the child may appeal to the Tribunal against the determination.

(2A) A notice under sub-paragraph (2)(a) must inform the parent of the right of appeal under sub-paragraph (2)(b) and contain such other information as may be prescribed.

(3) On an appeal under this paragraph the Tribunal may –

(a) dismiss the appeal, or
(b) order the local education authority to continue to maintain the statement in its existing form or with such amendments of –

(i) the description in the statement of the authority's assessment of the child's special educational needs, or
(ii) the special educational provision specified in the statement, and such other consequential amendments, as the Tribunal may determine.

(4) Except where the parent of the child appeals to the Tribunal under this paragraph, a local education authority may only cease to maintain a statement under this paragraph within the prescribed period beginning with the service of the notice under sub-paragraph (2).

(5) A local education authority may not, under this paragraph, cease to maintain a statement if –

(a) the parent of the child has appealed under this paragraph against the authority's determination to cease to maintain the statement, and
(b) the appeal has not been determined by the Tribunal or withdrawn.

The Education (Special Educational Needs) (England) (Consolidation) Regulations 2001
(S.I. 2001 No. 3455)
ARRANGEMENT OF REGULATIONS

PART I
General

1. Citation and commencement
2. Interpretation
3. Delegation of functions
4. Notices
5. Service of documents

PART II
Assessments

6. Notices relating to assessment
7. Advice to be sought
8. Educational advice
9. Medical advice
10. Psychological advice
11. Matters to be taken into account in making an assessment
12. Time limits and prescribed information
13. Children without statements in special schools

PART III
Statements

14. Notices accompanying a proposed statement or proposed amended statement
15. Notice accompanying an amendment notice
16. Statement of special educational needs
17. Time limits and prescribed information
18. Reviews of statements
19. Phase transfers
20. Review of statement of child attending school (other than a review in respect of a child in his tenth year of compulsory education)
21. Reviews of statements where child in his tenth year of compulsory education attends school
22. Review of statement where child does not attend school
23. Transfer of statements
24. Restriction on disclosure of statements

PART IV
Compliance with Tribunal Orders

25. Compliance with Tribunal Orders
26. Compliance with parents' requests when an authority concedes an appeal to the Tribunal

PART V
Revocation and transitional provisions

27. Revocation of the 1994 Regulations
28. Transitional provisions

SCHEDULES

Schedule 1.

Part A – Notice to Parent (proposed statements and proposed amended statements)

Part B – Notice to Parent (amendment notices)

Schedule 2.

Statement of Special Educational Needs

In exercise of the powers conferred on the Secretary of State by sections 316A(2), 322(4), 324(2), 325(2A) and (2B), 326A(4), 328(1), (3A), and (3B), 329(2A), 329A(9), 336A(1) and 569(1), (2), (4) and (5) of, and paragraphs 2, 3(1), (3) and (4) of Schedule 26, and paragraphs 2(3), 2B(3), 5(3), 6(3), 7(1) and (2), 8(3A) and (5), 11(2A) and (4) of Schedule 27 to, the Education Act 1996[1], the Secretary of State for Education and Skills hereby makes the following Regulations:

[1] 1996 c. 56. By virtue of the National Assembly for Wales (Transfer of Functions) Order 1999 (S.I. 1999/672), the powers conferred by sections 322(4), 324(2), 328(1), and 569, and by paragraphs 2(1) and (2) of Schedule 26 are exercisable by the Secretary of State only in relation to England. For the meaning of regulations see section 579(1) of the Act. Sections 316A(2), 325(2A), and 2(B), 326A(4), 328(3A) and (3B), 329A(9) and 336A(1) were inserted by the Special Educational Needs and Disability Act 2001 (c. 10), section 1, paragraph 6 of Schedule 8, section 5, paragraph 7 of Schedule 8, section 8 and section 4 respectively.

PART I

GENERAL

Citation and commencement

1. (1) These Regulations may be cited as the Education (Special Educational Needs) (England) (Consolidation) Regulations 2001.

(2) These Regulations shall come into force on 1st January 2002.

(3) These Regulations apply only in relation to England.

Interpretation

2. (1) In these Regulations –

'the Act' means the Education Act 1996;

'annual review' means a review of a child's statement of educational needs carried out within 12 months of making the statement or the previous review under section 328(5)(b) of the Act;

'assessment' means an assessment of a child's educational needs under section 323 of the Act;

'authority' means a local education authority;

'Careers Service' means a body established to provide careers services under sections 8 to 10 of the Employment and Training Act 1973[2];

'Connexions Service' means a person of any description with whom the Secretary of State has made an arrangement under section 114(2)(a) of the Learning and Skills Act 2000[3] and section 10(1) of the Employment and Training Act 1973 and any person to whom he has given a direction under section 114(2)(b) of the Learning and Skills Act 2000 and section 10(2) of the Employment and Training Act 1973;

'early education provider' means a provider of relevant nursery education except that it shall not include an authority in respect of a maintained nursery school;

'head of SEN' means the person responsible for co-ordinating the day-to-day provision of education for pupils with special educational needs;

---

[2] 1973 c. 50; sections 8, 9 and 10 were substituted by the Trade Union Reform and Employment Rights Act 1993 (c. 19), section 45.
[3] 2000 c. 21.

'head teacher' includes any person to whom the duties or functions of a head teacher under these Regulations have been delegated by the head teacher in accordance with regulation 3;

'health authority' has the same meaning as in the National Health Service Act 1977[4];

'parent partnership services' means the arrangements made by an authority under section 332A of the Act for the provision of advice and information about matters relating to special educational needs to parents of children with special educational needs;

'social services authority' means a local authority for the purposes of the Local Authority Social Services Act 1970[5] acting in the discharge of such functions as are referred to in section 1A of that Act;

'statement' means a statement of a child's special educational needs made under section 324 of the Act;

'target' means the knowledge, skills and understanding which a child is expected to have by the end of a particular period;

'tenth year of compulsory education' means the ninth school year after the school year in which a child reaches compulsory school age;

'transition plan' means a document which sets out the appropriate arrangements for a young person during the period beginning with the commencement of his tenth year of compulsory education and ending when aged 19 years, including arrangements for special educational provision and for any other necessary provision, for suitable employment and accommodation and for leisure activities, and which will facilitate a satisfactory transition from childhood to adulthood;

'Tribunal' means the Special Educational Needs Tribunal having the jurisdiction conferred on it by section 333 of the Act;

'working day' means a day other than a Saturday, Sunday, Christmas Day, Good Friday or Bank Holiday within the meaning of the Banking and Financial Dealings Act 1971[6];

'the 1994 Regulations' means the Education (Special Educational Needs) Regulations 1994[7].

---

[4] 1977 c. 49 amended by the Health Authorities Act 1995 (c. 17) and the Health Act 1999 (c. 32).
[5] 1970 c. 42; section 1A was inserted by the Local Government Act 2000 (c. 22), section 102(3).
[6] 1971 c. 80.
[7] S.I. 1994/1047.

(2) The expressions used in these Regulations set out in the first column of the table below have the meaning given by (or, as the case may be, are to be interpreted in accordance with), the provisions referred to in the second column of that table;

'compulsory school age'	section 85 of the Act;
'maintained school'	section 312 of the Act;
'parent'	section 576 of the Act;
'qualified teacher'	section 218 Education Reform Act 1988[8];
'relevant nursery eduction'	section 509A(5) of the Act;
'responsible body'	section 329A(13) of the Act;
'school day'	section 579(1) of the Act;
'school year'	section 579(1) of the Act;
'special school'	section 337 of the Act;
'young offender institution'	section 43 of the Prison Act 1952[9].

(3) In these Regulations any reference to the health authority or the social services authority is, in relation to a particular child, a reference to the health authority or social services authority in whose area that child lives.

(4) Where a thing is required to be done under these Regulations –

(a) within a period after an action is taken, the day on which that action was taken shall not be counted in the calculation of that period, and

(b) within a period and the last day of that period is not a working day, the period shall be extended to include the following working day.

(5) Unless the context otherwise requires references in these Regulations –

(a) to a section are references to a section of the Act,

(b) to a Schedule are references to a Schedule of the Act,

(c) to a regulation are references to a regulation in these Regulations, and

(d) to a paragraph and are references to a paragraph concerned.

Delegation of functions

3. Where a head teacher has any functions or duties under these Regulations he may delegate those functions or duties –

(a) generally to a member of the staff of the school who is a qualified teacher, or

(b) in a particular case to a member of the staff of the school who teaches the child in question.

---

[8] 1988 c. 40.
[9] 1952 c. 52.

Notices

4. Any notice required to be given by these Regulations shall be given in writing.

Service of documents

5. (1) Where any provision in Part IV of the Act or in these Regulations authorises or requires any document to be served or sent to a person or any notice to be given to a person the document may be served or sent or the notice may be given by properly addressing, pre-paying and posting a letter containing the document or notice.

(2) For the purposes of this regulation, the proper address of a person is –

(a) in the case of the child's parent, his last known address;
(b) in the case of a head teacher or other member of the staff of a school, the school's address, or
(c) in the case of any other person, the last known address of the place where he carries on his business, profession or other employment.

(3) Where first class post is used, the document or notice shall be treated as served, sent or given on the second working day after the date of posting, unless the contrary is shown.

(4) Where second class post is used, the document or notice shall be treated as served, sent or given on the fourth working day after the date of posting, unless the contrary is shown.

(5) The date of posting shall be presumed, unless the contrary is shown, to be the date shown in the post-mark on the envelope in which the document is contained.

PART II

ASSESSMENTS

Notices relating to assessment

6. (1) Paragraph (2) applies where –

(a) under section 323(1) or 329A(3) an authority serve notice on a child's parent that they are considering whether to make an assessment, or
(b) no notice has been given in relation to a particular assessment under section 323(1) or 329A(3), and under section 323(4) or 329A(7) an authority give notice to a child's parent of their decision to make an assessment.

(2) Where this paragraph applies an authority shall send copies of the relevant notice –

    (a) to the social services authority;

    (b) to the health authority;

    (c) if the child is registered at a school, to the head teacher of that school, or

    (d) if the child receives education from an early education provider, to the head of SEN in relation to that provider.

(3) Where a copy of a notice is sent under paragraph (2) an endorsement on the copy or a notice accompanying that copy shall inform the recipient what help the authority are likely to request.

(4) Where –

    (a) under section 328(2) or 329(1) a child's parent asks an authority to arrange for an assessment, and

    (b) no assessment has been made for that child within the period of six months ending with the date on which the request is made,

the authority shall give notice to the persons referred to in paragraph (2)(a) to (d) that the request has been made and inform them what help the authority are likely to request.

(5) Where –

    (a) under section 329A(1) a responsible body asks an authority to arrange for an assessment, and

    (b) no assessment has been made for that child within the period of six months ending with the date on which the request is made the authority shall give notice to the persons referred to in paragraph (2)(a) to (d) that the request has been made and inform them what help the authority are likely to request.

(6) Where the head teacher at a school or head of SEN in relation to an early education provider is the responsible body referred to at paragraph (5)(a) the authority may –

    (a) choose not to serve a notice on the head teacher or head of SEN under paragraph (5)(b), and

    (b) endorse the notice served on the responsible body under section 329A(7) or serve a further notice accompanying that notice informing the head teacher of the school or the head of SEN in relation to the early education provider of the help the authority are likely to request.

Advice to be sought

7. (1) For the purpose of making an assessment an authority shall seek –

    (a) advice from the child's parent;

    (b) educational advice as provided for in regulation 8;

    (c) medical advice from the health authority as provided for in regulation 9;

    (d) pyschological advice as provided for in regulation 10;

    (e) advice from the social services authority, and

    (f) any other advice which the authority consider appropriate for the purpose of arriving at a satisfactory assessment.

(2) The advice referred to in paragraph (1) shall be written advice relating to –

    (a) the educational, medical, psychological or other features of the case (according to the nature of the advice sought) which appear to be relevant to the child's educational needs (including his likely future needs);

    (b) how those features could affect the child's educational needs, and

    (c) the provision which is appropriate for the child in light of those features of the child's case, whether by way of special educational provision or non-educational provision, but not relating to any matter which is required to be specified in a statement by virtue of section 324(4)(b).

(3) A person from whom the advice referred to in paragraph (1) is sought may in connection therewith consult such persons as it appears to him expedient to consult; and he shall consult such persons, if any, as are specified in the particular case by the authority as persons who have relevant knowledge of, or information relating to, the child.

(4) When seeking the advice referred to in paragraphs (1)(b) to (f) an authority shall provide the person from whom it is sought with copies of –

    (a) any representations made by the parent, and

    (b) any evidence submitted by, or at the request of, the parent under section 323(1)(d) or section 329A(3)(d) as the case may be.

(5) The authority need not seek the advice referred to in paragraph (1)(b), (c), (d), (e) or (f) if –

    (a) the authority have obtained advice under paragraph (1)(b), (c), (d), (e) or (f) respectively within the preceding 12 months, and

    (b) the authority, the person from whom the advice was obtained and the child's parent are satisfied that the existing advice is sufficient for the purpose of arriving at a satisfactory assessment.

Educational advice

8. (1) The educational advice referred to in regulation 7(1)(b) shall, subject to paragraphs (2) to (5), be sought –

    (a) from the head teacher of any school which the child is currently attending;

    (b) if advice cannot be obtained from a head teacher of a school which the child is currently attending (because the child is not attending a school or otherwise) then from a person who the authority are satisfied has the experience of teaching children with special educational needs or knowledge of the differing provision which may be called for in different cases to meet those needs;

    (c) if the child is not currently attending a school and if advice obtained under sub-paragraph (b) is not advice from such a person, from a person responsible for educational provision for him, and

    (d) if any parent of the child is a serving member of Her Majesty's armed forces, from Service Children's Education.

(2) Subject to paragraph (3), the advice sought as provided in paragraphs (1)(a) to (c) shall not be sought from any person who is not a qualified teacher.

(3) If the advice sought as provided in paragraph 1(c) is to be obtained in respect of a child receiving education from an early educational provider and there is no person responsible for that child's educational provision who is a qualified teacher, advice shall be sought from a person responsible for his educational provision who is not a qualified teacher.

(4) The advice sought from a head teacher as provided in paragraph (1)(a) shall, if the head teacher has not himself taught the child within the preceding 18 months, be advice given after consultation with a teacher who has so taught the child.

(5) The advice sought from a head teacher as provided in paragraph (1)(a) shall include advice relating to the steps which have been taken by the school to identify and assess the special educational needs of the child and to make provision for the purpose of meeting those needs.

(6) The advice sought under paragraph (1)(b) or (1)(c) in relation to a child receiving education from an early education provider shall include advice relating to the steps which have been taken by the provider to identify and assess the special educational needs of the child and to make provision for meeting those needs.

(7) Where it appears to the authority, in consequence of medical advice or otherwise, that the child in question is –

(a) hearing impaired;

(b) visually impaired; or

(c) both hearing impaired and visually impaired,

and any such person from whom advice is sought as provided in paragraph (1) is not qualified to teach pupils who are so impaired then the advice sought shall be advice given after consultation with a person who is so qualified.

(8) For the purposes of paragraph (7) a person shall be considered to be qualified to teach pupils who are hearing impaired or visually impaired or who are both hearing impaired and visually impaired if he is qualified to be employed at a school as a teacher of a class for pupils who are so impaired otherwise than to give instruction in a craft, trade, or domestic subject.

(9) Paragraphs (4) and (7) are without prejudice to regulation 7(3).

Medical advice

9. The advice referred to in regulation 7(1)(c) shall be sought from the health authority, who shall obtain the advice from a fully registered medical practitioner.

Psychological advice

10. (1) The psychological advice referred to in regulation 7(1)(d) shall be sought from a person –

(a) regularly employed by the authority as an educational psychologist, or

(b) engaged by the authority as an educational psychologist in the case in question.

(2) The advice sought from a person as provided in paragraph (1) shall, if that person has reason to believe that another psychologist has relevant knowledge of, or information relating to, the child, be advice given after consultation with that other psychologist.

(3) Paragraph (2) is without prejudice to regulation 7(3).

Matters to be taken into account in making an assessment

11. When making an assessment an authority shall take into consideration –

(a) any representations made by the child's parent under section 323(1)(d) or section 329A(3)(d);

330

(b) any evidence submitted by, or at the request of, the child's parent under section 323(1)(d) or section 329A(3)(d), and

(c) the advice obtained under regulation 7.

Time limits and prescribed information

12. (1) Where section 323(1) an authority serve a notice on a child's parent informing him that they are considering whether to make an assessment they shall within 6 weeks of the date of service of that notice give notice to the child's parent of –

(a) their decision to make an assessment, and of their reasons for making that decision, or

(b) their decision not to assess the educational needs of the child and of their reasons for making that decision, and

in either case the availability to the parent of advice and information on matters related to his child's special educational needs from the parent partnership service.

(2) Where under section 328(2) or 329(1) a parent asks the authority to arrange for an assessment to be made they shall within 6 weeks of the date of receipt of the request give notice to the child's parent –

(a) of –

(i) their decision to make an assessment;

(ii) their reasons for making that decision, and

(iii) the availability to the parent of advice and information on matters related to his child's special educational needs from the parent partnership service,

(b) of –

(i) their determination not to comply with the parent's request;

(ii) their reasons for making that determination;

(iii) the availability to the parent of advice and information on matters related to his child's special educational needs from the parent partnership service;

(iv) the availability to the parent of arrangements for the prevention and resolution of disagreements between parents and authorities made by the authority under section 332B(1);

(v) the parent's right to appeal to the Tribunal against the determination not to make an assessment;

(vi) the time limit within which an appeal must be made to the Tribunal, and

(vii) the fact that the arrangements made under section 332B(1) cannot affect the parent's right to appeal to the Tribunal and that a parent may appeal to the Tribunal and enter into the arrangements made under section 332B(1).

(3) Where section 329A applies an authority shall, within 6 weeks of the date of a request from a responsible body that an assessment of a child be made, give notice to that body –

(a) of their decision to make an assessment, and of their reasons for making that decision, or

(b) of their decision not to assess the educational needs of the child, and of their reasons for making that decision.

(4) Where section 329A applies an authority shall, within 6 weeks of the date of receipt of a request from a responsible body that an assessment of a child be made, give notice to the child's parent –

(a) of –

(i)   their decision to make an assessment;

(ii) their reasons for making that decision, and

(iii) the availability to the parent of advice and information about matters related to his child's special educational needs from the parent partnership service, or

(b) of –

(i)   their decision not to assess the educational needs of the child;

(ii) their reasons for making that decision;

(iii) the availability to the parent of advice and information on matters related to his child's special educational needs from the parent partnership service;

(iv) the availability to the parent of arrangements for the prevention and resolution of disputes between parents and authorities made by the authority under section 332B(1);

(v)   the parent's right to appeal to the Tribunal against the decision not to make an assessment;

(vi) the time limit within which an appeal must be made to the Tribunal, and

(vii) the fact that the arrangements made under section 332B(1) cannot affect the parent's right to appeal to the Tribunal and that the parent may appeal to the Tribunal and enter into the arrangements made under section 332B(1).

(5) An authority need not comply with the time limits referred to in paragraphs (1) to (4) if it is impractical to do so because –

(a) the authority have requested advice from the head teacher of a school during a period beginning 1 week before any date on which that school was closed for a continuous period of not less than 4 weeks from that date and ending 1 week before the date on which it re-opens;

(b) the authority have requested advice from the head of SEN in relation to or other person responsible for a child's education at an early education provider during a period beginning 1 week before any date on which that early education provider was closed for a continuous period of not less than 4 weeks from that date and ending 1 week before the date on which it re-opens;

(c) exceptional personal circumstances affect the child or his parent during the 6 week period referred to in paragraphs (1) to (4), or

(d) the child or his parent are absent from the area of the authority for a continuous period of not less than 4 weeks during the 6 weeks period referred to in paragraphs (1) to (4).

(6) Subject to paragraph (7), where under section 323(4) or 329A(7) an authority have given notice to the child's parent of their decision to make an assessment they shall complete that assessment within 10 weeks of the date on which such notice was given.

(7) An authority need not comply with the time limit referred to in paragraph (6) if it is impractical to do so because –

(a) in exceptional cases after receiving the advice sought under regulation 7 it is necessary for the authority to seek further advice;

(b) the child's parent has indicated to the authority that he wishes to provide advice to the authority after the expiry of 6 weeks from the date on which a request for such advice under regulation 7(1)(a) was received, and the authority have agreed to consider such advice before completing the assessment;

(c) the authority have requested advice from the head teacher of a school under regulation 7(1)(b) during a period beginning 1 week before any date on which that school was closed for a continuous period of not less than 4 weeks from that date and ending 1 week before the date on which it re-opens;

(d) the authority have requested advice from the head of SEN in relation to or other person responsible for a child's education at an early education provider under regulation 7(1)(b) during a period beginning 1 week before any date on which that early education provider was closed for a continuous period of not less than 4 weeks from that date and ending 1 week before the date on which it re-opens;

(e) the authority have requested advice from a health authority or a social services authority under regulation 7(1)(c) or (e) respectively and the health authority or the social services authority have not complied with that request within 6 weeks from the date on which it was made;

(f) exceptional personal circumstances affect the child or his parent during the 10 week period referred to in paragraph (6);

(g) the child or his parent are absent from the area of the authority for a continuous period of not less than 4 weeks during the 10 week period referred to in paragraph (6); or

(h) the child fails to keep an appointment for an examination or a test during the 10 week period referred to in paragraph (6).

(8) Subject to paragraphs (9), (10) and (11), where an authority have requested advice from a health authority or a social services authority under regulation 7(1)(c) or (e) respectively the health authority or social services authority shall comply with that request within 6 weeks of the date on which they receive it.

(9) A health authority or a social services authority need not comply with the time limit referred to in paragraph (8) if it is impractical to do so because –

(a) exceptional personal circumstances affect the child or his parent during the 6 week period referred to in paragraph (8);

(b) the child or his parent are absent from the area of the authority for a continuous period of not less than 4 weeks during the 6 week period referred to in paragraph (8), or

(c) the child fails to keep an appointment for an examination or a test made by the health authority or the social services authority respectively during the 6 week period referred to in paragraph (8).

(10) A health authority need not comply with the time limit referred to in paragraph (8) if they have not before the date on which a copy of a notice has been served on them in accordance with regulation 6(2), 6(4) or 6(5) produced or maintained any information or records relevant to the assessment of the child.

(11) A social services authority need not comply with the request referred to in paragraph (8) if they have not before the date on which a copy of a notice has been served on them in accordance with regulation 6(2), 6(4) or 6(5) produced or maintained any information or records relevant to the assessment of the child.

Children without statements in special schools

13. If a child without a statement has been admitted to a special school for the purposes of an assessment, as provided for in section 316A(2), he may remain at that school –

(a) until the expiry of ten school days after the authority serve a notice under section 325 informing the child's parent that they do not propose to make a statement, or

(b) until a statement is made[10].

10 Once a statement has been made for a child that statement will determine whether he will be educated in a special school or elsewhere.

335

PART III

STATEMENTS

Notices accompanying a proposed statement or proposed amended statement

14. The notice which shall be served by an authority on a parent pursuant to paragraph 2B(2) of Schedule 27 to accompany –

   (a) a copy of a proposed statement (served under paragraph 2(1) of Schedule 27), or

   (b) a copy of a proposed amended statement (served under paragraph 2A(2) of Schedule 27),

shall contain the information as specified in Part A of Schedule 1 to these Regulations.

Notice accompanying an amendment notice

15. The notice which shall be served by an authority on a parent pursuant to paragraph 2B(2) of Schedule 27 to accompany an amendment notice (served under paragraph 2A(4) of Schedule 27) shall contain the information as specified in Part B of Schedule 1 to these Regulations.

Statement of special educational needs

16. A statement shall –

   (a) be in a form substantially corresponding to that set out in Schedule 2 to these Regulations;

   (b) contain the information therein specified;

   (c) be dated and authenticated by the signature of a duly authorised officer of the authority concerned;

   (d) set out whether it is the first statement made by the authority for the child or a subsequent statement;

   (e) indicate on the front page if it is –

   (i) amended pursuant to an annual review and the date of any such annual review;

   (ii) amended pursuant to a review other than an annual review, and the date of any such review;

   (iii) amended pursuant to an order of the Tribunal, and the date of any such order, or

   (iv) amended pursuant to a direction of the Secretary of State, and the date of any such direction.

Time limits and prescribed information

17. (1) Where an authority have made an assessment of a child for whom no statement is maintained they shall within 2 weeks of the date on which the assessment was completed either –

    (a) serve a copy of a proposed statement and a notice on the child's parent under paragraphs 2(1) and 2B(2) of Schedule 27 respectively, or

    (b) give notice to the child's parent –

    (i) under section 325(1) that they have decided not to make a statement;

    (ii) of their reasons for that decision;

    (iii) of the parent's right of appeal against that decision to the Tribunal, and

    (iv) of the time limit within which an appeal to the Tribunal must be made.

(2) Where an authority have made an assessment of a child for whom a statement is maintained they shall within 2 weeks of the date on which the assessment was completed –

    (a) serve on the child's parent a copy of a proposed amended statement and a notice under paragraphs 2A(2) and 2B(2) of Schedule 27 respectively, or

    (b) give notice to the child's parent –

    (i) under paragraph 11(2) of Schedule 27 that they have determined to cease to maintain the statement;

    (ii) of the parent's right of appeal against that determination to the Tribunal, and

    (iii) of the time limit within which an appeal to the Tribunal must be made, or

(c) serve on the child's parent a notice –

    (i) which informs him that they have determined not to amend the statement;

    (ii) which informs him of their reasons for that determination;

    (iii) which is accompanied by copies of the professional advice obtained during the assessment;

    (iv) which informs him that under section 326(1)(c) he may appeal to the Tribunal against the description in the statement of the authority's assessment of the child's special educational needs, the special educational provision specified in the statement (including the name of a school so specified) or, if no school is named in the statement, that fact, and

(v) which informs him of the time limit within which an appeal to the Tribunal must be made.

(3) Subject to paragraph (4), where an authority have served a copy of a proposed statement or proposed amended statement on the child's parent under paragraph 2(1) or 2A(2) of Schedule 27 the authority shall within 8 weeks of the date on which the proposed statement or proposed amended statement was served a copy of the completed statement or completed amended statement and a written notice on the child's parent under paragraphs 6(1) and 6(2) respectively of Schedule 27.

(4) The authority need not comply with the time limit referred to in paragraph (3) if it is impractical to do so because –

(a) exceptional personal circumstances affect the child or his parent during the 8 week period referred to in paragraph (3);

(b) the child or his parent are absent from the area of the authority for a continuous period of not less than 4 weeks during the 8 week period referred to in paragraph (3);

(c) the child's parent indicates that he wishes to make representations to the authority about the content of the statement under paragraph 4(1) of Schedule 27 after the expiry of the 15 day period for making such representations provided for in paragraph 4(4) of that Schedule;

(d) a meeting between the child's parent and an officer of the authority has been held pursuant to paragraph 4(1) of Schedule 27 and the child's parent under paragraph 4(2) of that Schedule has either required that another such meeting be arranged or has required a meeting with the appropriate person be arranged, or

(e) the authority have sent a written request to the Secretary of State seeking her consent under section 347(5) to the child being educated at an independent school which is not approved by him and such consent has not been received by the authority within 2 weeks of the date on which the request was sent.

(5) Where under paragraph 8(1) of Schedule 27 the child's parent asks the authority to substitute for the name of a school or institution specified in a statement the name of another school specified by him and where the conditions referred to in paragraph 8(1)(b) of Schedule 27 have been satisfied the authority shall within 8 weeks of the date on which the request was received either –

(a) comply with the request, or

(b) give notice to the child's parent under paragraph 8(3) of Schedule 27 that they have determined not to comply with the request, their reasons for that decision, and of his right to appeal against that determination to the Tribunal.

(6) Where under paragraph 2A(4) of Schedule 27 an authority serve an amendment notice on the child's parent informing him of their proposal to amend a statement they shall amend the statement before the expiry of 8 weeks from the date on which the notice was served.

(7) The authority need not comply with the time limit in paragraph (6) where –

  (a) the amendment notice contained an amendment about the type or name of a school or institution or the provision made for the child concerned under arrangements made under section 319, and
  (b) it is impractical to do so because any of the circumstances referred to in paragraph 4(a) to (e) apply in relation to the 8 week period referred to in paragraph 6.

(8) Where under paragraph 11(1) of Schedule 27 an authority give notice to the child's parent that they have determined to cease to maintain a statement, the authority shall not cease to maintain the statement before the expiry of the prescribed period during which the parent may appeal to the Tribunal against the determination[11].

(9) Any notice given in accordance with this regulation shall inform the parent on whom it is served of –

  (a) the availability to the parent of arrangements for the prevention and resolution of disagreements between parents and authorities made by the authority under section 332B, and
  (b) the fact that the arrangements made under section 332B cannot affect any right the parent has to appeal to the Tribunal and that the parent may appeal to the Tribunal and take up the arrangements made under section 332B.

Reviews of statements

18. (1) Not less than two weeks before the first day of every school term an authority shall serve a notice on the head teacher of every school listing those pupils with statements registered at that school –

  (a) for whom the authority is responsible, and
  (b) whose annual reviews fall to be carried out before the commencement of the second term after the notice is given.

---

[11] The Special Educational Needs Tribunal Regulations 2001 (S.I. 2001/600) provide that an appeal must be made no later than the first working day after the expiry of two months from which the authority notify a parent of his right of appeal. Under paragraph 11(5) of Schedule 27 to the Act an authority may not cease to maintain a statement if a parent has appealed against the authority's determination to cease to maintain a statement and that appeal has not been determined by the Tribunal or withdrawn.

(2) In this regulation 'school' means –

   (a) a community, voluntary, foundation, community or foundation special school;
   (b) a maintained nursery school;
   (c) a pupil referral unit;
   (d) a school approved by the Secretary of State under section 342 or section 347, and
   (e) a City Technology College, a City College for Technology and the Arts, or a City Academy,

at which a pupil for whom the authority is responsible is a registered pupil.

(3) The notice served in accordance with paragraph (1) shall –

   (a) require the head teacher to submit a report to the authority in respect of each child mentioned in it which shall be prepared by the head teacher and reviewed by the authority in accordance with –

     (i) paragraphs (4) to (15) of Regulation 20 in respect of a child, other than a child in his tenth year of compulsory education, or
     (ii) paragraphs (4) to (15) of Regulation 21 in respect of a child in his tenth year of compulsory education, and

   (b) specify for each child any person from whom the authority consider advice should be sought for the purpose of arriving at a satisfactory report.

(4) The report referred to in paragraph (3) shall be prepared by the head teacher –

   (a) by the end of the term which follows service of the notice, or if earlier
   (b) within ten school days of the review meeting referred to in regulation 20(6), on in the case of a child in his tenth year of compulsory education, regulation 21(6).

(5) Not less than two weeks before the first day of a school year an authority shall serve on the Connexions Service for their area, or where no Connexions Service has been established at that date, the Careers Service for their area, a notice –

   (a) listing all the children with statements for whom the authority is responsible and who will be in their tenth year of compulsory education in that school year, and
   (b) indicating the school attended by each of those children or the educational provision made in respect of them.

(6) Not less than two weeks before the first day of every school term an authority shall serve a notice on the health authority and on the social services authority –

(a) listing –

(i) those children with statements of special educational needs living in the area of the health authority or social services authority;
(ii) for whom the authority is responsible, and
(iii) whose annual reviews fall to be carried out before the commencement of the second term after the notice is given, and

(b) indicating the school attended by those children or the educational provision made in respect of them.

Phase transfers

19. (1) This Regulation applies where –

(a) a statement is maintained for a child, and
(b) the child is within twelve calendar months of a transfer between phases of his schooling.

(2) In this Regulation a transfer between phases of schooling means a transfer from –

(a) primary school to middle school;
(b) primary school to secondary school;
(c) middle school to secondary school, or
(d) secondary school to an institution specified in section 2A of the Act.

(3) Where this Regulation applies an authority must ensure that the child's statement is amended so that before 15th February in the calendar year of the child's transfer the statement names the school or other institution which the child will be attending following that transfer.

Review of statement of child attending school (other than a review in respect of a child in his tenth year of compulsory education)

20. (1) This Regulation applies where –

(a) an authority carry out an annual review of a child's statement;
(b) the child concerned attends a school, and
(c) the child is not in his tenth year of compulsory education.

(2) Subject to paragraph (3) the authority shall by notice in writing require the head teacher of the child's school to submit a report to them under this Regulation by a specified date not less than two months from the date the notice is given.

(3) If the name of the child is included in the notice served under paragraph (1) of regulation 18 no further notice need be served on the head teacher in respect of that child under paragraph (2) of this Regulation.

(4) The head teacher shall for the purpose of preparing the report referred to in paragraph (2) of this Regulation or paragraph (3) of regulation 18 seek the advice referred to in paragraph (5) from –

(a) the child's parent (in relation to all the matters referred to in paragraph (5));

(b) any person whose advice the authority consider appropriate for the purpose of arriving at a satisfactory report and whom they specify in the notice referred to in paragraph (2) of this regulation or in paragraph (1) of regulation 18 in relation to the particular child (in relation to such of the matters referred to in paragraph (5) as the head teacher considers are within that person's knowledge or expertise), and

(c) any person whose advice the head teacher considers appropriate for the purpose of arriving at a satisfactory report (in relation to such of the matters referred to in paragraph (5) as the head teacher considers are within that person's knowledge or expertise).

(5) The advice referred to in paragraph (4) shall be written advice as to –

(a) the child's progress towards meeting the objectives specified in the statement;

(b) the child's progress towards attaining any targets established in furtherance of the objectives specified in the statement;

(c) where the school is a community, foundation or voluntary school or a community or foundation special school other than a special school established in a hospital, the application of the provisions of the National Curriculum to the child, and the progress made in relation to those provisions by the child since the statement was made or the last review under section 328;

(d) the application of any provisions substituted for the provisions of the National Curriculum in order to maintain a balanced and broadly based curriculum and the progress made in relation to those provisions by the child since the statement was made or the last review under section 328;

(e) the progress made by the child since the statement was made or the last review under section 328 in his behaviour and attitude to learning;

(f) where appropriate, and in any case where a transition plan exists, any matters which are the appropriate subject of such a plan;

(g) whether the statement continues to be appropriate;

(h) any amendments to the statement which would be appropriate, and

(i) whether the authority should cease to maintain the statement.

(6) The notice referred to in paragraph (2) of this regulation or paragraph (1) of regulation 18 shall require the head teacher to invite the following persons to attend a meeting in respect of each child specified in the report to be held on a date before the report referred to in that paragraph is to be submitted –

(a) the representative of the authority specified in the notice;

(b) the child's parent;

(c) a member or members of the staff of the school who teach the child or who are otherwise responsible for the provision of education for the child whose attendance the head teacher considers appropriate;

(d) any other person whose attendance the head teacher considers appropriate, and

(e) any person whose attendance the authority consider appropriate and who is specified in the notice.

(7) The head teacher shall not later than two weeks before the date on which a meeting referred to in paragraph (6) is to be held send to all the persons invited to that meeting and who have not informed the head teacher that they will not be attending it copies of the advice he has received pursuant to his request under paragraph (4) and by written notice accompanying the copies shall request the recipients to submit to him before or at the meeting written comments on that advice and any other advice which they think appropriate.

(8) The meeting referred to in paragraph (6) shall consider –

(a) the matters referred to in paragraph (5), and

(b) any significant changes in the child's circumstances since the date on which the statement was made or last reviewed.

(9) The meeting shall recommend –

(a) any steps which it concludes ought to be taken, including whether the authority should amend or cease to maintain the statement;

(b) any targets to be established in furtherance of the objectives specified in the statement which it concludes the child ought to meet during the period until the next review, and

(c) where a transition plan exists, the matters which it concludes ought to be included in that plan.

(10) If the meeting cannot agree the recommendations to be made under paragraph (9) the persons who attended the meeting shall make differing recommendations as appears necessary to each of them.

(11) The report to be submitted under paragraph (2) of this Regulation or paragraph (3) of regulation 18 shall be completed after the meeting is held and shall include the head teacher's assessment of the matters referred to in paragraph (8) and his recommendations as to the matters referred to in paragraph (9), and shall refer to any difference between his assessment and recommendations and those of the meeting.

(12) When the head teacher submits his report to the authority under paragraph (2) of this Regulation or paragraph (3) of regulation 18 he shall at the same time send copies to –

(a) the child's parent;
(b) any other person who submitted advice under paragraph (4) or paragraph (7);
(c) any other person to whom the authority consider it appropriate that a copy be sent and to whom they direct him to send a copy, and
(d) any other person to whom the head teacher considers it appropriate that a copy be sent.

(13) The authority shall review the statement under section 328 in light of the report and any other information or advice which they consider relevant, record in writing their decisions on the matters referred to in paragraphs 9(a) and (b) and, where a transition plan exists, shall make written recommendations for amendments to the plan as they consider appropriate.

(14) The authority shall within one week of completing the review under section 328 send copies of their decisions and recommendations to –

(a) the child's parent;
(b) the head teacher, and
(c) any other person to whom the authority consider it appropriate that a copy be sent.

(15) The head teacher shall be responsible for ensuring that any necessary amendments to any transition plan are made.

(16) In this Regulation the term 'school' shall have the same meaning as it does in regulation 18.

Reviews of statements where child in his tenth year of compulsory education attends school

21. (1) This Regulation applies where –

(a) an authority carry out an annual review of a child's statement;

(b) the child concerned attends a school, and

(c) the review is the first review after the child has commenced his tenth year of compulsory education.

(2) Subject to paragraph (3) the authority shall by notice in writing require the head teacher of the child's school to submit a report to them under this Regulation by a specified date not less than two months from the date when the notice is given.

(3) If the name of the child is included in the notice served under paragraph (1) of regulation 18 no further notice need to be served on the head teacher in respect of that child under paragraph (2) of this Regulation.

(4) The head teacher shall for the purposes of the report referred to in paragraph (2) of this Regulation or paragraph (3) of regulation 18 seek the advice referred to in paragraph (5) from –

(a) the child's parent (in relation to all the matters referred to in paragraph (5));

(b) any person whose advice the authority consider appropriate for the purpose of arriving at a satisfactory report and whom they specify in the notice referred to in paragraph (2) or in paragraph (1) of regulation 18 in relation to a particular child (in relation to such of the matters referred to in paragraph (5) as the head teacher considers are within that person's knowledge or expertise);

(c) a representative of the Connexions Service, or if no Connexions Service has been established at the date the advice is requested, a representative of the Careers Service (in relation to the matters referred to in sub-paragraph (5)(f) and such other matters referred to in paragraph (5) as the head teacher considers are within the representative's knowledge or expertise), and

(d) any person whose advice the head teacher considers appropriate for the purpose of arriving at a satisfactory report (in relation to such of the matters referred to in paragraph (5) as the head teacher considers are within that person's knowledge or expertise).

(5) The advice referred to in paragraph (4) shall be written advice as to –

(a) the child's progress towards meeting the objectives specified in the statement;

(b) the child's progress towards attaining any targets established in furtherance of the objectives specified in the statement;

(c) where the school is a community, foundation or voluntary school or a community or foundation special school other than a special school established in a hospital, the application of the provisions of the National Curriculum to the child, and the progress made in relation to those provisions by the child since the statement was made or the last review under section 328;

(d) the application of any provisions substituted for the provisions of the National Curriculum in order to maintain a balanced and broadly based curriculum and the progress made in relation to the provisions by the child since the statement was made or the last review under section 328;

(e) the progress made by the child since the statement was made or the last review under section 328 in his behaviour and attitude to learning;

(f) any matters which are the appropriate subject of a transition plan;

(g) whether the statement continues to be appropriate;

(h) any amendments to the statement which would be appropriate, and

(i) whether the authority should cease to maintain the statement.

(6) The notice referred to in paragraph (2) of this Regulation or paragraph (1) of regulation 18 shall require the head teacher to invite the following persons to attend a meeting to be held on a date before the report referred to in that paragraph is required to be submitted –

(a) the child's parent;

(b) a member or members of the staff of the school who teach the child or who are otherwise responsible for the provision of education for the child whose attendance the head teacher considers appropriate;

(c) a representative of the social services authority;

(d) a representative of the Connexions Service or, if no Connexions Service has been established at the date of the request, a representative of the Careers Service;

(e) any person whose attendance the head teacher considers appropriate;

(f) any person whose attendance the authority consider appropriate and who is specified in the notice, and

(g) a representative of the authority.

(7) The head teacher shall not later than two weeks before the date on which the meeting referred to in paragraph (6) is to be held serve on all the persons invited to attend that meeting and who have not informed the head teacher that they will not be attending it copies of the advice he has received pursuant to his request under paragraph (4) and shall by written notice request the recipients to submit to him before or at the meeting written comments on that advice and any other advice which they think appropriate.

(8) The meeting referred to in paragraph (6) shall consider –

(a) the matters referred to in paragraph (5), in all cases including the matters referred to in paragraph (5)(f), and

(b) any significant changes in the child's circumstances since the date on which the statement was made or last reviewed under section 328.

(9) The meeting shall recommend –

(a) any steps which it concludes ought to be taken, including whether the authority should amend or cease to amend the statement;

(b) any targets to be established in furtherance of the objectives specified in the statement which it concludes the child ought to meet during the period until the next review, and

(c) the matters which it concludes ought to be included in a transition plan.

(10) If the meeting cannot agree the recommendations to be made under paragraph (9) the persons who attended the meeting shall make differing recommendations as appears necessary to each of them.

(11) The report to be submitted under paragraph (2) of this Regulation or paragraph (3) of regulation 18 shall be completed after the meeting is held, shall include the head teacher's assessment of the matters referred to in paragraph (8) and his recommendations as to the matters referred to in paragraph (9), and shall refer to any difference between his assessment and recommendations and those of the meeting.

(12) When the head teacher submits his report to the authority under paragraph (2) of this Regulation or paragraph (3) of regulation 18 he shall at the same time send copies to –

(a) the child's parent;

(b) any other person to whom the authority considers it appropriate that a copy be sent and to whom they direct him to send a copy, and

(c) any other person to whom the head teacher considers it appropriate that a copy be sent.

(13) The authority shall review the statement under section 328 in light of the report and any other information or advice which they consider relevant and shall make written recommendations as to the matters referred to in paragraph 9(a), (b) and (c).

(14) The authority shall within one week of the completing the review under section 328 send copies of the recommendations and the transition plan to –

(a) the child's parent;

(b) the head teacher, and

(c) any other person to whom they consider it appropriate to send a copy.

(15) The head teacher shall be responsible for ensuring that a transition plan is drawn up.

(16) In this Regulation the term 'school' shall have the same meaning as it does in regulation 18.

Review of statement where child does not attend school

22. (1) This Regulation applies where an authority carry out an annual review of a statement and the child concerned does not attend a school.

(2) The authority shall prepare a report addressing the matters referred to in regulation 20(5), including the matters referred to in regulation 20(5)(f) in any case where the review referred to in paragraph (1) is commenced after the child begins his tenth year of compulsory education, and for that purpose shall seek advice on those matters from the child's parent and on such of those matters from any other person whose advice they consider appropriate in the case in question for the purpose of arriving at a satisfactory report.

(3) The authority shall invite the following persons to attend a meeting to be held on a date before the review referred to in paragraph (1) is required to be completed –

    (a) the child's parent;

    (b) where the review referred to in paragraph (1) is the first review commenced after the child has begun his tenth year of compulsory education, a representative of the social services authority;

    (c) where sub-paragraph (b) applies, a representative of the Connexions Service, or if no Connexions Service has been established at the date the invitation is made, a representative of the Careers Service, and

    (d) any person or persons whose attendance the authority consider appropriate.

(4) The authority shall not later than two weeks before the date on which the meeting referred to in paragraph (3) is to be held send to all the persons invited to that meeting a copy of the report which they propose to make under paragraph (2) and by written notice accompanying the copies shall request the recipients to submit to the authority written comments on the report and any other advice which they think appropriate.

(5) A representative of the authority shall attend the meeting.

(6) The meeting shall consider the matters referred to in regulation 20(5), and in any case where the review is commenced after the child has begun his tenth year of compulsory education, the matters referred to in regulation 20(5)(f), and shall make recommendations in accordance with

regulation 20(9), and in any case where the child has begun his tenth year of compulsory education, recommendations as to the matters which it concludes ought to be included in a transition plan.

(7) The report prepared by the authority under paragraph (2) shall be completed after the meeting referred to in paragraph (3) is held, shall contain the authority's assessment of the matters required to be considered by the meeting and their recommendations as to the matters required to be recommended by it, and shall refer to any difference between their assessment and recommendations and those of the meeting.

(8) The authority shall within one week of the date on which the meeting referred to in paragraph (3) was held send copies of the report completed under paragraph (7) to

    (a) the child's parent;
    (b) any person to whom they consider it appropriate to send a copy.

(9) The authority shall review the statement under section 328 in light of the report and any other information or advice which it considers relevant, shall make written recommendations as to the matters referred to in regulation 20(9) and in any case where the review is the first review commenced after the child has commenced his tenth year of compulsory education prepare a transition plan, and in any case where a transition plan exists amend the plan as they consider appropriate.

(10) The authority shall within one week of completing the review under section 328 send copies of the recommendations and any transition plan referred to in paragraph (9) to the persons referred to in paragraph (8).

(11) In this Regulation the term 'school' shall have the same meaning as it does in regulation 18.

Transfer of statements

23. (1) This Regulation applies where a child in respect of whom a statement is maintained moves from the area of the authority which maintains the statement ('the old authority') into that of another ('the new authority').

(2) The old authority shall transfer the statement to the new authority.

(3) From the date of the transfer –

    (a) the statement shall be treated for the purposes of the new authority's duties and functions under Part IV of the Act and these Regulations as if it had been made by the new authority on the date on which it was made by the old authority, and

(b) where the new authority make an assessment and the old authority have supplied the new authority with advice obtained in pursuance of a previous assessment regulation 7(5) shall apply as if the new authority had obtained the advice on the date on which the old authority obtained it.

(4) The new authority shall within 6 weeks of the date of the transfer serve a notice on the child's parent informing him –

(a) that the statement has been transferred;
(b) whether they propose to make an assessment, and
(c) when they propose to review the statement in accordance with paragraph (5).

(5) The new authority shall review the statement under section 328(5)(b) before the expiry of whichever of the following two periods expires later –

(a) the period of 12 months beginning with the making of the statement, or as the case may be, with the previous review, or
(b) the period of 3 months beginning with the date of the transfer.

(6) Where by virtue of the transfer the new authority come under a duty to arrange the child's attendance at a school specified in the statement but in light of the child's move that attendance is no longer practicable the new authority may arrange for the child's attendance at another school appropriate for the child until such time as it is possible to amend the statement in accordance with the procedure set out in Schedule 27.

(7) In this Regulation 'the new authority' shall include a local education authority in Wales for the purposes of paragraphs (1) and (2) only.

(8) An authority to whom a statement is transferred from a local educational authority in Wales shall treat the statement as having been transferred by an old authority for the purposes of paragraphs (3) to (6).

Restriction on disclosure of statements

24. (1) Subject to the provisions of the Act and of these Regulations, a statement in respect of a child shall not be disclosed without the child's consent except –

(a) to persons to whom, in the opinion of the authority concerned, it is necessary to disclose the statement in the interests of the child;
(b) for the purposes of any appeal under the Act;
(c) for the purposes of educational research which, in the opinion of the authority, may advance the education of children with special educational needs, if, but only if, the person engaged in that research undertakes not to publish anything contained in, or

derived from, a statement otherwise than in a form which does not identify any individual concerned including, in particular, the child concerned and his parent;

(d) on the order of any court or for the purposes of any criminal proceedings;

(e) for the purposes of any investigation under Part III of the Local Government Act 1974[12] (investigation of maladministration);

(f) to the Secretary of State when he requests such disclosure for the purposes of deciding whether to give directions or make an order under section 496, 497 or 497A;

(g) for the purposes of an assessment of the needs of the child with respect to the provision of any statutory services for him being carried out by officers of a social services authority by virtue of arrangements made under section 5(5) of the Disabled Persons (Services, Consultation and Representation) Act 1986[13];

(h) for the purposes of a local authority in the performance of their duties under sections 22(3)(a), 85(4)(a), 86(3)(a) and 87(3) of the Children Act 1989[14];

(i) to Her Majesty's Chief Inspector of Schools, one of Her Majesty's Inspectors of Schools, or to a registered inspector or a member of an inspection team, who requests the right to inspect or take copies of a statement in accordance with section 2(8) or 3(3) of or paragraph 7 of Schedule 3 to the School Inspections Act 1996[15] respectively;

(j) to the Connexions Service for the purposes of writing or amending a transition plan, or

(k) to a Young Offender Institution for the purposes of the performance of its duties under rule 38 of the Young Offender Institution Rules 2000[16].

(2) A child may consent to the disclosure of a statement for the purposes of this Regulation if his age and understanding are sufficient to allow him to understand the nature of that consent.

(3) If a child does not have sufficient age or understanding to allow him to consent to disclosure of his statement his parent may consent on his behalf.

---

[12] 1974 c. 7.

[13] 1986 c. 33; section 5 is amended by the Special Education Needs and Disability Act 2001; paragraphs 16 to 18 of Schedule 8.

[14] 1989 c. 41; section 87(3) is prospectively amended by the Care Standards Act 2000 (c. 14), section 105.

[15] 1996 c. 57; section 28 is amended by the Education Act 1997 (c. 44), section 42 and Schedule 6 and paragraph 7 of Schedule 3 is amended by the Education Act 1977, section 42 and Schedule 6, paragraph 12.

[16] S.I. 2000/3371.

(4) The arrangements for keeping such statements shall be such as to ensure, so far as is reasonably practicable, that unauthorised persons do not have access to them.

(5) In this regulation any reference to a statement includes a reference to any representations, evidence, advice or information which is set out in the appendices to a statement.

PART IV

COMPLIANCE WITH TRIBUNAL ORDERS

Compliance with Tribunal Orders

25. (1) Subject to paragraph (4), if the Tribunal, following an appeal to it by a parent, makes an order requiring an authority to perform an action referred to in paragraph (2) the authority shall perform that action within the period specified in paragraph (2).

(2) In the case of an order –

(a) to make an assessment, the authority shall notify the child's parent that it will make an assessment under section 323(4) or 329A(7) as the case may be within 4 weeks;

(b) to make and maintain a statement, the authority shall make a statement within 5 weeks;

(c) remitting a case back to the authority under section 325(3)(c), the authority shall take the action referred to in regulation 17(1)(a) or 17(1)(b) within 2 weeks;

(d) to amend a statement, the authority shall serve an amendment notice on the child's parent under paragraph 2A of Schedule 27 within 5 weeks;

(e) to continue to maintain a statement, the authority shall continue to maintain a statement with immediate effect;

(f) to continue to maintain and to amend a statement, the authority shall continue to maintain the statement with immediate effect and shall serve an amendment notice on the child's parent under paragraph 2A of Schedule 27 within 5 weeks;

(g) to substitute the name of the school or other institution specified in a child's statement with the name of a school specified by a parent, the authority shall specify the school specified by the parent within 2 weeks, and

(h) dismissing an appeal against a determination to cease to maintain a statement, the authority shall cease to maintain that statement immediately or on a date proposed by the authority, whichever is the later.

(3) In each case the period shall begin on the day after the issue of the Order in question.

(4) The authority need not comply with the time limits referred to in paragraph (2) if it is impractical to do so because –

(a) exceptional personal circumstances affect the child or his parent during the relevant time period;

(b) the child or his parent are absent from the area of the authority for a continuous period of not less than 2 weeks during the relevant time period;

(c) the child's parent indicates that he wishes to make representations to the authority about the content of the statement under paragraph 4(1) of Schedule 27 after the expiry of the 15-day period for making such representations provided for in paragraph 4(4) of that Schedule;

(d) a meeting between the child's parent and an officer of the authority has been held pursuant to paragraph 4(1) of Schedule 27 and the child's parent under paragraph 4(2) of that Schedule has either required that another such meeting be arranged or has required that a meeting with the appropriate person be arranged, or

(e) the authority have sent a written request to the Secretary of State seeking her consent under section 347(5) to the child being educated at an independent school which is not approved by him and such consent has not been received by the authority within 3 weeks of the day on which the request was sent.

Compliance with parents' requests when an authority concedes an appeal to the Tribunal

26. (1) Subject to paragraph (3) if, under section 326A(2), an appeal to the Tribunal is treated as having been determined in favour of the parent making the appeal, the authority shall –

(a) in the case of an appeal under section 325, make a statement within 5 weeks;

(b) in the case of an appeal under section 328, 329, or 329A, the authority shall make an assessment within 4 weeks, and

(c) in the case of an appeal under paragraph 8(3) of Schedule 27 against a determination not to comply with the parent's request to substitute the name of a maintained school for the name of the school or institution specified in the statement, comply with that request within 2 weeks.

(2) In each case the period shall begin on the day after the authority notifies the Tribunal that they have determined that they will not, or will no longer, oppose the appeal.

(3) The authority need not comply with the time limits referred to in paragraph (1) if it is impractical to do so because –

(a) exceptional personal circumstances affect the child or his parent during the relevant time period;

(b) the child or his parent are absent from the area of the authority for a continuous period of not less that 2 weeks during the relevant time period;

(c) the child's parent indicates that he wishes to make representations to the authority about the content of the statement under paragraph 4(1) of Schedule 27 after the expiry of the 15 day period for making such representations provided for in paragraph 4(4) of that Schedule;

(d) a meeting between the child's parent and an officer of the authority has been held pursuant to paragraph 4(1) of Schedule 27 and the child's parent under paragraph 4(2) of that Schedule has either required that another such meeting be arranged or has required that a meeting with the appropriate person be arranged, or

(e) the authority have sent a written request to the Secretary of State seeking her consent under section 347(5) to the child being educated at an independent school which is not approved by him and such consent has not been received by the authority within 3 weeks of the day on which the request was sent.

PART V

REVOCATION AND TRANSITIONAL PROVISIONS

Revocation

27. (1) Subject to regulation 28, the 1994 Regulations are revoked.

(2) The Education (Special Educational Needs) (England) Regulations 2001, the Education (Special Educational Needs) (England) (Amendment) Regulations 2001, and the Education (Special Educational Needs) (England) (Amendment No 2) Regulations 2001, are hereby revoked.

Transitional provisions

28. (1) Subject to the following provisions of this Regulation references in these Regulations to anything done under these Regulations shall be read in relation to the times, circumstances or purposes in relation to which a corresponding provision of the 1994 Regulations had effect and so far as the nature of the reference permits as including a reference to that corresponding provision.

(2) Regulations 6 to 11 of the 1994 Regulations shall continue to apply in relation to any assessment where before 1st January 2002 in pursuance of section 323(4) the authority notify the parent that they have decided to make an assessment, and regulations 6 to 12 of these Regulations shall not apply in relation to any such assessment.

(3) Where regulations 6 to 11 of the 1994 Regulations continue to apply in relation to any assessment but the authority have not before 1st May 2002 –

(a) notified the parent of their decision that they are not required to determine the special educational provision of the child in accordance with section 325(1);

(b) served on the parent a copy of a proposed statement in accordance with paragraph 2 of Schedule 27, or

(c) served on the parent a copy of a proposed amended statement under paragraph 3 of Schedule 27

regulations 6 to 12 of these Regulations shall apply in relation to the assessment from 1st May 2002 as if on that date the authority had given notice to the parent under section 323(4) of their decision to make an assessment.

(4) Where in accordance with paragraph (3) above regulations 6 to 12 of these Regulations apply in relation to an assessment the authority shall obtain advice in accordance with Part II, but advice obtained in accordance with the 1994 Regulations shall be considered to have been obtained under Part II of these Regulations if such advice is appropriate for the purpose of arriving at a satisfactory assessment under that Part.

(5) Where before 1st January 2002 in accordance with section 323(1) the authority have served notice on the child's parent that they propose to make an assessment but they have not before that date notified the parent under section 323(4) Act that they have decided to make the assessment or notified him under section 323(6) that they have decided not make the assessment, regulation 11 of the 1994 Regulations shall continue to apply for the purpose of any such notification under section 323(4) or 323(6) only.

(6) Where before 1st January 2002 in accordance with section 328 or 329 a parent has asked the authority to arrange for an assessment to be made of his child's educational needs but the authority have not before that date notified the parent under section 323(4) that they have decided to make the assessment or notified him under section 328(3) or 329(2) that they have decided not to make the assessment, regulation 11 of the 1994 Regulations shall continue to apply for the purpose of any notification under section 323(4), 328(3) or 329(2) only.

(7) Regulations 13 and 14 of the 1994 Regulations shall continue to apply to the making of any statement where before 1st January 2002 the authority have served on the parent a copy of a proposed statement in accordance with paragraph 2 of Schedule 27.

(8) Regulation 14 of the 1994 Regulations shall continue to apply in relation to a proposal to amend or cease to maintain a statement where an authority serve a notice under paragraphs 10(1) or 11(2) of Schedule 27 before 1st January 2002.

(9) Regulation 15 of the 1994 Regulations shall continue to apply to a review of a statement in respect of which an authority serve a notice as required by regulation 15(2) of the 1994 Regulations before 1st January 2002.

(10) Regulation 16 of the 1994 Regulations shall continue to apply to a review of a statement in respect of which an authority serve a notice as required by regulation 16(2) of the 1994 Regulations before 1st January 2002.

(11) Regulation 17 of the 1994 Regulations shall continue to apply to a review in respect of which an authority in accordance with regulation 17(3) of the 1994 Regulations have before 1st January 2002 invited the attendance of the persons specified in that regulation to a meeting.

SCHEDULE 1
Regulation 14
PART A

NOTICE TO PARENT

Name and address of authority

Date

Address of Parents

Dear [*here insert name of parents*]

I am pleased to enclose a copy of [*child's name*] proposed statement of special educational needs/proposed amended statement of special educational needs. We have attached to it copies of all the advice we were given during [*child's name*] assessment for the statement.

If you want to meet us to talk about the statement you need to tell us within 15 days of receiving this letter. This is not the final statement. You can ask for changes to be made to it. The rest of this letter tells you how you can do this.

As you will see the statement is in six parts:

Part 1 Introduction

Part 2 Special Educational Needs

Part 3 Special Educational Provision, including objectives and monitoring arrangements

Part 4 Placement

Part 5 Non-educational Needs

Part 6 Non-educational Provision

We have left part 4 blank so that you can tell us where you think [*child's name*] should be educated. You can tell us which maintained (Local Education Authority) school, including an LEA-maintained special school, you would like [*child's name*] to go to and tell us the reasons. To help you decide, a list of all the maintained [*primary/secondary*] schools in the area is attached.

357

[A list of all primary or secondary schools, depending on whether the child requires primary or secondary education must be attached to this letter.]

If you suggest the name of a maintained school, including a maintained special school, we must name the school in part 4 of the statement unless –

(a) the school is unsuitable to [*child's name*] age, ability or aptitude or to his/her special educational needs, or

(b) the attendance of [*child's name*] at the school would be incompatible with the provision of efficient education for the children with whom he/she would be educated or the efficient use of resources.

If you think that [*child's name*] should attend a non-maintained special school or an independent school you can suggest the name of a school and tell us why you think that school should be named in [*child's name*] statement. A list of non-maintained special schools and independent schools approved by the Secretary of State [*and if such a list is produced by the National Assembly of Wales*] and the National Assembly of Wales is attached to help you.

[Such lists of independent and non-maintained special schools as the Secretary of State and the National Assembly of Wales may issue from time to time must be attached to this letter.]

If you want to tell us the name of a school you want [*child's name*] to go to you must do so within 15 days of getting this letter. However, if you attend a meeting with us to discuss this statement after getting this letter you will have another 15 days from that meeting to suggest a school. You can also tell us if you disagree with what the statement says. If you do disagree with the statement you must also tell us within 15 days of getting this letter, or 15 days from when you meet us to talk about the statement. If you still disagree with the statement, or any of the advice given during the assessment after you meet us, you can ask us for another meeting to discuss the advice you disagree with but you must ask us within 15 days of the first meeting. We will arrange for the person who gave the advice, or someone else they suggest, to attend this new meeting. We can arrange more than one meeting if necessary, if you disagree with more than one part of the advice.

Once all these stages are finished we will send you a final statement that will have part 4 completed.

If you have any concerns or questions about this process, or disagree with any part of the statement you may wish to get advice or support from the local parent partnership service. They can be contacted at [*contact address and telephone number*].

They can also put you in touch with the informal arrangements set up to help resolve or prevent any disagreements between you and the authority.

Using either of these services does not prevent you from appealing to the Special Educational Needs Tribunal about Parts 2, 3 or 4 of the Statement at the same time; your rights are not affected and an appeal to the Tribunal can run at the same time as any disagreement resolution.

When you receive the final statement, if you disagree with parts 2, 3 or 4 you can appeal to the Special Educational Needs Tribunal. The Tribunal can hold a hearing to decide what should be in these parts of [*child's name*] statement. You have to appeal to the Tribunal within two months of getting the final statement. The address of the Tribunal is 50 Victoria Street, London, SW1H 0HW.

If you have any questions, now or at any time, about this process or about the statement itself, our case officer [*name*] can be contacted at [*address and telephone number*].

Please do not hesitate to get in touch.

Yours sincerely

[Signature of officer responsible]

PART B

Regulation 15

Name and address of authority

Date

Address of Parents

Dear [*here insert name of parents*]

As you know [*child's name*] has a statement of special educational needs dated [*here insert date of statement*].

We propose amending [*child's name*] statement [*please insert reasons e.g. following an annual review*]. Details of the amendments are in the amendment notice attached.

If you disagree with the suggested changes and want to meet us to talk please tell us within 15 days.

(when amendment to part 4 is recommended)

We [*also*] want to amend part 4 of the statement [*explain reasons why e.g. so that a child can go to secondary school*].

You can tell us which maintained (LEA) school, including an LEA-maintained special school, you would like [*child's name*] to go to and tell us the reasons. To help you decide, a list of all the maintained [*primary/secondary*] schools in the area is attached.

[*A list of all primary or secondary schools, depending on whether the child requires primary or secondary education must be attached to this letter.*]

If you suggest the name of a maintained school, including a maintained special school, we must name the school in part 4 of the statement unless –

(a) the school is unsuitable to [*child's name*] age, ability or aptitude or to his/her special educational needs, or

(b) the attendance of [*insert child's name*] at the school would be incompatible with the provision of efficient education for the children with whom he/she would be educated or the efficient use of resources.

If you think that [*child's name*] should attend a non-maintained special school or an independent school you can suggest the name of a school and tell us why you think that school should be named in [*child's name*] statement. A list of non-maintained special schools and independent schools approved by the Secretary of State [*and if such a list is produced by the National Assembly of Wales*] and the National Assembly of Wales is attached to help you.

[*Such lists of independent and non-maintained special schools as the Secretary of State and the National Assembly of Wales may issue from time to time must be attached to this letter.*]

If you want to tell us the name of a school you want [*child's name*] to go to you must do so within 15 days of getting this letter. However, if you attend a meeting with us to discuss the suggested changes to this statement after getting this letter you have another 15 days from that meeting to name a school. You can also tell us if you disagree with the changes to the statement that we are suggesting. If you do disagree with the suggested changes you must also tell us within 15 days of getting this letter.

Once all these stages are finished we will send you an amended final statement. If you have any concerns or disagree with any part of the amended final statement you may wish to get advice or support from the local parent partnership service. They can be contacted [*here insert contact address and telephone number*]. They can also put you in touch with the informal arrangements set up to help resolve or prevent any disagreements between you and the authority. Using either of these services does not prevent you from appealing to the Special Educational Needs Tribunal about parts 2, 3, or 4 of the statement at the same time; your rights are not affected and an appeal to the Tribunal can run at the same time as any disagreement resolution.

When you receive the amended final statement, if you disagree with parts 2, 3 or 4 of the statement you can appeal to the Special Educational Needs Tribunal. The Tribunal can hold a hearing to decide what should be in these parts of [*child's name*] statement. You have to appeal to the Tribunal within two months of getting the final statement. The address of the Tribunal is 50 Victoria Street, London SW1H 0HW.

If you have any questions, now or at any time, about this process or about the statement itself, our case office [*name*] can be contacted at [*address and telephone number*].

Please do not hesitate to get in touch.

Yours sincerely

[Signature of officer responsible]

SCHEDULE 2
Regulation 16

Set out name of Authority

STATEMENT OF SPECIAL EDUCATIONAL NEEDS

Part 1: Introduction

1. In accordance with Section 324 of the Education Act 1996 ('the Act'), and Educational (Special Educational Needs) (England) (Consolidation) Regulations 2001, the following statement is made on [*here set out date*] by [*here set out name of authority*] ('the education authority') in respect of [*here set out name of child*] whose particulars are set out below

Child	
Surname:	Other Names:
Home Address:	
	Sex:
Date of Birth:	Religion:
	Home Language:
Child's Parent or person responsible	
Surname:	Other Names:
Home Address:	Relationship to Child:
Telephone Number:	

2. When assessing [*child's name*] educational needs under Section 323 of the Education Act 1996 the authority took into consideration, in accordance with regulation 11 of the Regulations, the evidence and advice set out in Appendices A to F to this statement.

Name of parent:	Parental Advice	Dated:
Name of head teacher/ head of SEN or other person responsible:	Educational Advice	Dated:
Name of Doctor:	Medical Advice	Dated:
Name of Educational Psychologist:	Psychological Advice	Dated:
Name of Social Worker:	Advice for Social Services Authority	Dated:
Name of persons providing other advice:	Advice from others	Dated:

362

(In making this statement the authority has taken into account the additional representations, evidence and advice set out in Appendix G to this statement.)

Part 2: Special Educational Needs

[*Here set out child's special educational needs, in terms of the child's learning difficulties which call for special educational provision, as assessed by the authority.*]

Part 3: Special Educational Provision

Objectives

[*Here specify the objectives which the special educational provision for the child should aim to meet.*]

Educational provision to meet needs and objectives

[*Here specify the special educational provision which the authority consider appropriate to meet the needs specified in Part 2 and to meet the objectives specified in this Part, and in particular specify –*]

(a) any appropriate facilities and equipment, staffing arrangements and curriculum,

(b) any appropriate modifications to the application of the National Curriculum,

(c) any appropriate exclusions from the application of the National Curriculum, in detail, and the provision which it is proposed to substitute for any such exclusions in order to maintain a balanced and broadly based curriculum; and

(d) where residential accommodation is appropriate, that fact.]

Monitoring

[*Here specify the arrangements to be made for –*]

(a) regularly monitoring progress in meeting objectives specified in this Part,

(b) establishing targets in furtherance of those objectives,

(c) regularly monitoring the targets referred to in (b),

(d) regularly monitoring the appropriateness of any modifications to the application of the National Curriculum, and

(e) regularly monitoring the appropriateness of any provision substituted for exclusions from the application of the National Curriculum.

Here also specify any special arrangements for reviewing this statement.]

Part 4: Placement

[Here specify

(a) the type of school which the authority consider appropriate for the child and if the authority are required to specify the name of a school for which the parent has expressed a preference, the name of that school, or, where the authority are otherwise required to specify the name of a school or institution, the name of the school or institution which they consider would be appropriate for the child and should be specified, or

(b) any provision for his education otherwise than at a school which the authority make under section 319 and consider it appropriate to specify.]

Part 5: Non-Educational Needs

[Here specify the non-educational needs of the child for which the authority consider provision is appropriate if the child is to properly benefit from the special educational provision specified in Part 3.]

Part 6: Non-Educational Provision

[Here specify the non-education provision which the authority propose to make available or which they are satisfied will be made available by a district health authority, a social services authority or some other body, including the arrangements for its provision. Also specify the objectives of the provision, and the arrangements for monitoring progress in meeting those objectives.]

Date

A duly authorised officer of the authority

Appendix A: Parental Advice

[Here set out

(1) any written representations made by the child's parents under section 323(1)(d) or 329A(3)(d) of or paragraph 4(1) of Schedule 27 to the Act and a summary which the parent has accepted as accurate of any oral representations so made or record that no such representations were made.

(2) any written evidence either submitted by the parent of the child under section 323(1)(d) or 329A(3)(d) of the Act or record that no such evidence was submitted, and

(3) the advice obtained under regulation 7(1)(a).]

Appendix B: Educational Advice
[Here set out the advice obtained under regulation 7(1)(b).]

Appendix C: Medical Advice
[Here set out the advice obtained under regulation 7(1)(c).]

Appendix D: Psychological Advice
[Here set out the advice obtained under regulation 7(1)(d).]

Appendix E: Advice from the Social Services Authority
[Here set out the advice obtained under regulation 7(1)(e).]

Appendix F: Other Advice Obtained by the Authority
[Here set out the advice obtained under regulation 7(1)(f).]

Appendix G: Advice Obtained by the Authority since the last assessment of the child under section 323 of the Education Act 1996 was made
[Here set out the advice about the child obtained by the authority since the last assessment of the child under section 323 of the Education Act 1996 was made.]

The Special Educational Needs Tribunal Regulations 2001
(S.I. 2001 No. 600)

ARRANGEMENT OF REGULATIONS

PART 1
General

1. Citation and application commencement
2. Interpretation
3. Members of lay panel
4. Establishment of tribunals
5. Membership of tribunal
6. Proof of documents and certification of decisions

PART 2
Making an appeal to the tribunal and statements of case

(A) THE PARENT

7. Notice of appeal
8. Reasons for appealing
9. Statement of parent's case and supplementary provisions
10. Withdrawal of appeal
11. Further action by parent
12. Parent's representatives

(B) THE AUTHORITY

13. Statement of authority's case, and supplementary provisions
14. Authority's representative
15. Failure to deliver a statement of case and absence of opposition
16. Representation at hearing and further action by the authority

PART 3
Preparation for a hearing

17. Acknowledgement of appeal and service of documents by the Secretary of the Tribunal
18. Statements of case

19. Copy of documents for parties
20. Enquiries by the Secretary of the Tribunal
21. Directions in preparation for a hearing
22. Varying or setting aside directions
23. Particulars and supplementary statements
24. Disclosures of documents and other material
25. Failure to comply with directions
26. Summoning witnesses
27. Consolidating appeals
28. Notice of place and time of hearings and adjournments

PART 4
Determination of appeals

29. Power to determine an appeal without a hearing
30. Hearings to be in private: exceptions
31. Failure of parties to attend hearing
32. Procedure at hearing
33. Late written evidence
34. Evidence at hearing
35. Adjournments and directions
36. Decision of the tribunal
37. Application or proposal for review of tribunal's decision
38. Review of tribunal's decision
39. Review of the President's decision
40. Orders for costs and expenses

PART 5
Additional powers of and provisions relating to the Tribunal

41. Transfer of proceedings
42. Miscellaneous powers of the tribunal
43. Change of authority
44. Power to strike out
45. Power to exercise powers of President and chairmen
46. Power to exercise the functions of a lay member
47. The Secretary of the Tribunal
48. Orders of the Court
49. Irregularities
50. Method of sending, delivering or serving notices and documents
51. Extensions of time
52. Revocation and saving

9

In exercise of the powers conferred by sections 333(5), 334(2), 336(2) and 569(4) of the Education Act 1996, the Secretary of State for Education and Employment, with the agreement of the National Assembly for Wales in accordance with Article 5 of the National Assembly for Wales (Transfer of Functions) Order 1999 and after consultation with the Council on Tribunals in accordance with section 8 of the Tribunals and Inquiries Act 1992, hereby make the following Regulations:

PART 1

GENERAL

9

Citation, commencement and application

1. (1) These Regulations may be cited as the Special Educational Needs Tribunal Regulations 2001 and shall come into force on 1st September 2001.

(2) These Regulations apply to all appeals to the Tribunal where the notice of appeal is entered in the records of the Tribunal on or after 1st September 2001.

Interpretation

2. (1) In these Regulations, unless the context otherwise requires –

'the 1996 Act' means the Education Act 1996;

'authority' means the local education authority which made the disputed decision;

'the case statement period' is the period specified in the notice given under regulation 18(1), including any extension ordered by the President under regulation 51(1);

'child' means the child in respect of whom the appeal is brought;

'child's statement' means the statement of special educational needs relating to the child made under section 324 of the 1996 Act;

'disputed decision' means the decision or determination in respect of which the appeal is brought;

'the clerk to the tribunal' means the person appointed by the Secretary of the Tribunal to act in that capacity at one or more hearings;

'hearing' means a sitting of the tribunal duly constituted for the purpose of receiving evidence, hearing addresses and witnesses or doing anything lawfully requisite to enable the tribunal to reach a decision on any question;

'parent' means, except in regulations 7, 30(2) and (8) and 39(6), a parent who has made an appeal to the Tribunal under the 1996 Act;

'records' means the records of the Tribunal;

'the Secretary of the Tribunal' means the person for the time being acting as the Secretary of the office of the Tribunal;

'the tribunal' means the Special Educational Needs Tribunal but where the President has determined pursuant to regulation 4(1) that the jurisdiction of the Tribunal is to be exercised by more than one tribunal, it means, in relation to any proceedings, the tribunal to which the proceedings have been referred by the President;

'working day', except in Regulation 28, means any day other than –

    (a) a Saturday, a Sunday, Christmas Day, Good Friday or a day which is a bank holiday within the meaning of the Banking and Financial Dealings Act 1971; or

    (b) a day in August.

'written evidence' includes evidence recorded in any way.

(2) Nothing in these Regulations authorises a body corporate to take any steps in proceedings or to attend a hearing other than by a representative.

Members of lay panel

3 No person may be appointed as a member of the lay panel unless the Secretary of State in respect of England, and the National Assembly for Wales in respect of Wales, is satisfied that he has knowledge and experience of children with special educational needs and that he is not eligible for appointment to the chairmen's panel.

Establishment of tribunals

4. (1) The President may from time to time determine the number of tribunals to exercise the jurisdiction of the Tribunal.

(2) The tribunals shall sit at such times and in such places as may from time to time be determined by the President.

Membership of tribunal

5. (1) Subject to the provisions of regulation 32(5), the tribunal shall consist of a chairman and two other members.

(2) For each hearing –

    (a) the chairman shall be the President or a person selected by him from the chairman's panel; and

(b) the two other members of the tribunal shall be selected from the lay panel by the President.

Proof of documents and certification of decisions

6. (1) A document purporting to be a document issued by the Secretary of the Tribunal on behalf of the Special Educational Needs Tribunal shall, unless the contrary is proved, be deemed to be a document so issued.

(2) A document purporting to be certified by the Secretary of the Tribunal to be a true copy of a document containing a decision of the tribunal shall, unless the contrary is proved, be sufficient evidence of its contents.

PART 2

MAKING AN APPEAL TO THE TRIBUNAL AND STATEMENTS OF CASE

(A) THE PARENT

Notice of appeal

7. (1) An appeal to the Tribunal shall be made by notice which –

(a) shall state –

(i) the name and address of the parent making the appeal and if more than one address is given, the address to which the tribunal should send replies or notices concerning the appeal;
(ii) the name and date of birth of the child;
(iii) that the notice is a notice of appeal;
(iv) the name of the authority which made the disputed decision and the date on which the parent was notified of it;
(v) if the parent seeks an order that the child's statement be amended, to which Part or Parts of the statement the appeal relates;
(vi) if the parent seeks an order that a school (other than one already named in the child's statement) be named in it, either the name and address of that school or a sufficient description of the type and nature of the school which the parent considers would constitute an appropriate placement for the child;

(b) shall be accompanied by –

(i) a copy of the notice of the disputed decision;
(ii) where the appeal is made under section 326 of, or paragraph 8 of Schedule 27 to, the 1996 Act, a copy of the child's statement.

(iii) where the notice of appeal states the name of a school in accordance with paragraph (a)(vi) above, written confirmation that the parent has informed the school that he proposes to request that it be named in the statement;

(c) shall include or be accompanied by a statement of the parent's reasons for appealing;

(d) may appoint a representative in accordance with regulation 12.

(2) The parent shall sign the notice of appeal.

(3) The parent must deliver the notice of appeal to the Secretary of the Tribunal so that it is received no later than the first working day after the expiry of two months from the date on which the authority gave him notice, under Part IV of the 1996 Act, that he had a right of appeal.

(4) In this regulation 'parent' means a person to whom the 1996 Act gives the right to appeal to the Tribunal.

Reasons for appealing

8. (1) If the notice of appeal does not include, and is not accompanied by, reasons for appealing which the President considers sufficient to enable the authority to respond to the appeal, he shall direct the parent to send particulars of the reasons to the Secretary of the Tribunal within 10 working days of his direction.

(2) Regulations 21 and 25 shall apply to a direction under paragraph (1).

(3) Particulars of reasons sent in response to a direction made in accordance with paragraph (1) shall be treated as part of the notice of appeal.

Statement of parent's case, and supplementary provisions

9. (1) During the case statement period, the parent may deliver to the Secretary of the Tribunal a written statement of his case, which may include the views of the child, and all written evidence which he wishes to submit to the Tribunal.

(2) In exceptional circumstances, the parent may amend the notice of appeal, deliver a supplementary statement of reasons for appealing or statement of case or amend a supplementary statement of reasons for appealing or statement of case, if permission is given by –

(a) the President, at any time before the hearing; or
(b) the tribunal at the hearing.

372

(3) The parent shall deliver to the Secretary of the Tribunal a copy of every amendment and supplementary statement for which permission was given.

(4) If the President gives permission under paragraph 2(a) he shall consider extending the case statement period.

Withdrawal of appeal

10. The parent may withdraw his appeal –

(a) at any time before the hearing of the appeal by sending to the Secretary of the Tribunal a notice signed by him;

(b) at the hearing of the appeal.

Further action by parent

11. (1) The parent shall give the Secretary of the Tribunal the information requested in the enquiry made under regulation 20.

(2) If the parent does not intend to attend or be represented at the hearing, he may, not less than five working days before the hearing, send to the Secretary of the Tribunal additional written representations in support of his appeal.

Parent's representatives

12. (1) The parent may in the notice of appeal or by giving written notice to the Secretary of the Tribunal at any later time –

(a) appoint a representative;

(b) appoint another representative to replace the representative previously appointed, whose appointment is cancelled by the later appointment;

(c) state that no person is acting as the parent's representative, which cancels any previous appointment.

(2) To appoint a representative, the parent must give the name, address and profession of the representative.

(3) If a person whom the parent has appointed as a representative notifies the Secretary of the Tribunal in writing that he is not prepared, or is no longer prepared, to act in that capacity –

(a) the Secretary of the Tribunal shall notify the parent;

(b) the appointment of that representative is cancelled.

(4) Subject to paragraph (5), at any time after the parent has appointed a representative, and until that appointment is cancelled –

(a) the Secretary of the Tribunal shall send all documents and notices concerning the appeal to the representative instead of the parent;

(b) references in these Regulations (however expressed) to sending documents to, or giving notice to, the parent shall be construed as references to sending documents to, or giving notice to, the representative.

(5) Paragraph (4) applies:

(a) unless the parent notifies the Secretary of the Tribunal that he does not wish it to apply;

(b) subject to regulations 36(6) and 49(5).

(6) At a hearing, the parent may conduct his case himself (with assistance from one person if he wishes) or may appear and be represented by one person whether or not legally qualified:

Provided that, if the President gives permission before the hearing or the tribunal gives permission at the hearing, the parent may obtain assistance or be represented by more than one person.

(B) THE AUTHORITY

Statement of authority's case, and supplementary provisions

13. (1) During the case statement period, the authority shall deliver to the Secretary of the Tribunal a written statement of its case and all written evidence which it wishes to submit to the Tribunal.

(2) The statement of the authority's case shall be signed by an officer of the authority who is authorised to sign such documents, and shall state whether or not the authority intends to oppose the appeal, and if it does intend to oppose the appeal shall state –

(a) the grounds on which it relies;

(b) the name and profession of the representative of the authority and the address for service of the authority for the purposes of the appeal;

(c) a summary of the facts relating to the disputed decision;

(d) the reasons for the disputed decision, if they are not included in the decision;

(e) the views of the child concerning the issues raised by the appeal, or the reasons why the authority has not ascertained those views.

(3) In exceptional circumstances the authority may amend its statement of case, deliver a supplementary statement of case or amend a supplementary statement of case if permission is given by –

(a) the President, at any time before the hearing; or

(b) the tribunal at the hearing.

(4) The authority shall deliver to the Secretary of the Tribunal a copy of every amendment and supplementary statement for which permission was given.

(5) If the President gives permission under paragraph (3) he shall consider extending the case statement period.

Authority's representative

14. (1) The authority may at any time change its representative for the purposes of the appeal by notifying the Secretary of the Tribunal of the name and profession of its new representative.

(2) References in these Regulations (however expressed) to sending documents to, or giving notice to, the authority shall be construed as references to sending documents to, or giving notice to, the representative named in accordance with regulation 13(2)(b) or paragraph (1) above.

Failure to deliver a statement of case and absence of opposition

15. (1) If the Secretary of the Tribunal does not receive a statement of case from the authority within the case statement period or if the authority states in writing that it does not resist the appeal, or withdraws its opposition to the appeal, the tribunal shall –

(a) determine the appeal on the basis of the notice of appeal without a hearing; or

(b) without notifying the authority hold a hearing at which the authority is not represented.

(2) Where the parent's appeal relates to the contents of the child's statement, no statement that the authority does not resist the appeal or that it withdraws its opposition shall take effect until the authority sends the Tribunal a written statement of the amendments (if any) to the statement which it agrees to make.

Representation at hearing and further action by the authority

16. (1) At a hearing or part of a hearing the authority may be represented by one person whether or not legally qualified:

Provided that if the President gives permission before the hearing or the tribunal gives permission at the hearing the authority may be represented by more than one person.

(2) The authority shall give the Secretary of the Tribunal the information requested in the enquiry made under regulation 20.

(3) If the authority does not intend to be represented at the hearing it may, not less than five working days before the hearing, send to the Secretary of the Tribunal additional representations in support of its case.

PART 3

Preparation of a Hearing

Acknowledgement of appeal and service of documents by the Secretary of the Tribunal

17. (1) Upon receiving a notice of appeal the Secretary of the Tribunal shall –

(a) enter particulars of it in the records;
(b) send to the parent –

(i) an acknowledgement of its receipt and a note of the case number entered in the records;
(ii) a note of the address to which notices and communications to the Tribunal or to the Secretary of the Tribunal should be sent;
(iii) notification that advice about the appeals procedure may be obtained from the office of the Tribunal; and
(iv) subject to regulation 18(2), a notice stating the time for submitting a statement of the parent's case and written evidence under regulation 18(1);

(c) subject to paragraph 18(2), send to the authority –

(i) a copy of the notice of appeal and any accompanying papers;
(ii) a note of the address to which notices and communications to the Tribunal to the Secretary of the Tribunal should be sent; and
(iii) a notice stating the time for submitting a statement of the authority's case and written evidence under regulation 18(1) and the consequences of failing to do so;

(d) if, in accordance with regulation 7(1)(a)(vi), the notice of appeal names a maintained school, other than one maintained by the authority, give the head teacher of that school notice of the appeal, stating the name and date of birth of the child and the name of the authority.

(2) Where the Secretary of the Tribunal is of the opinion that, on the basis of the notice of appeal, the parent is asking the Tribunal to do something which it cannot do, he may give notice to the parent –

(a) stating the reasons for his opinion; and
(b) informing the parent that the notice of appeal will not be entered in the records unless, within a specified time (which shall not be less than five working days), the parent notifies the Secretary of the Tribunal that he wishes to proceed with it.

(3) Where the Secretary of the Tribunal is of the opinion that there is an obvious error in the notice of appeal –

(a) he may correct that error and if he does so shall notify the parent accordingly and such notification shall state the effect of paragraph (b); and
(b) unless within five working days the parent notifies the Secretary of the Tribunal that he objects to the correction, the notice of appeal so corrected shall be treated as the notice of appeal for the purposes of these Regulations.

(4) If the Secretary of the Tribunal has given a notice under paragraph (2), the notice of appeal shall only be treated as having been received for the purposes of paragraph (1) when the parent notifies the Secretary of the Tribunal that he wishes to proceed with the appeal.

Statements of case

18. (1) Both parties shall be allowed the same period of 30 working days, from the date on which notification is taken to have been delivered in accordance with regulation 50(6), to send statement of their respective cases and written evidence to the Secretary of the Tribunal.

(2) Where the President makes a direction in accordance with regulation 8, the period specified in paragraph (1) shall not start, and the Secretary of the Tribunal shall not send a notice as required by regulation 17(1)(b)(iv), or any documents as required by regulation 17(1)(c), until particulars of reasons are received in response to the direction.

Copy documents for parties

19. (1) Subject to paragraph (2), the Secretary of the Tribunal shall –

(a) forthwith send to the authority a copy of any amendment to the notice of appeal received during the case statement period;
(b) at the end of the case statement period send a copy of each party's statement of case and written evidence to the other party;

(c) forthwith send copies of any amendments or supplementary statements, written representations, written evidence (other than written evidence of which a copy is received in accordance with regulation 33(2)(b)) or other documents received from a party after the end of the case statement period to the other party to the proceedings.

(2) If a notice of appeal, a statement of case, amendment, supplementary statement, written representation, written evidence or other document is delivered to the Secretary of the Tribunal after the time prescribed by these Regulations, the Secretary of the Tribunal shall not send a copy of it to the other party unless the President extends the time limit pursuant to regulation 51.

(3) If a notice of appeal is amended in accordance with regulation 9(2) so that the parent seeks an order that a maintained school, or a different maintained school, other than the one already named in the child's statement be named in the statement, the Secretary of the Tribunal shall give the head teacher of that school notice of appeal, stating the name and the date of birth of the child and the name of the authority unless the school is maintained by the authority.

Enquiries by the Secretary of the Tribunal

20. The Secretary of the Tribunal shall, at any time after he has received the notice of appeal –

(a) ask each party –

(i) whether or not the party intends to attend the hearing;
(ii) whether the party wishes to be represented at the hearing in accordance with regulation 12(6) or 16(1) and if so the name of the representative;
(iii) whether the party wishes the hearing to be in public;
(iv) whether the party intends to call witnesses and if so the names of the proposed witnesses;
(v) whether the party or a witness will require the assistance of an interpreter;

(b) enquire of the parent whether he wishes any persons (other than a person who will represent him or any witness whom he proposes to call) to attend the hearing if the hearing is in private and if so the name of such persons; and
(c) inform each party of the effect of regulation 30(4)(c).

Directions in preparation for a hearing

21. (1) The President may, on the application of a party or on his own initiative, at any time before the hearing give such directions as are provided in regulations 23 and 24 to enable the parties to prepare for the hearing or to assist the tribunal to determine the issues.

(2) An application by a party for directions shall be made in writing to the Secretary of the Tribunal and, unless it is accompanied by the written consent of the other party, shall be served by the Secretary of the Tribunal on that other party. If the other party objects to the directions sought, the President shall consider the objection and, if he considers it necessary for the determination of the application, shall give the parties an opportunity of appearing before him.

(3) If in the opinion of the President there would not be a reasonable time before a hearing of which notice has been given under regulation 28(1) to comply with a direction for which a party applies, he shall refuse the application.

(4) A direction shall –

(a) include a statement of the possible consequences for the appeal, as provided by regulation 25, of a party's failure to comply with the requirement within the time allowed by the President;

(b) if made under regulation 24(2), contain a reference to the fact that, under section 336 of the 1996 Act, any person who without reasonable cause fails to comply with requirements regarding disclosure or inspection of documents shall be liable on summary conviction to a fine not exceeding level 3 on the standard scale; and

(c) unless the person to whom the direction is addressed had an opportunity to object to the direction, or he gave his written consent to the application for it, contain a statement to the effect that that person may apply to the President under regulation 22 to vary or set aside the direction.

Varying or setting aside directions

22. Where a party to whom a direction is addressed had no opportunity to object to the giving of such direction and he did not give his written consent to the application for it, he may apply to the President, by notice to the Secretary of the Tribunal, to vary it or set it aside, but the President shall not do so without first notifying the other party and considering any representations made by him.

Particulars and supplementary statements

23. The President may give directions requiring any party to provide in or with that party's statement of case, such particulars or supplementary statements as may reasonably be required for the determination of the appeal.

Disclosures of documents and other material

24. (1) The President –

(a) may give directions requiring a party to deliver to the tribunal any document or other material which the tribunal may require and which it is in the power of that party to deliver;

(b) shall impose a condition on the supply of a copy of any document or other material delivered in compliance with a direction given under this paragraph that the party receiving it shall use such document only for the purposes of the appeal; and

(c) may require a written undertaking to observe that condition before supplying a copy.

(2) The President may grant to a party an order for such disclosure or inspection of documents (including the taking of copies) as might be granted under the Civil Procedure Rules 1998.

Failure to comply with directions

25. (1) If a party has not complied with a direction within the time specified in the direction the tribunal may –

(a) where the party in default is the parent, dismiss the appeal without a hearing;

(b) where the party in default is the authority, determine the appeal without a hearing; or

(c) (i) hold a hearing (without notifying the party in default) at which the party in default is not present or represented; or

(ii) where the parties have been notified of the hearing in accordance with regulation 28(1), direct that neither the party in default nor any person whom he intends should represent him or give evidence on his behalf be entitled to attend the hearing.

(2) In this regulation 'the party in default' means the party which has failed to comply with the direction.

Summoning witnesses

26. (1) The President may by summons require any person in England and Wales to attend as a witness at a hearing of an appeal at such time and place as may be specified in the summons, and at any adjournment of that hearing, and at the hearing to answer any questions or produce any documents or other material in his custody or under his control which relate to any matter in question in the appeal:

Provided that –

(a) no person shall be compelled to give any evidence or produce any document or other material that he could not be compelled to give or produce at a trial of an action in a Court of law;

(b) in exercising the power conferred by this regulation, the President shall take into account the need to protect any matter that relates to intimate personal or financial circumstances or consists of information communicated or obtained in confidence;

(c) no person shall be required to attend in obedience to such a summons unless he has been given at least five working days' notice of the hearing or, if less than five working days, he has informed the President that he accepts such notice as he has been given: and

(d) no person shall be required in obedience to such a summons to attend and give evidence or to produce any document unless the necessary expenses of his attendance are paid or tendered to him.

(2) A party seeking a witness summons shall apply in writing to the Secretary of the Tribunal at least eight working days before the hearing, or later if the person to whom the summons is to be addressed consents in writing.

(3) A witness summons shall contain –

(a) a reference to the fact that, under section 336 of the 1996 Act, any person who without reasonable excuse fails to comply with any requirement to attend to give evidence and, if the summons so requires, to produce documents shall be liable on summary conviction to a fine not exceeding level 3 on the standard scale; and

(b) a statement of the effect of paragraph (4).

(4) A person to whom a witness summons is addressed may apply to the President, by notice to the Secretary of the Tribunal, to vary it or set it aside, but the President shall not do so without first notifying the party who applied for the issue of the summons and considering any representations made by him.

Consolidating appeals

27. (1) Where more than one appeal relates to the same child, or requires a decision on substantially the same issue, the President may order that they be heard at the same hearing.

(2) The President may make an order varying or revoking an earlier order made under paragraph (1).

(3) An order made under this regulation shall only be made if it appears to be just and convenient to do so, and before an order is made the parties to every appeal affected shall be given an opportunity to be heard.

Notice of place and time of hearing and adjournments

28. (1) Subject to the provisions of regulation 29, the Secretary of the Tribunal shall, after consultation with the parties, fix the time and place of the hearing and send to each party a notice that the hearing is to be at such time and place.

(2) The notice referred to in paragraph (1) above shall be sent –

   (a) not less than five working days before the date fixed for the hearing where the hearing is held under regulation 15, 37, 38 or 44;
   (b) not less than 10 working days before the date fixed for the hearing in any other case;
   (c) or in any case within such shorter period before the date fixed for the hearing as the parties may agree.

(3) The Secretary of the Tribunal shall include in or with the notice of hearing –

   (a) information and guidance, in a form approved by the President, as to attendance at the hearing of the parties and witnesses, the bringing of documents, and the right of representation or assistance as provided by regulation 12(6) or 16(1); and
   (b) a statement explaining the possible consequences of non-attendance and the right to make representations in writing enjoyed by –

   (i) the parent if he does not attend and is not represented; and
   (ii) the authority if it is not represented and if it has submitted a statement of its case, unless it stated in writing that it did not resist the appeal or withdrew its opposition to the appeal.

(4) The tribunal may alter the time and place of any hearing and the Secretary of the Tribunal shall give the parties not less than 5 working days (or such shorter time as the parties agree) notice of the altered hearing date:

Provided that any altered hearing date shall not (unless the parties agree) be before the date notified under paragraph (1).

(5) If the time and place of an adjourned hearing are announced at the hearing before the adjournment, no further notice shall be required.

(6) Nothing in paragraphs (1) and (4) shall oblige the Secretary of the Tribunal to consult, or send a notice to any party who is not entitled to be represented at the hearing.

In this regulation 'working day' means any day other than a Saturday, a Sunday, Christmas Day, Good Friday or a day which is a bank holiday within the meaning of the Banking and Financial Dealings Act 1971.

PART 4

DETERMINATION OF APPEALS

Power to determine an appeal without a hearing

29. (1) The tribunal may determine an appeal or any particular issue without a hearing –

(a) if the parties so agree in writing; or
(b) in the circumstances described in regulations 15 or 25.

(2) The provisions of regulation 31(2) shall apply in respect of the determination of an appeal, or any particular issue, under this regulation.

Hearings to be in private: exceptions

30. (1) A hearing shall be in private unless –

(a) both the parent and the authority request that the hearing be in public; or
(b) the President, at any time before the hearing, or the tribunal at the hearing, orders that the hearing should be in public.

(2) The following persons (as well as the parties and their representatives and witnesses) shall be entitled to attend the hearing of an appeal, even though it is in private –

(a) the child;
(b) subject to the provisions of paragraph (8) below, any person named by the parent in response to the enquiry under regulation 20(b) unless the President has determined that any such person should not attend the hearing and has notified the parent accordingly;

   (c) a parent of the child who is not a party to the appeal;

   (d) the clerk to the tribunal and the Secretary of the Tribunal;

   (e) the President and a member of the chairmen's or lay panel (when not sitting as a member of the tribunal);

   (f) a member of the Council on Tribunals;

   (g) a person undergoing training as a member of the chairmen's or lay panel or as a clerk to the tribunal;

   (h) a person acting on behalf of the President in the training or supervision of clerks to tribunals;

   (i) an interpreter.

(3) The tribunal, with the consent of the parties or their representatives actually present, may permit any other person to attend the hearing of an appeal which is held in private.

(4) Without prejudice to any other powers it may have, the tribunal may exclude fom the hearing, or part of it –

   (a) a person whose conduct has disrupted or is likely, in the opinion of the tribunal, to disrupt the hearing;

   (b) a person, including the child, whose presence is likely, in the opinion of the tribunal to make it difficult for any person to adduce the evidence or make the representations necessary for the proper conduct of the appeal;

   (c) a representative or witness whom a party omitted to name, without reasonable cause, in response to the enquiry by the Secretary of the Tribunal under regulation 20.

(5) For the purposes of arriving at its decision a tribunal shall, and for the purposes of discussing a question of procedure may, notwithstanding anything contained in these Regulations, order all persons to withdraw from the sitting of the tribunal other than the members of the tribunal and any of the persons mentioned in paragraph 2(d) to (g).

(6) Except as provided in paragraphs (7) and (8) below none of the persons mentioned in paragraphs (2)(a) to (i) or (3) above shall, save in the case of the clerk to the tribunal or an interpreter as their respective duties require, take any part in the hearing or (where entitled or permitted to remain) in the deliberations of the tribunal.

(7) The tribunal may permit the child to give evidence and to address the tribunal on the subject matter of the appeal.

(8) The tribunal may permit a parent of the child who is not a party to the appeal to address the tribunal on the subject matter of the appeal.

(9) Where the parent has named more than two persons in response to the enquiry under regulation 20(b) only two persons shall be entitled to attend the hearing unless the President has given permission before the hearing or the tribunal gives permission at the hearing for a greater number to attend.

(10) Section 576 of the 1996 Act (which defines the word 'parent' applies to paragraphs (2) and (8) of this regulation.

Failure of parties to attend hearing

31. (1) If a party fails to attend or be represented at a hearing of which he has been duly notified, the tribunal may –

    (a) unless it is satisfied that there is sufficient reason for such absence, hear and determine the appeal in the party's absence; or

    (b) adjourn the hearing.

(2) Before disposing of an appeal in the absence of a party, the tribunal shall consider any representations in writing submitted by that party in response to the notice of hearing and, for the purpose of this regulation the notice of appeal, and the parties' statements of their cases shall be treated as representations in writing.

Procedure at hearing

32. (1) At the beginning of the hearing the chairman shall explain the order of proceedings which the tribunal proposes to adopt.

(2) The tribunal shall conduct the hearing in such manner as it considers most suitable to the clarification of the issues and generally to the just handling of the proceedings; it shall, so far as appears to it appropriate, seek to avoid formality in its proceedings.

(3) The tribunal shall determine the order in which the parties are heard and the issues determined.

(4) The tribunal may, if it is satisfied that it is just and reasonable to do so, permit –

    (a) the parent to rely on grounds not stated in his notice of appeal or the statement of his case and to adduce evidence not presented to the authority before or at the time it took the disputed decision;

    (b) the authority to rely on grounds not specified in the statement of its case.

(5) If, at or after the beginning of a hearing a member of the tribunal other than the chairman is absent, the hearing may, with the consent of the parties, be conducted by the other two members and in that event the tribunal shall be deemed to be properly constituted and the decision of the tribunal shall be taken by those two members.

Late written evidence

33. (1) At the beginning of the hearing, a party may submit further written evidence which satisfies the conditions set out in paragraph (2) below unless the tribunal, after considering any representations from the other party, is of the opinion that that would be contrary to the interests of justice.

(2) The conditions referred to in paragraph (1) are that –

(a) the evidence was not, and could not reasonably have been, available to that party before the end of the case statement period;

(b) a copy of the evidence was sent or delivered to the Secretary of the Tribunal and to the other party to arrive at least 5 working days before the hearing; and

(c) the extent and form of the evidence is such that, in the opinion of the tribunal, it is not likely to impede the efficient conduct of the hearing.

(3) If the paragraph (1) does not apply, the tribunal may give a party permission to submit further written evidence at the hearing if it is of the opinion that –

(a) the case is wholly exceptional; and

(b) unless the evidence is admitted, there is a serious risk of prejudice to the interests of the child.

(4) Before the hearing the tribunal may refer to copies of evidence sent to the Secretary of the Tribunal under paragraph (2)(b) above for the purpose of considering whether or not it satisfies the conditions in paragraph (2); but if the evidence is not admitted the tribunal shall disregard it in determining the appeal.

Evidence at hearing

34. (1) In the course of the hearing the parties shall be entitled to give evidence, to call witnesses, to question any witnesses and to address the tribunal both on the evidence, including the written evidence submitted before the hearing, and generally on the subject matter of the appeal:

Provided that neither party shall be entitled to call more than two witnesses to give evidence orally (in addition to any witnesses whose attendance is required pursuant to paragraph (2) below) unless the President has given permission before the hearing or the tribunal gives permission at the hearing.

(2) Evidence before the tribunal may be given orally or by written statement, but the tribunal may at any stage of the proceedings require the personal attendance of any maker of any written statement:

Provided that a party shall only be entitled to give evidence by written statement if such evidence is submitted with the notice of appeal or the statement of his case or in accordance with regulation 33.

(3) The tribunal may receive evidence of any fact which appears to the tribunal to be relevant.

(4) The tribunal may require any witness to give evidence on oath or affirmation, and for that purpose there may be administered an oath or affirmation in due form, or may require any evidence given by written statement to be given by statement of truth.

Adjournments and directions

35. (1) The tribunal may from time to time adjourn the hearing.

(2) When a hearing is adjourned –

(a) the tribunal may give directions to be complied with before or at the resumed hearing;
(b) the chairman may announce provisional conclusions reached by the tribunal. The provisional conclusions are not a decision of the tribunal.

(3) A direction under paragraph (2)(a) may require a party to provide such particulars, evidence or statements as may reasonably be required for the determination of the appeal.

(4) If a party fails to comply with such a direction, the tribunal shall take account of that fact when determining the appeal or deciding whether to make an order for costs.

Decision of the tribunal

36. (1) A decision of the tribunal may be taken by a majority and where the tribunal is constituted by two members under regulation 32(5) the chairman shall have a second or casting vote.

(2) The decision of the tribunal may be given orally at the end of the hearing or reserved and, in any event, whether there has been a hearing or not, shall be recorded forthwith in a document which save in the case of a decision by consent, shall also contain, or have annexed to it, a statement of the reasons (in summary form) for the tribunal's decision, and each such document shall be signed and dated by the chairman.

(3) Neither a decision given orally nor the document referred to in paragraph (2) shall contain any reference to the decision being by majority (if that be the case) or to any opinion of a minority.

(4) Every decision of the tribunal shall be entered in the records.

(5) As soon as may be the Secretary of the Tribunal shall send a copy of the document referred to in paragraph (2) to each party, accompanied by guidance, in a form approved by the President, about the circumstances in which there is a right to appeal against a tribunal decision and the procedure to be followed.

(6) Where, under regulation 12 a parent has appointed a representative the Secretary of the Tribunal shall send a copy of the documents referred to in paragraph (5) to the parent as well as to the representative.

(7) Every decision shall be treated as having been made on the date on which a copy of the document recording it is sent to the parent (whether or not the decision has been previously announced at the end of the hearing).

Application or proposal for review of tribunal's decision

37. (1) A party may apply to the Secretary of the Tribunal for the decision of the tribunal to be reviewed on the grounds that–

(a) its decision was wrongly made as a result of an error on the part of the tribunal staff;
(b) a party, who was entitled to be heard at the hearing but failed to appear or to be represented, had good and sufficient reason for failing to appear;
(c) there was an obvious error in the decision; or
(d) the interests of justice require.

(2) An application that a decision of the tribunal be reviewed shall –

(a) be made not later than 10 working days after the date on which the decision was sent to the parties;
(b) be in writing stating the grounds in full.

(3) An application that a decision of the tribunal be reviewed may be refused by the President, or by the chairman of the tribunal which decided the case, if in his opinion it has no reasonable grounds of success.

(4) Unless an application that a decision of the tribunal be reviewed is refused in accordance with paragraph (3), it shall be determined, after the parities have had an opportunity to be heard, by the tribunal which made the decision or, where that is not practicable, by a tribunal appointed by the President.

(5) The tribunal may on its own initiative propose to review its decision on any of the grounds referred to in paragraph (1), in which case –

    (a) the Secretary of the Tribunal shall serve notice on the parents not later than 10 working days after the date on which the decision was sent to them; and

    (b) the parties shall have opportunity to be heard.

(6) If, on the application of a party or on its own initiative, the tribunal is satisfied as to any of the grounds referred to in paragraph (1) –

    (a) it shall order that whole or a specified part of the decision be reviewed; and

    (b) it may give directions to be compiled with before or at the hearing of the review.

(7) A direction under paragraph (6) may require a party to provide such particulars, evidence or statements as may reasonably be required for the determination of the review.

(8) If a party fails to comply with such a direction, the tribunal shall take account of that fact when determining the review or deciding whether to make an order for costs.

Review of tribunal's decision

38. (1) A tribunal which reviews all or part of a decision may –

    (a) by certificate under the chairman's hand set aside or vary that decision and substitute such other decision as it thinks fit; or

    (b) order a rehearing before the same or a differently constituted tribunal.

(2) If the decision is set aside or varied, the Secretary of the Tribunal shall alter the entry in the records to conform to the chairman's certificate and shall notify the parties accordingly.

Review of the President's decision

39. (1) On the application of a party to the Secretary of the Tribunal or on his own initiative, the President may review and set aside or vary any decision of his if he is satisfied that –

  (a) the decision was wrongly made as a result of an error on the part of tribunal staff;
  (b) there was an obvious error in the decision; or
  (c) the interests of justice so require.

(2) An application by party for a review under paragraph (1) shall be made –

  (a) in writing stating the grounds in full;
  (b) not later than 10 working days after the date on which he was notified of the decision.

(3) Where the President proposes to review his decision on his own initiative he shall serve notice of that proposal on the parties not later than 10 working days after they were notified of the decision.

(4) The parties shall have an opportunity to be heard on any application or proposal for review under this regulation and the review shall be determined by the President.

(5) If any decision is set aside or varied under this regulation the Secretary of the Tribunal shall alter the entry in the records and shall notify the parties accordingly.

(6) A decision by the President not to extend the parent's time for delivering notice of appeal under regulation 7(3) shall be capable of being reviewed under this regulation on the application of the parent as if he were party to an appeal. In such a case, the authority shall not be entitled to be heard or notified.

Orders for costs and expenses

40. (1) The tribunal shall not normally make an order in respect of costs and expenses, but may, subject to paragraph (3), make such an order–

  (a) against a party (including a parent who has withdrawn his appeal or an authority which has withdrawn its opposition to the appeal) if it is of the opinion that that party has acted frivolously or vexatiously or that his conduct in making, pursuing or resisting an appeal was wholly unreasonable;
  (b) against a party who has failed to attend or be represented at a hearing of which he has been duly notified;

(c) against the authority where it has not delivered a written reply under regulation 13; or

(d) against the authority, where it considers that the disputed decision was wholly unreasonable.

(2) Any order in respect of costs and expenses may be made –

(a) as respects any costs or expenses incurred, or any allowances paid; or

(b) as respects the whole, or any part, of any allowance (other than allowances paid to members of tribunals) paid by the Secretary of State under section 336 of the 1996 Act to any person for the purposes of, or in connection with, his attendance at the tribunal.

(3) No order shall be made under paragraph (1) above against a party without first giving that party an opportunity of making representations against the making of the order.

(4) An order under paragraph (1) above may require the party against whom it is made to pay the other party either a specified sum in respect of the costs and expenses incurred by that other party in connection with the proceedings or the whole or part of such costs as assessed if not otherwise agreed.

(5) An order under this regulation for costs to be assessed shall allow the county court to make a detailed assessment of fast track trial costs either on the standard or indemnity basis as the order may specify in accordance with the Civil Procedure Rules 1998.

PART 5

Additional Powers of and Provisions Relating to the Tribunal

Transfer of proceedings

41. Where it appears to the President that an appeal pending before a tribunal could be determined more conveniently in another tribunal he may at any time, upon the application of a party or on his own initiative, direct that the proceedings be transferred so as to be determined in that other tribunal:

Provided that no such direction shall be given unless notice has been sent to all parties concerned giving them an opportunity to make representations against the giving of the direction.

Miscellaneous powers of the tribunal

42. (1) Subject to the provisions of the 1996 Act and these Regulations, a tribunal may regulate its own procedure.

(2) A tribunal may, if it thinks fit, make a decision in terms agreed in writing by the parties.

Change of authority

43. (1) This regulation applies if, after the date on which the disputed decision is taken, the child becomes the responsibility, within the meaning of section 321(3) of the 1996 Act, of a local education authority ('the new authority') other than the authority which made the disputed decision ('the old authority').

(2) On receiving evidence that this regulation applies, the President may order that, for all the purposes of the appeal, the name of the new authority be substituted for the old authority.

(3) The old authority, the new authority and the parent shall have an opportunity to be heard before an order is made under paragraph (2).

(4) When an order is made under paragraph (2) –

    (a) the Secretary of the Tribunal shall notify the old authority, the new authority and the parent;

    (b) the old authority shall no longer be party to the appeal;

    (c) the new authority shall be a party to the appeal;

(d) these regulations shall apply as if the new authority had made the disputed decision;

(e) the Secretary of the Tribunal shall send to the new authority copies of all the documents and written evidence relating to the appeal duly received by the Tribunal from the parent and from the old authority;

(f) the procedure for determining the appeal shall re-start, and regulation 17 shall apply as if the documents and written evidence sent in accordance with paragraph (e) above were the notice of appeal referred to in regulation 17(1).

Power to strike out

44. (1) The Secretary of the Tribunal shall, at any stage of the proceedings if the authority applies or the President so directs serve a notice on the parent stating that it appears that the appeal should be struck out on one or both of the grounds specified in paragraph (2) or for want of prosecution.

(2) The grounds referred to in paragraph (1) are that –

(a) the appeal is not, or is no longer, within the jurisdiction of the Tribunal;

(b) the notice of the appeal is, or the appeal is or has become, scandalous, frivolous or vexatious.

(3) The notice under paragraph (1) shall invite the parent to make representations.

(4) The tribunal may, after considering any representations duly made by the parent, order that the appeal should be struck out on one or both of the grounds specified in paragraph (2) or for want of prosecution.

(5) The tribunal may make such an order without holding a hearing unless the parent requests the opportunity to make oral representations, and if the tribunal holds a hearing it may be held at the beginning of the hearing of the substantive appeal.

(6) The President may, if he thinks fit, at any stage of the proceedings order that a party's case should be struck out or amended on the grounds that it is scandalous, frivolous or vexatious.

(7) Before making an order under paragraph (6) above, the President shall give to the party against whom he proposes to make the order a notice inviting representations and shall consider any representations duly made.

(8) For the purposes of this regulation –

(a) a notice inviting representations must inform the recipient that he may, within a period (not being less than 5 working days) specified in the notice, either make written representations or request an opportunity to make oral representations;

(b) representations are duly made if –

(i) in the case of written representations, they are made within the period so specified; and

(ii) in the case of oral representations, the party proposing to make them has requested an opportunity to do so within the period so specified.

Power to exercise powers of President and chairman

45. (1) An act which these Regulations require or authorise the President to do may be done by a member of the chairmen's panel authorised by him.

(2) Where a member of the chairmen's panel authorised under paragraph (1) –

(a) selects the chairman of the tribunal, he may select himself;

(b) makes a decision, regulation 39 applies in relation to that decision as if it referred to the member of the chairmen's panel in place of the President.

(3) Subject to regulation 49(6), in the event of the death or incapacity of the chairman, or if he ceases to be a member of the chairmen's panel, following the decision of the tribunal, the functions of the chairman for the completion of the proceedings, including any review of the decision, may be exercised by the President or any member of the chairmen's panel.

Power to exercise the functions of the lay member

46. (1) In the event of the death or incapacity of a member of the tribunal other than the chairman, or if he ceases to be a member of the lay panel, following the decision of the tribunal, the functions of the tribunal in relation to any review of that decision may be undertaken by the other two members.

(2) This regulation shall not apply to a tribunal –

(a) which is constituted of two members in accordance with regulation 32(5);

(b) of which any person is authorised to act in place of the chairman in accordance with regulation 44(3).

The Secretary of the Tribunal

47. A function of the Secretary of the Tribunal may be performed by another member of the staff of the Tribunal authorised by the President.

Orders of the Court

48. (1) If any decision of the tribunal is set aside, varied or altered in any way by order of the court, the Secretary of the Tribunal shall alter the entry in the records to conform to that order and shall notify the parties accordingly.

(2) If an appeal is remitted to the tribunal by order of the Court to be reheard, the Secretary of the Tribunal shall notify both parties that, during a period of 15 working days (or such shorter period as the parties may agree in writing) each may submit a supplementary statement of his case and further written evidence.

(3) If an order to strike out an appeal is quashed or set aside by the court, the Secretary of the Tribunal shall notify the parties –

(a) in the case where the case statement period has not expired before the order to strike out took effect, that regulation 18(1) applies;

(b) in any other case, that each party has a period of 15 working days (or such shorter period as the parties may agree in writing) to submit a supplementary statement of his case and further written evidence.

(4) The Secretary of the Tribunal shall forthwith send a copy of all statements and written evidence received from a party during that period to the other party.

Irregularities

49. (1) An irregularity resulting from failure to comply with any provisions of these Regulations or of any direction of the tribunal before the tribunal has reached its decision shall not of itself render the proceedings void.

(2) Where any such irregularity comes to the attention of the tribunal, the tribunal may, and shall, if it considers that any person may have been prejudiced by the irregularity, give such directions as it thinks just before reaching its decision to cure or waive the irregularity.

(3) Clerical mistakes in any document recording a decision of the tribunal or a direction or decision of the President produced by or on behalf of the tribunal or errors arising in such documents from accidental slips or omissions may at any time be corrected by the chairman or the President (as the case may be) by certificate under his hand.

(4) The Secretary of the Tribunal shall as soon as may be send a copy of any corrected document containing reasons for the tribunal's decision, to each party.

(5) Where a parent has appointed a representative in accordance with regulation 12, the Secretary of the Tribunal shall (notwithstanding regulation 12(4)) send a copy of the document referred to in paragraph (4) above to the parent as well as the representative.

(6) Where these Regulations require the chairman to sign a document, but by reason of death or incapacity he is unable to do so, the other members of the tribunal shall sign it and certify that the chairman is unable to sign.

Method of sending, delivering or serving notices and documents

50. (1) A notice given under these Regulations shall be in writing and a party whom the Regulations require to notify a matter to the Secretary of the Tribunal shall do so in writing.

(2) Notices and documents required by these Regulations to be sent or delivered to the Secretary of the Tribunal or to the Tribunal may be sent by post, by facsimile transmission or by electronic mail to or delivered at the office of the Tribunal or such other office as the Secretary of the Tribunal may notify to the parties.

(3) Notices and documents which these Regulations authorise or require the President or the Secretary of the Tribunal to send may (subject to paragraph (5)) either be sent by first class post or by facsimile transmission to or delivered at –

    (a) in the case of a party –

    (i) his address for service specified in the notice of appeal or in a written reply or in a notice under paragraph (4), or
    (ii) if no address for service has been so specified his last known address; and

    (b) in the case of any other person, his place of residence or business or if such person is a corporation, the corporation's registered or principal office.

(4) A party may at any time by notice to the Secretary of the Tribunal change his address for service under these Regulations.

(5) The recorded delivery service shall be used instead of first class post for service of a summons issued under regulation 26 requiring the attendance of a witness.

(6) A notice or document sent by the Secretary of the Tribunal by post in accordance with these Regulations, and not returned, shall be taken to have been delivered to the addressee on the second day for normal postal deliveries after it was posted.

(7) A notice or document sent by facsimile transmission or electronic mail shall be taken to have been delivered when it is received in legible form.

(8) Where for any sufficient reason service of any document or notice cannot be effected in the manner prescribed under this regulation, the President may dispense with service or make an order for substituted service in such manner as he may deem fit and such service shall have the same effect as service in the manner prescribed under this regulation.

Extensions of time

51. (1) Where these Regulations or a direction made under them requires or authorises a person to do something within a period of time, the President may, on the application of that person or on his own initiative, in exceptional circumstances extend that period of time.

(2) Where the President has extended a period of time reference in these Regulations to that period of time shall be construed as a reference to the period of time as so extended.

Revocation and saving

52. The Special Educational Needs Tribunal Regulations 1995 are hereby revoked, except in relation to any appeal where the notice of appeal was entered in the records of the Tribunal before 1st September 2001, and those Regulations shall continue to apply to such an appeal.

Part 10

Glossary

Glossary

10

Advice. This is the name given to the reports which professionals write when a child is being assessed for special education provision. The local education authority must get advice, or written reports, from a child's school (the educational advice), an educational psychologist (the psychological advice), a medical officer (the medical advice) and the social services department (social service advice).

When parents receive a copy of a proposed statement of special educational needs, they must also be sent copies of all the advice which the LEA has obtained.

Assessment. An assessment under the 1996 Education Act should take no more than ten weeks. This is what it involves: the local education authority asks for advice (see above) from a number of professionals, as well as a written contribution from the parent. Sometimes a child will be examined by a professional before a report is written. After reading all of the reports, the LEA decides whether or not to write a statement of special education needs. If they decide not to, they must write and tell the parents why not, and must inform them of their right to appeal to the Special Educational Needs Tribunal. If they decide to write a statement, they must send a proposed (or draft) version of the statement to the parents and ask them for their comments. An assessment under the 1996 Education Act is sometimes called a 'formal assessment' or a 'statutory assessment.'

Code of Practice. This is a book published by the Government. It advises schools on the arrangements they must make to provide for children with special educational needs who do not have a statement. The Code also advises local education authorities on how they should fulfil their legal duties towards children with special educational needs. Although the Code is not legally binding on an LEA or school, they must have a good reason to act contrary to its advice. You can get a free copy by ringing 0845–602 2260.

DfES. The Department for Education and Skills. This is the government department which is responsible for ensuring that local education authorities fulfil their legal duties. If you believe that your LEA is not obeying the law on special education you can make a formal complaint to the DfEE (see Part 7 of the guide).

Individual education plan. The plan is produced by the school's SENCO (see below) and should set out clearly a child's needs, the action to be taken to meet these needs and a date for a review of progress being made.

LEA (Local education authority). This is the part of the local authority which has the legal responsibility to ensure that children with special educational needs receive the provision they need. LEAs are named after the counties or boroughs they serve, e.g. Lancashire Local Education Authority; London Borough of Merton Local Education Authority. If you are not sure of the name of your LEA, ask in your local library.

Maintained schools. These are schools which are paid for out of public money, i.e. community, foundation or voluntary schools (e.g. church schools). Some are special schools, some are mainstream schools.

Note in lieu. Sometimes LEAs send parents a note in lieu of a statement after an assessment when they decide not to issue a statement. It should describe a child's needs and the provision necessary to meet them. It should also have attached to it all the professional advice collected as part of the assessment. The main difference between a note in lieu and a statement is that the note in lieu is not binding in law. This means that LEAs do not have to arrange the provision set out in them.

School-based stages. The Code of Practice advises schools to adopt a system which places children who have special educational needs, but who do not have a statement, on one of two stages. Children on School Action will be helped by the special educational needs co-ordinator, who will draw up an individual education plan (see above) for them. Children on School Action Plus will also receive support of some kind from an outside specialist. This may be in the form of teaching or therapy from a visiting specialist or advice and support for their teacher.

Secretary of State. The Secretary of State for Education and Skills is the government minister who is responsible for the Department for Education and Skills (see above).

Special educational needs. These are learning difficulties which cause a child to have significantly greater difficulty in learning than other children of the same age, and which call for different or additional provision. A disability which prevents or hinders a child from making use of the facilities generally available in an LEA school is also called a special educational need. If a child under 5 is likely to have a learning difficulty or a disability when they start school, they are also said to have special educational needs.

Special educational needs co-ordinator (SENCO). This is the teacher in a school who has responsibility for co-ordinating special educational provision. In a small school, the headteacher may take on this role.

Special educational needs officer. This is the officer who acts on behalf of the LEA when a child is assessed and when a statement is issued. He or she is sometimes called the 'named officer'.

Special Educational Needs Tribunal. This is an independent body set up under the 1996 Education Act to hear parents' appeals against decisions made by LEAs. The Tribunal can summon witnesses and place them on oath. Its decisions are binding. See part 3 of this guide for advice on appealing to the Tribunal.

Special educational provision. This is the provision required by a child who has special educational needs. It is provision which is additional to, or different from, provision which is made generally for children of the same age in the LEA.

Statement of special educational needs. This is a document issued by an LEA following an assessment when the LEA believes that a child needs provision over and above what is available in a school. Part 3 of a statement specifies the special education provisions to be made and an LEA is legally bound to arrange this provision.

Part 11

Index

Note: Page numbers in **bold** refer to the Glossary.

administrative law 204–5
  bias 218–9
  discretionary powers 207, 211–4
  duty to act fairly 217–8
  error of law 207, 208–10
  excess of power 207, 208
  fair hearing 219–20
  irrationality 207, 214–6
  natural justice 217–8
  precedent 205
  principles 206–208
  procedural errors 207, 216–20
  Regulations 216–7
  Wednesbury unreasonable 215–6
advice **400**
  appeals to Special Educational
  Needs Tribunal 191–2
  Code of Practice 74
  help in mainstream school 75–6
  insufficient detail 71–4, 121–6
  law 311, 328–30
  notes in lieu **401**
  time limits 53–6, 331–4
annual reviews *see* statement of
  special educational needs:
  reviews
appeals to court of appeal 232–3
appeals to Special Educational
  Needs
  Tribunal 135–8, 187–92
  advice on 187–92
  ceasing to maintain 182–5, 190,
  320, 339
  challenging decision of 187–92,
  192, 234
  costs and expenses 390–1
  how to appeal 190, 285
  law 299–301
  LEA amendments to statement
  150–4, 189
  LEA refusal to amend statement
  189, 299
  LEA refusal to assess 12–15, 36–
  42, 188
  LEA refusal to issue statement
  68–70, 299–300

legal 'aid' 191, 235–9
  McKenzie advisers 237
  named school 71–80, 84–95,
  188–9
  needs description 96–9, 121–6,
  188–9
  Notice of Appeal 121–6, 188–9,
  371–2
  professional advice 191–2
  provision 100–4, 121–6, 188–9
  Regulations 366–97
  right to appeal 188–90
  solicitors 191, 238–9
  success rate 190–1
  time limits on appealing 68–70,
  190
  time limit on implementation of
  Order 139–43, 352–3
appeals to the High Court
  see High Court appeals
assessment **400**
  calling off 63–7
  Code of Practice 14, 31, 38–9, 40,
  42, 51, 57, 59
  delay 49–56
  law 297, 311–2, 326–34
  LEA duty 12–5, 303–6
  LEA refusal 12–5, 188
  parental consent 28–32, 312
  parental request 12–5, 40–2,
  302–3
  pre-school 8–15, 305–6
  school request 43–8, 303–5
  school-based stages 16–8, 21, 401
  time limits 49–52, 331–4
  wrong information 57–60
  see also psychological assessment
Attendance Orders 155–7

barristers 191, 231–2
behavioural difficulties 28–32
bullying 25–7
*B vs Harrow London Borough Coun-
  cil and the Special Educational
  Needs Tribunal [2000] ELR 110*
  265–8

case law 241–68
children under 2 8–11, 305–6
church schools 168–72, 401
citations viii
City of Bradford Metropolitan Council vs A [1997] ELR 417
C vs Special Educational Needs Tribunal and London Borough of Greenwich [1999] ELR 5 260–1
Code of Practice 289, **400**
   denominational considerations 171
   English as a second language 38–9
   home education 180–1
   named school 170–1
   non-educational provision 140
   speech and language therapy 111
   statement amendment proposals 153
   statement reviews 176
   statements 69–70, 98, 104
   transfer to new school 170–1
   wishes and feelings of child 27
complaining to the Secretary of State
   acting 'unreasonably' 273–4
   failure to fulfil legal duty 270–2
complaints
   see complaining to the Secretary of State; Local Authority Monitoring Officer; Ombudsman
conductive education 135–8
court of appeal 232–3
   see also High Court appeals
court orders 222–7
Crane vs Lancashire County Council [1997] ELR 377 121, 219
C vs Lancashire County Council [1997] ELR 377 248

deadlines
   see time limits
DfEE (Department for Education and Employment) **400**
discipline 28–32
divisional courts 231
dyslexia 244, 254

Education Act 1996, Sections 312 to 336A and Schedules 26 and 27 288–320
Education (School Information) Regulations 1998 9
Education (Special Educational Needs) Regulations 2001 321–65
educational advice 329–30
educational psychologists 57–60, 71–4
   see also psychological assessment
emergency placements 155–7
English as a second language 38–9
exclusion from school 61–7, 158–63
   see also refusal to attend school

fairness 217–8
formal assessment *see* assessment

gender viii

Hackney London Borough Council vs Silyadin [1988] ELR 571 259–60
head teachers 173–6
health authorities 53–6
hearing (tribunal) 190
hearing (judicial review) 231–2
High Court appeals 234
home education 177–81

inclusion 75–80, 84–95
Inclusive Schooling = DfES Guidance 87–94
individual education plans **400**, 19–21
injunctions 224–5
injustice 275

judicial review 204–6
   administrative law 206–8
   application for permission 228–31
   costs 235–6
   court orders 221–7

L vs Clarke and Somerset County Council [1998] ELR 244
law

guides to 285
see also administrative law; case law;
Education Act 1996; Education (School Information) Regulations 1998; Education (Special Educational Needs) Regulations 1994; judicial review.
LEA (Local Education Authority) **400**
  acting 'unreasonably' 273–4
  duty of assessment 10–1, 305–6
  duty to arrange provision 147–9, 298
  duty to review statements 173–6, 341–9
  duty towards pre-school children 8–11, 305–6
  failure to fulfil legal duty 270–2
  proposed amendments to statements 150–4, 318–9
  provision of goods and services 294–5
  refusal to amend statement 318–9
  refusal to issue statement 68–70, 188
  transfer of schools 168–72, 341
  transfer of statements 349–50
  see also assessment; statement of special educational needs
learning difficulties 288
  see also provision of special educational needs
Legal Help 236–9
Local Authority Monitoring Officer 278–80
Local Commissioner for Administration *see* Ombudsman
Local Education Authority *see* LEA
London Borough of Bromley and Special Educational Needs Tribunal and Others, QBD and CA [1999] ELR 260 262–4

maintained schools **401**
maladministration 274–5
McKenzie advisers 237
medical advice 330

moving home 349–50
multi-professional assessment *see* assessment

named officer *see* special educational needs officer
named school *see* statement of special educational needs: Part 4 (placement)
non-educational needs 144–6, 364
non-educational provision 144–6, 364
notes in lieu 68–70, **401**
Notice of Appeal 190, 371–2

occupational therapy 262–4
Ombudsman 274–8
  compensation 278
  injustice 275
  maladministration 274–5
  three months rule 275
  time 274

parents' choice of school
  'full' 117–20
  independent 105–8
  mainstream 75–80, 84–95
  neighbouring LEA 117–20
  refusal by LEA 127–34
  religious grounds 168–72
  see also home education; schools: outside England and Wales; statement of special educational needs: Part 4 (placement)
P vs Hillingdon London Borough Council [1998] ELR 38 254
physiotherapy 262–4
precedent 205
pre-school children
  LEA duty 8–15
proposed statements *see* statement of special educational needs: proposed statements
provision for special educational needs 121–6, **402**
  law 288–397
  otherwise than in schools 177–81

see also LEA (Local Education Authority): duty to arrange provision; schools: provision for special needs; statement of special educational needs

provision of goods and services 294–5

psychological advice 330

R vs Chair of Governors and Headteacher of A & S School ex parte T [2000] ELR 274 264

R vs Cumbria County Council ex parte P [1995] COD 267 251–2

R vs Dorsel County Council and Further Education Funding Council ex parte M [1995] ELR 109 253

R vs East Sussex County Council ex parte T [1998] ELR 251 256–8

R vs Hereford and Worcester County Council ex parte P [1992] 2 ELR 732 244–5

R vs Hillingdon London Borough Council ex parte the Governing Body of Queensmead School [1997] ELR 331 254–5

R vs Lancashire County Council ex parte M [1989] 2 ELR 279 245–7

R vs London Borough of Barnet ex parte G [1998] ELR 281 258–9

R vs London Borough of Harrow ex parte M [1997] ELR 62 247–8

R vs Oxfordshire County Council ex parte B, Court of Appeal [1997] ELR 90 253–4

R vs Oxfordshire County Council ex parte Pittick [1996] 249–50

R vs Surrey County Council Education Committee ex parte H (1985) 83 LGR 219 245

R vs The Secretary of State for Education and Science ex parte E [1992] 1 ELR 242–3

refusal to attend school 155–7

religious concerns 168–72

reviews *see* statement of special educational needs: reviews

school placement *see* parents' choice of school; statement of

special educational needs: Part 4 (placement)

school-based stages 16–27, **401**

schools
governors' duties 16–8, 292–3
numbers of pupils 117–20
outside England and Wales 295
responsibility for special needs 16–8, 292–3
see also maintained schools; parents' choice of school; special schools; specialist independent schools; statement of special educational needs: Part 4 (placement); transfers

Secretary of State **401**
see also complaining to the Secretary of State

SENCO (special educational needs co-ordinator) **401**

social services departments 54–6

solicitors 236–9
Special Educational Needs Tribunal 191

special educational needs **401**

special educational needs officer **401**

Special Educational Needs Tribunal **401–2**
challenging decisions of 192
Regulations 2001 366–97
see also appeals to Special Educational Needs Tribunal

special schools
exclusion from 158–63
transfer to 33–5

specialist independent schools 105–8

speech and language therapy 109–6
case law 245–7
Code of Practice 111

statement of special educational needs 298–9, 336–52, **402**

support organisations 282–4

S vs Essex County Council and the Special Educational Needs Tribunal, 19 April 2000 (unreported) 268

407

transfer to new LEA 349–50
travel to school 168–72
Tribunal
    see appeals to Special Educa-
    tional Needs Tribunal; Special
    Educational Needs Tribunal

Wednesbury unreasonable 215
wishes and feelings of child 27
withdrawal support 25–7
witness statements 229–30